# Modern Techniques in Watershed Management: Its Uses and Effects

# Modern Techniques in Watershed Management: Its Uses and Effects

**Parikshit Ballabh**

**CYBER TECH PUBLICATIONS**
4264/3, Ansari Road, Daryaganj, New Delhi-110002 (India)
Ph.: 011-23244078, 011-43559448 Fax: 011-23280028
E-Mail: cyberpublicationsdelhi@yahoo.com
Website: www.cybertechpublications.com

**MODERN TECHNIQUES IN WATERSHED MANAGEMENT: ITS USES AND EFFECTS**

**Parikshit Ballabh**



First Edition 2010



*Published by* : Asian Offset Printers

**G.S. Rawat** for **Cyber Tech Publications**
4264/3, Ansari Road, Daryaganj, New Delhi-110002 (India)
Ph.: 011-23244078, 011-43559448 Fax: 011-23280028
E-Mail: cyberpublicationsdelhi@yahoo.com
Website: www.cybertechpublications.com

# Preface

The Watershed Approach is a decision making process that reflects a common strategy for information collection and analysis as well as a common understanding of the roles, priorities, and responsibilities of all stakeholders within a watershed. The Watershed Approach is based on the concept that many water quality problems, like the accumulation of pollutants or nonpoint source pollution, are best addressed at the watershed level. In addition, a watershed focus helps identify the most cost-effective pollution control strategies to meet clean water goals.

A watershed can be defined as the entire land area that ultimately drains into a particular watercourse or body of water. Watersheds can be many different shapes or sizes. Everyone lives in a watershed. Tennessee refers to watersheds by their proper name as well as by a grouping of numbers. This set of numbers is called the watershed's Hydrologic Unit Code, or HUC. The HUC can range from 2 to 16 digits long, more digits indicating a smaller and smaller portion of the watershed is represented.

Watersheds are appropriate as organizational units because they are readily identifiable landscape units with readily identifiable boundaries that integrate terrestrial, aquatic, and geologic features. Focusing on the whole watershed helps reach the best balance among efforts to control point source pollution and polluted runoff as well as protect drinking water sources and sensitive natural resources such as wetlands.

— *Author*

# Preface

# CONTENTS

# 1

# BACKDROP

India receives 4000 $Km^3$ of water through rainfall. Of this 3/4 part occur only during monsoon. The surface flow is estimated as 1880 $Km^3$. The annual replenishable ground water resources are assessed to be about 600 $Km^3$ of which the annual usable resources are estimated at 420 $Km^3$.

Inland water resources of the country are classified as rivers and canals; reservoirs; tanks and ponds; beels, oxbow lakes, derelict water; and brackish water. Other than rivers and canals, total water bodies cover an area of about 7 million hectare.

Statewise details of inland water resources are given in table; there are few desert rivers, which flow for some distance and get lost in deserts. There are complete arid areas where evaporation equals rainfall and hence no surface-flow. The medium and minor river basins are coastal rivers.

The Brahmaputra, Ganga, Indus and Godavari putting together cover more than half of the area of the country. The whole of the west coast stretching 1500 km between Surat in Gujarat and Cape Comorin in Tamilnadu are fed by fourteen medium and eighteen minor river basins leaving important cities like Bombay, Panaji, Cochin, Trivandrum out of major river basins.

On the east coast of Peninsular India there are three pockets, which are out of any major river basins. These three pockets are: the area south of River Cauvery starting from Madurai to Cape Comorin; the area between Pennar and Cauvery basin wherein Chennai and Pondicherry are located; and the area between Mahanadi and Godavari basins in Orissa coast. There is a tremendous variation both in the quantity of discharge from a major basin to minor one and also in the quality of discharge from region to region.

## SURFACE WATER

All the major river basins are not perennial. Only four of the thirteen major basin posses areas of high rainfall, i.e. Brahmaputra, Ganga, Mahanadi and Brahmini having annual average discharge of a minimum of 0.47 million cubic meter per $Km^2$, and they are perennial.

Six basins (Krishna, Indus, Godavari, Narmada, Tapi and Subernrekha) occupy the area of medium rainfall and have annual average discharge of a minimum of 0.26 million cubic meter per $Km^2$, and the remaining four (Cauvery, Mahi, Sabarmati and Pennar) occupy the area of low rainfall and have annual average discharge between of 0.06 and 0.24 million cubic meter per $Km^2$.

Thus, many of the major river basins also goes dry during summer leaving no available water for dilution of waste water discharged in them.

The revirine length in Uttar Pradesh is inclusive of Uttaranchal. Similarly, the Chattisgarh is covered under Madhya Pradesh ; and Jharkhand under Bihar.

## GROUND WATER

Total replenishable ground water potential of the country, has been estimated by Ministry of Water Resources as 431 $Km^3$ cubic kilometer per year.

After making provision for drinking, industrial and other purposes (other than irrigation), which is about 16 percent of total potential, the potential available for irrigation is 360 $Km^3$ per year.

The figure for net draft of ground water considering the present utilisation indicates that substantial portion of total potential (about 68 percent) is still remaining untapped.

## WATER QUALITY MONITORING PROGRAMME

Water quality monitoring is an important exercise, which helps in evaluating the nature and extent of pollution control required, and effectiveness of pollution control measures already in existence. It also helps in drawing the water quality trends and prioritising pollution control efforts. The pollution control boards in India are responsible for restore and maintain the wholesomeness of aquatic resources. To ensure that the water quality is being maintained or restored at desired level it is important that the pollution control boards regularly monitor the water quality. The water quality monitoring is performed with following main objectives in mind.

- For rational planning of pollution control strategies and their prioritisation;
- To assess nature and extent of pollution control needed in different water bodies or their part;
- To evaluate effectiveness of pollution control measures already is existence;
- To evaluate water quality trend over a period of time;
- To assess assimilative capacity of a water body thereby reducing cost on pollution control;
- To understand the environmental fate of different pollutants.
- To assess the fitness of water for different uses.

## MONITORING NETWORK

The Central Pollution Control Board has been monitoring water quality of national aquatic resources in collaboration with concerned State Pollution Control Boards at 784 stations. Out of which 707 stations are under MINARS (Monitoring of Indian National Aquatic Resources), 50 stations are under GEMS (Global Environmental Monitoring Systems) and 27 stations are under YAP (Yamuna Action Plan) programs. Out of 784 stations, 514 stations are on rivers, 181 stations on ground water, 57 stations on lakes and 32 stations on canals, creeks, drains, ponds and tanks. Monitoring under YAP is being carried by CPCB, Head Office. For remaining stations the monitoring is being carried out by respective SPCB's/PCC's. The monitoring of water quality at 254 stations is being done on monthly basis, 349 stations on quarterly basis, 178 on half yearly basis and 3 stations on yearly basis. The monitoring is done on monthly or quarterly basis in surface waters and on half yearly basis in case of groundwaters. The water quality-monitoring network is covering 26 States and 5 Union Territories spread over the country. The monitoring network covers 168 Rivers, 53 Lakes, 5 Tanks, 2 Ponds, 3 Creeks, 3 Canals, 12 Drains and 181 Wells. The collected samples are analysed for physico-chemical and bacteriological parameters.

CPCB initiated water quality monitoring in 1976-77 with 18 stations on Yamuna River and the number of stations in water quality monitoring network at present is 784. Number of stations gradually increased based on available resources and water quality problems.

***State wise and water body wise Distribution of Water Quality Monitoring Stations***

| State | River | Well | Lake | Other | Total |
|---|---|---|---|---|---|
| Andhra pradesh | 28 | 24 | 4 | 3 | 59 |
| Assam | 17 | 10 | - | 2 | 29 |
| Bihar | 7 | - | - | - | 7 |
| Chhatissgarh | 11 | 4 | - | - | 15 |
| Dadra and Nagar Haveli | - | 1 | - | - | 1 |
| Daman | 3 | 1 | - | - | 4 |
| Delhi | 4 | - | - | 8 | 12 |
| Goa | 10 | - | 1 | - | 11 |
| Gujarat | 34 | 3 | 4 | - | 41 |
| Haryana | 5 | - | 2 | 11 | 18 |
| Himachal pradesh | 26 | 8 | 3 | - | 37 |
| Jammu & kashmir | 7 | - | 2 | - | 9 |
| Jharkhand | 8 | - | - | - | 8 |
| Karnataka | 34 | - | 2 | - | 36 |

| | | | | | |
|---|---|---|---|---|---|
| Kerala | 30 | 15 | 10 | - | 55 |
| Lakshdweep | - | 15 | - | 1 | 16 |
| Madhya Pradesh | 40 | 5 | 3 | - | 48 |
| Maharashtra | 35 | - | - | 3 | 38 |
| Manipur | 8 | - | 4 | - | 12 |
| Meghalaya | 5 | 5 | 3 | - | 13 |
| Nagaland | 5 | - | - | - | 5 |
| Orissa | 39 | 15 | - | - | 54 |
| Pondicherry | 1 | 7 | 2 | - | 10 |
| Punjab | 35 | - | 2 | - | 37 |
| Rajasthan | 7 | 18 | 7 | - | 32 |
| Sikkim | 9 | - | - | - | 9 |
| Tamil nadu | 27 | 2 | 3 | - | 32 |
| Tripura | 3 | 7 | 2 | 1 | 13 |
| Uttar pradesh | 45 | 25 | 1 | 3 | 74 |
| Uttranchal | 13 | 1 | 1 | - | 15 |
| West Bengal | 18 | 15 | 1 | - | 34 |
| Total : - | 514 | 181 | 57 | 32 | 784 |

Frequency of monitoring station on surface water bodies such as rivers, lakes, ponds, canals and creeks is either monthly or quarterly whereas the groundwater monitoring stations are monitored on half yearly basis. Three river stations in upper Ganga and Yamuna river are monitored on yearly basis.

## Approach to Water Quality Management

The water quality management in India is performed under the provision of Water (Prevention and Control of Pollution) Act, 1974. The basic objective of this Act is to maintain and restore the wholesomeness of national aquatic resources by prevention and control of pollution. The Act does not define the level of wholesomeness to be maintained or restored in different water bodies of the country. The Central Pollution Control Board (CPCB) has tried to define the wholesomeness in terms of protection of human uses, and thus, taken human uses of water as base f or identification of water quality objectives for different water bodies in the country.

It was considered ambitious to maintain or restore all natural water body at pristine level. Planning pollution control activities to attain such a goal is bound to be deterrent to developmental activities and cost prohibitive. Since the natural water bodies have got to be used for various competing as well as conflicting demands, the objective is aimed at restoring and/or maintaining natural water bodies or their parts to such a quality as needed for their best uses.

Thus, a concept of "designated best use" (DBU) was developed. According to this concept, out of several uses a water body is put to, the use which demands highest quality of water, is termed as "designated best use", and accordingly the water body is designated. Primary water quality criteria for different uses have been identified.

The entire water resources of the country were classified according to their designated best uses and a "Water Use Map" was prepared. For identification of the water bodies or their parts where water quality is at variance with water quality criteria, it was felt important to measure water quality of that water body or its part. It would help in preparation of "Water Quality Map" of India. The idea was to superimpose "Water Quality Map" on "Water Use Map" to identify the water bodies or their parts which are in need of improvement (restoration). Subsequently through a wide network of water quality monitoring, water quality data are acquired. A large number of water bodies were identified as polluted stretches for taking appropriate measures to restore their water quality. Today almost all policies and programmes on water quality management are based on this concept including the Ganga Action Plan and National River Action Plans.

## TREND IN INDIA

The water quality monitoring results obtained during 2002 and 2003 indicate that the organic and bacterial contamination are continued to be critical in water bodies. This is mainly due to discharge of domestic wastewater mostly in untreated form from the urban centres of the country. The municipal corporations at large are not able to treat the increasing load of municipal sewage flowing into water bodies without treatment. Secondly the receiving water bodies also do not have adequate water for dilution. Therefore, the oxygen demand and bacterial pollution is increasing day by day. This is mainly responsible for water borne diseases.

The water quality monitoring results were analysed with respect to indicator of oxygen consuming substances (Bio-chemical demand) and indicator of pathogenic bacteria (total coliform and faecal coliform).

## BIOCHEMICAL OXYGEN DEMAND (BOD)

The number of observed BOD values less than 3 mg/l were between 58-67% during year 1994 to 2003. The maximum value of 67% was observed during 2003. This shows that there is a gradual improvement in number of locations meeting the level of desired criteria. The number of observed BOD values ranges from 3-6 mg/l were between 18-28% during year 1994 to 2003, the maximum value of 28% was observed in the year 1998. It was observed that there was a gradual decrease in number of observations having BOD between 3-6 mg/l.

The number of observed BOD value> 6 mg/l were between 15 and 19% during year 1994-2003 and the maximum value of 19% was observed in the year 1998. It was observed that there was a gradual decrease in number of observations having BOD >6 mg/l.

## TOTAL COLIFORM (TC)

The number of observed TC values < 500 MPN/100 ml were between 40-63% during 1994-2003, the values gradually increases to 63% in year 1999 which decreases to 45% in 2003. It was observed that first the values gradually increases and then decreases in number of observations having TC < 500 MPN/100 ml.

The number of observed TC values ranges from 500-5000 were between 28-37% during year 1994-2003 the maximum value of 37% was observed in 1994 and this % was gradually decreases to 33% in 2003. It was also observed that there was a gradual decrease in number of observations having TC between 500-5000 MPN/100 ml.

The number of observed TC values > 5000 MPN/100 ml were between 9-23% during year 1994-2003. The maximum value of 23% was observed in the year 1994 that gradually decreases to 9% in the year 1999 which again rose to 22% in 2003.

## FAECAL COLIFORM (FC)

The number of observed FC values < 5000 MPN/100 ml were between 46-67% during year 1994-2003. The maximum value of 67% was observed in the year 1998 that gradually decreases to 48% in 1999 which rose to 58% in 2003.

The number of observed FC values ranges from 500-5000 MPN/100 ml were between 22-35% during year 1994 to 2003. The maximum value of 35% was observed in the year 1999, which decreases to 28% in the year 2003.

The number of observed FC values ranges > 5000 MPN/100 ml were between 7-19% during year 1994-2003. The maximum value of 19% was observed in 1994, which gradually decreases to 7% in 1998 and again rose to 14% in the year 2003.

## RIVERS AT A GLANCE

The monitoring results reflect that organic matter & bacterial population of fecal origin continue to dominate the water pollution problem in India. The major water quality concerns as revealed from the monitoring results are : pathogenic pollution as reflected through indicators i.e. Total Coliforms (TC) & Faecal Coliform (FC) organic matter as reflected through BOD, salinity as reflected through conductivity & other inorganic parameters & nutrients as reflected through nitrates & phosphates.

## ORGANIC AND PATHOGENIC POLLUTION

The Organic pollution as measured through Biochemical Oxygen Demand (BOD) and Chemical Oxygen Demand (COD) is considerably high, water bodies are saprobic followed by eutrophicated near large urban centres due to the discharge of partly treated or untreated wastewater. This results in depletion of oxygen in these stretches of water bodies. The rivers and lakes in hilly part of the country are not affected significantly by such pollution, as there are no large urban centres. Although, high BOD is associated with low Dissolved Oxygen (DO), but many times the DO measurement does not reflect such conclusion due to the fact that the DO is measured during daytime when the photosynthetic effects are prominent. In such stretches of water bodies, the diurnal variation in dissolved oxygen is quite large. The dissolved oxygen during daytime increases to super saturation level (sometimes as high as 300% saturation) whereas at night at the same place the dissolved oxygen goes as low as zero mg/l. The pathogenic pollution is one of the major water pollutants in Indian water bodies the main cause for water borne disease. The majority of surface water monitoring locations are found contaminated with high levels of Faecal Coliform bacteria, which are indicators of pathogenic pollution.

The water quality of major rivers varied widely with respect to DO, BOD, Total Coliform (TC) and Faecal Coliform (FC). The level of DO is observed more than 4 mg/l in river Tapi, Narmada, Brahmini, Brahmaputra, Subarnrekha and Beas throughout the year, whereas the lowest values are observed in stretches of river Yamuna (0.1 mg/l), Sabarmati (0.6 mg/l), Mahanadi (1.3 mg/l) Ghaggar (2.6 mg/l) and Godavari (3.1 mg/l) at few locations downstream of urban settlements due to discharge of untreated/partially treated municipal wastewater, which is responsible for high oxygen demand. Very high values of Biochemical Oxygen Demand (BOD) are observed in river(s) Sabarmati (475 mg/l) followed by Ghaggar (180 mg/l), Godavari (78mg/l), Satluj (45 mg/l),Yamuna (36 mg/l), Cauvery (27mg/l), Ganga (17mg/l), Krishna and Tapi (10 mg/l each), Mahanadi (8 mg/l) and Brahmani (6 mg/l). The relatively low values of BOD are measured in river(s) Mahi, Narmada, Brahmaputra and Beas.

In respect of Total Coliform and Faecal Coliform Numbers, river Yamuna is leading with highest count of 2.6 billion MPN/

100 ml and 1.7 million MPN/100 ml respectively, followed by Sabarmati (28 million and 2.8 million), Ganga (25 million and 11 million), Brahmaputra (240,000 and 24,000), Cauvery (160,000 and 28,000), Brahmani(90,000 and 60,000),Satluj (35,000 and 3500),Krishna (33,300 and 10,000), Mahanadi (30,000 and 17,000), Baitarni (22,000 and 11,000), Ghaggar (14,000 and 2500) and Godavari (5260 and 3640) at certain locations. The river Mahi, Tapi and Narmada are relatively clean rivers as the number of Total Coliform and Faecal Coliform count are relatively less than 2400 MPN/100 ml and 210 MPN/100 ml respectively.

## NUTRIENTS & OTHER PARAMETERS

The results of conductivity, pH, temperature, nitrogen, phosphate and major ions measurement revealed that conductivity is conforming to the irrigation requirement in most of the rivers except esturine parts. The minimum level of conductivity observed in upper stretches of the rivers ranging between 28-320 mhos/cm. In esturine region due to tidal influence the conductivity shoots up ranging between 11050 mhos/cm for Krishna estury to 53100 mhos/cm for Cauvery estuary. The nutrients like nitrates & phosphate are enriched downstream of major towns along the rivers due to discharge of wastewater & solids. In such stretches eutrophication at various level was observed. The pH was observed in the range of 6-9 in all the rivers except Sabarmati & Amlakhadi, where it was abnormally low 1.5 to 2.5 due to discharge of industrial wastewater.

The hardness varies between 50-300 mg/L in most of the rivers. However, some river stretches are having hardness as high as 1000 to 3000 (Ambika, Mandovi, Khari, Par & Bhadar). Similarly, alkalinity varies between 50-200 mg/L. Conductivity, total dissolved solid, sodium & chloride showed parallel pattern in most of the rivers. The conductivity in Himalayan rivers & upper stretches of rivers in Kerala is observed very low (20 to 150 mhos/cm). The rivers in plane are having conductivity in the range of 150-700 mhos/cm. However, some stretches of the river or their tributaries showed high level of conductivity

(800-2800 mhos/cm). Similarly, rivers in Kerala, Himachal Pradesh & Upper Stretches of most of the rivers are having dissolved solids, sodium & chloride in the range of 50 to 700 mg/L, 6 to 400 mg/L & 10 to 500 mg/L respectively. However in some minor rivers like Ambika, Amlakhadi, Bhadar, Khari, Mandovi & Par they were found abnormally high.

## RIVERS IN INDUS BASIN

The Indus Basin is bounded on the east by the Great Himalayas, on the north by the Karakoram and Haramosh ranges, on the west by the Sulaiman and Kirthar ranges and on the south by the Arabian Sea. The basin in Indian Territory has a maximum east-west length of about 855 km and maximum north south width of about 560 km.

The Indus rises near Manasarowar lake in Tibet Plateau (China). The river has five tributaries in India, they are the Jhelum, the Chenab, the Ravi, the Beas, and the Sutlaj. The Jhelum, the Ravi and the Sutluj rivers each has a considerable length running along the international boundary.

The basin area of Indus is covering the States of Jammu & Kashmir, Haryana, Himachal Pradesh, Punjab, Chandigarh and Rajasthan., The important urban centres in these States are Ambala, Shimla, Jalandhar, Moga, Pathankot, Ludhiana, Batala, Patiala, Hoshiarpur, Amritsar, Bathinda, Abohar, Ganganagar, Chandigarh, Barnala, Faridkot, Fazilka, Firozpur, FirozpurCantt., Gurdaspur, Kapurthala, Khanna, KotKapura, Malerkotla, Malout, Mansa, Muktsar, Phagwara, Rajpura, S.A.S.Nagar, (Mohali), Sangrur, Nabha, Panchkula Urban Estate, Hanumangarh

The State Pollution Control Boards of Himachal Pradesh, Punjab, Haryana and Rajasthan at 52 locations carry out the water quality monitoring of tributaries of River Indus in the basin. The ranges of water quality observed in rivers Beas, Satluj and Ravi with respect to pH, Conductivity, DO, BOD, COD, Total Coliform(TC) and Faecal Coliform(FC) are presented as minimum, maximum and mean value to assess the extent of water quality variation throughout the year.

The Water quality of river Beas indicates that pH, DO and Conductivity are meeting the water quality criteria. The dissolved oxygen(D.O) is observed in the range of 6.0-11.5 mg/l. The BOD value ranges from 1-5mg/l. The highest value of 5 mg/l of BOD is observed at D/S Pathankot and D/s Mukerian. The COD value ranges from 1-13 mg/l. The count of Fecal Coliforms ranges from 2 to 1600 MPN/100 ml whereas Total Coliforms ranges from 2-2400 MPN/100 ml. The TC and FC are satisfying the water quality criteria.

The water quality of river Satluj is conforming to water quality criteria with respect to pH, DO and Conductivity. The DO varies from 3.8 to 11.4 mg/l. The BOD ranges from 1-45 mg/l. The maximum value of 45 mg/l of BOD is observed at D/s of Budhanala in Ludhiana.The other locations having high level of BOD are at Boat Bridge Dharmkotnakodar Road (11 mg/l) and at D/S of East Bein(22 mg/l). The values of COD ranges from 1-80 mg/l, Fecal coliform value ranges from 2-3500MPN/100 ml whereas the Total Coliform value ranges from 8 to 35000 MPN/100 ml.The Total and Faecal Coliforms count is considerably high and does not meet the criteria at number of locations such as U/s of Headworks Nangal,D/s of Budhanala in Ludhiana and at D/s of East Bein in Jallandhar.

The water quality of river Ravi, Parvati, Largi and Sirsa are meeting the water quality criteria for pH, Conductivity, DO, BOD, TC, and FC at all occasions in the year during the period of monitoring.

The Water quality of river Beas indicates that pH and DO are meeting the water quality criteria. The BOD value ranges from 0.1-6 mg/l. The highest value of 6 mg/l of BOD is observed at D/S of effluent discharge point at Mukerian. The COD value ranges from 1-18 mg/l. The count of Fecal Coliforms ranges from 2 to 1600 MPN/100 ml whereas Total Coliforms ranges from 2-2400 MPN/100 ml. The TC and FC are meeting the water quality criteria.

The water quality of river Satluj is conforming to water quality criteria with respect to pH and Dissolved Oxygen(DO). The DO varies from 3.4 to 11.5 mg/l. The lowest value of D.O is observed at downstream of Buddha Nala in Lidhiana. The

BOD ranges from 0.1-24 mg/l. The maximum value of 24 mg/l of BOD is observed at D/s of Budhanala in Ludhiana.The other locations having high level of BOD are at Boat Bridge Dharmkotnakodar Road (16 mg/l) and at U/S of Head works Ropar (12 mg/l). The Fecal coliform value ranges from 1 to 1300 MPN/100 ml whereas the Total Coliform value ranges from 3 to 30000 MPN/100 ml.The Total and Faecal Coliforms count are considerably high and does not meet the criteria at number of locations such as at Boat Bridge, Dharmkotnakodar in Jalandhar, D/s of Budhanala in Ludhiana and at D/s of United Paper Mills at Arson. The concentration of Nitrite (NO2-) is observed in the range of 0.06-0.6 mg/l, whereas Ammonical Nitrogen (NH4-N) is in the range of 0.1-2 mg/l.

The water quality of river Ravi, Parvati, Largi and Sirsa and Jhelum are meeting the water quality criteria for pH, DO, BOD, TC, and FC at all occasions in the year during the period of monitoring.

In the catchment area of river Satluj, sewage generated from the municipal corporation of Ludhiana and Jalandhar alongwith industrial wastewater generated from these industrial cities are the major source of pollution. The river Beas is polluted by the wastewater generated from Mukerian town and Mukerian Paper Mill.The river Satluj is polluted at D/S of Ludhiana, Dharamkotnakodar, D/s of East Bein, Harike, and the river Beas is polluted D/s of Mukerian. These stretches of rivers are considered under under National River Action Plan (NRAP) for restoration of water quality to the desired level.

## RIVERS IN GANGA BASIN

The Ganga basin covers slightly more than one-fourth (26.3 per cent) of the country's total geographical area, and is the biggest river basin. In India the basin covers the whole of Uttaranchal, Uttar Pradesh, Bihar and the Union Territory of Delhi and parts of Punjab, Haryana, Himachal Pradesh, Rajasthan, Madhya Pradesh and West Bengal. The main river, rising in the northern most part of Uttaranchal, flows through Uttar Pradesh, Bihar and West Bengal and finally falls into the Bay of Bengal. The Ganga Basin is bound on the north by the

Himalays and on the south by the Vindhyas. The ridge between the Indus system and the Ganga system, the Great desert of Rajasthan and the Aravalli hills form the boundary on the west. After traversing a length of 1450 km in Uttaranchal and Uttar Pradesh and 110 km in the boundary between U.P. and Bihar the river then enters Bihar and flows 445 km more or less through the middle of the State. The length of the river measured along the Bhagirathi and the Hugli during its course in West Bengal is about 520 km.

The Ganga has a large number of tributaries. Some of these are of Himalayan origin having considerably large water wealth. The important tributaries within India are, the Kali, the Ramganga, the Yamuna, the Gomti, the Ghaghara, the Gandak and the Kosi. The Yamuna although a tributary of the Ganga, is virtually a river by itself. Its major tributaries are the Chambal, the Sind, the Betwa and the Ken. The main plateau tributaries of the Ganga are the Tons, the Son, the Damodar and the Kasai-Haldi.

The water quality-monitoring of the river Ganga and its several tributaries are being done in the basin by the State Pollution Control Boards of Uttaranchal, Uttar Pradesh, Bihar, West Bengal, Haryana, Himachal Pradesh, Rajasthan, Madhya Pradesh and Central Pollution Control Board at 120 locations.

**River Ganga**

The Water quality of river Ganga indicates that pH and DO are meeting the water quality criteria at majority of locations. Dissolved Oxygen range from 2.7 to 11.5 mg/l. The lowest value of 2.7 mg/l DO is observed at Kannauj downstream. The BOD value ranges from 1-17mg/l. The highest value of 17mg/l of BOD is observed at D/S of Varanasi and the other locations having high value of BOD are, Kanpur D/s (6mg/l) and 5mg/l of BOD is observed at several other locations are, Narora, Bahrampur, Dakshineshwar, Uluberia and Palta. The COD value ranges from 1-30mg/l. The count of Faecal Coliforms ranges from 20 to 11,00,000 MPN/100 ml whereas Total Coliforms ranges from 280-80,00,000 MPN/100 ml. The highest value of Faecal and Total Coliform are observed at Serampore and Dakshineshwar respectively in West Bengal. The Water quality of river Ganga indicates that pH and DO are meeting the water quality criteria at majority of locations. Dissolved Oxygen range from 4.0 to 11.0 mg/l. The lowest value of 4.0 mg/l DO is observed at Uluberia in West Bengal. The BOD value ranges from 0.8-24.8 mg/l. The highest value of 24.8 mg/l of BOD is observed at D/S of Varanasi. The COD value ranges from 2-47.2 mg/l. The count of Faecal Coliforms(FC) ranges from 26 to 12,00,000 MPN/100 ml whereas Total Coliforms(TC) ranges from 47-45,00,000 MPN/100 ml. The highest value of Faecal and Total Coliform are observed at Dakshineshwar in West Bengal. The concentration of Nitrate (NO3-) varies from 0.002-7.0 mg/l whereas Nitrite (NO2-) ranges from 0.002-1.8 mg/l; the Ammonical Nitrogen (NH4-N) is observed in the range of 0.006-5.0 mg/l, the highest value found at Garhmukteshwar.

## RIVER YAMUNA

The river Yamuna is a major tributary of river Ganges. In the upper course of 200 km stretch it draws water from several major streams namely Rishi-Ganga, Unta and Hanuman Ganga, Tons, Giri, and Ashan. The combined stream flows through the shivalik range of hills of Uttaranchal, Himachal Pradesh, Uttar Pradesh and enters into the plains in the Dak Phatthar in Haryana where this river regulated through weir and diverted into canal for power generation. From Tajewala barrage in Yamunanagar district of Haryana, river again diverted into Western Yamuna Canal and Eastern Yamuna Canal for irrigation. River regain its water from ground water accrual and feeding canal through Som nadi (seasonal stream) just upstream of Kalanaur and traverses a route of about 1150 km through three states i.e. Haryana, Delhi and U.P. and finally to its confluence with Ganges at Allahabad. It receives major tributaries like Chambal, Betwa, Sindh and Ken from right bank and Hindon from left bank.

The availability of water in Yamuna river is greatly varied with time and space. Precipitation is confined to only three months in a year and varies greatly. Most of the water flows in the Yamuna (nearly 80%) in monsoon period (July, August, September) only. Whatever water flows in non-mosoon period (October to June) is extensively used for irrigation and drinking leaving very little or no water in the river to flow.

It is observed that about 500 km long stretch of the river is in bad shape, having water quality, most of the time, below desired level for "designated best use". In the dry season four distinct gradients of pollutional load can be discerned in the river stretch between Wazirabad and Etawah. The stretch between Wazirabad and Okhla is the most heavily polluted one, carrying the massive input of wastewater from Delhi. This input has sets off a progressive series of chemical and biological events in the downstream water. This stretch is characterised by high bacterial population, cloudy appearance high BOD and strong disagreeable odour-all indicating general depletion of oxygen. Masses of gasseous sludge rising from the bottom are often noticed floating near the surface of the water. During monsoon due to flood the sludge deposited in this stretch is flushed and stay in suspensioncauses rise in oxygn uptake in the downstream. This causes heavy fish mortality every year during first flushing after onset of monsoon.

Though there are number of bathing "Ghats along the river in Delhi stretch, the quality of water is far below the bathing standards. Even in this short stretch, remarkable purification takes place due to high temperature and long retention time in this stretch due to the two barrages one at Okhla and another at ITO (nearly 10 km upstream of Okhla Barrage). The ITO Barrage is used divert the Yamuna water for cooling purpose of the two Thermal Power Plants located near ITO. In the stetch between Okhla and Agra (225 km) the same assimilative capacity can be observed after the sewage input at Okhla, Mathura and Agra. After a few kilometers the repeated additions of sewage are mainly noticeable by a higher state of eutrophication leading to the formation of algal mats in the River. Excessive algal can cause problems associated with the oxygen balance in the water (daytime supersaturation and nighttime oxygen depletion). The water quality from DO, BOD, and bacterial point of view is not fit for designated best uses of this streach. The Agra Water Works is drawing its raw water from this only.

The 210 km long stretch from Agra to the confluence with the Chambal river at Etawah is characterized by self-purification processes of the Agra effluents. The confluence with relatively clean Chambal river is of great value in diluting the pollution load of Yamuna river before it joins the Ganga at Allahabad.

During the monsoon period due to huge mass of water flows in the river the barrages are opened leading to a more or less continuous system. The high load of untreated biodegradable material (domestic sewage) leads several gradients in saprobic and eutrophic conditions; major part of the Yamuna can hardly fulfill the designated uses.

The water quality of river Yamuna is conforming to water quality criteria with respect to pH only throughout its length. The DO varies from 0.1 to 22.7 mg/l, which indicates that the river is highly septic or eutrophicated at a number of locations. The lowest and highest values of DO are observed at Nizamuddin Bridge in Delhi and at Agra upstream respectively. The BOD ranges from 1-36mg/l. The maximum value of 36 mg/l of BOD is observed at Nizamuddin Bridge in Delhi. The other locations having high level of BOD are at Mazahuli (32mg/l) and at D/S of Agra (28mg/l). The Fecal coliform value ranges from 11 to 17,20,000 MPN/100 ml whereas the Total Coliform value ranges from 27 to 2,61,00,000 MPN/100 ml.The Total and Faecal Coliforms count is considerably high and does not meet the criteria at number of locations in Delhi and downstream reach of Delhi upto Etawah downstream.

The water quality of river Yamuna is conforming to water quality criteria with respect to pH only throughout its length. The DO varies from 0.3 to 22.8 mg/l, which indicates that the river is highly septic or eutrophicated at a number of locations. The lowest and highest values of DO are observed at Okhla Bridge in Delhi and at Agra upstream respectively. The BOD ranges from 1-58mg/l. The maximum value of 58 mg/l of BOD is observed at Okhla after meeting of Shahdara drain in Delhi. The other locations having high level of BOD are at Downstream of Agra (43mg/l) in U.P and at Nizamuddin (36mg/l) in Delhi.

The Fecal coliform value ranges from 40 to 20,30,00,000 MPN/100 ml whereas the Total Coliform value ranges from 110 to 1,71,00,00,000 MPN/100 ml.The Total and Faecal Coliforms count is considerably high and does not meet the criteria at number of locations in Delhi and downstream reach of Delhi upto Etawah downstream.

### *Kalinadi, Ramganga, Gomti, Saryu, Ghaghara, Hindon, Kali-Hindon, Rihand, Rapti and Gandak*

The water quality of the tributary streams Kalinadi, Ramganga, Gomti, Saryu, Ghaghara, Hindon, Kali-Hindon, Rihand, Rapti and Gandak with respect to pH, Conductivity and D.O are meeting the water quality criteria. The DO varies from 1.5 to 11.9 mg/l. The lowest and highest values of DO are observed at Hindon near Binauli town, Meerut and at Kalinadi at downstream of Muzzafarrnagar. The BOD ranges from 1-176 mg/l. The maximum value of 176 mg/l of BOD is observed at Kalinadi downstream of Mujaffar Nagar in Uttar Pradesh. The other locations having high level of BOD are at Kalinadi in Bulandshar (67mg/l) and at Hindon near binauli town in Meerut (33mg/l). The Fecal coliform (FC) value ranges from 50 to 3,60,000 MPN/100 ml whereas the Total Coliform (TC) value ranges from 40 to 4,80,00,000 MPN/100 ml. The highest values of Fecal (36x104 MPN/100 ml) and Total (48x106 MPN/100 ml) Coliforms count is observed at Kalinadi at Upstream of Gulaothi town in Bulandsahar of Uttar Pradesh. The coliforms count (FC and TC) is considerably high and does not meet the criteria at number of locations in Uttar Pradesh.

### *Chambal, Khan, Kshipra, Parvati, Betwa, Sind, Tons, Sone Johila, Sankh, Mandakini and Dohad*

The water quality of the tributary streams Chambal, Khan, Kshipra, Parvati, Betwa, Sind, Tons, Sone Johila, Sankh, Mandakini and Dohad with respect to pH, Conductivity and D.O are meeting the water quality criteria. The DO varies from 1.4 to 11.0 mg/l. The lowest values of DO are observed at Chambal at Nagda in Madhya Pradesh and at Rameshwarghat (Sawaimadhopur) in Rajasthan. The BOD ranges from 1-110 mg/l. The maximum value of 110 mg/l of BOD is observed at

Khan at Kabit Khedi, near Indore in Madhya Pradesh. The other locations having high level of BOD are Chambal at Nagda Downstream in Madhya Pradesh (30mg/l), Kshipra at Ramghat (Ujjain), Triveni Sangam, Tons at Madhavgarh, Mandakini at Chitrakoot, Chambal at Kota downstream. The Fecal coliform (FC) value ranges from 3 to 9000 MPN/100 ml whereas the Total Coliform (TC) value ranges from 4 to 93000 MPN/100 ml. the highest value of Total (93x103 MPN/100 ml) Coliforms count is observed at Chambal at Etawah before confluence to river Yamuna, Khan at Kabit Khedi, Betwa before confluence to Yamuna at Hamirpur and Sone at Koelwar in Bihar.

**Damodar and Rupnarayan**

The water quality of the tributary streams Damodar and Rupnarayan with respect to pH, Conductivity and D.O are meeting the water quality criteria. The DO varies from 1.5 to 9.8 mg/l. The lowest value of DO are observed at Damodar near Mujher mana village, after confluence of Tamla Nallah in West Bengal. The BOD ranges from 1-7 mg/l. The highest values are observed in Damodar at Haldia Downstream (7 mg/l), Damodar after confluence of Tamla Nala and the Rupnarayan at Geonkhali before confluence to River Ganga. The Fecal coliform (FC) value ranges from 4000 to 95000 MPN/100 ml whereas the Total Coliform (TC) value ranges from 92 to 25x105 MPN/100 ml. the highest value of Total and Fecal Coliforms count is observed at Damodar at Haldia downstream and Rupnarayan at Geonkhali before confluence to River Ganga in West Bengal.

**Kalinadi, Ramganga, Gomti, Saryu, Ghaghara, Hindon, Kali-Hindon, Rihand, Rapti and Gandak**

The water quality of tributaries namely, Kalinadi, Ramganga, Gomti, Saryu, Ghaghara, Hindon, Kali-Hindon, Rihand, Rapti and Gandak, is conforming to water quality criteria with respect to pH, conductivity throughout its length. The DO varies from 0.8 to 11.5 mg/l. The lowest value of D.O is observed at Hindon at Saharanpur Downsteram in Uttar Pradesh, Ramganga at Kannuj, Gomti at Lucknow downstream, Hindon at Binauli and Gaziabad. The BOD ranges from 0.7-149 mg/l. The high BOD values were observed at Kalinadi at upstream of Gulaothi town in Bulandsahar (149 mg/l), Kalinadi at downstream of Mujaffarnagar (102 mg/l) and Hindon at Saharanpur downstream in Uttar Pradesh (69 mg/l), Hindon at Binauli (56 mg/l), Ramganga at Kannuj (12.4 mg/l), Hindon at Gaziabad (9.6 mg/l), Gomti at Lucknow downstream (8.0 mg/l) and Rihad at Renukoot downstream (6.3 mg/l). The Fecal coliform (FC) value ranges from 40 to 46x106 MPN/100 ml whereas the Total Coliform (TC) value ranges from 52 to 19x107 MPN/100 ml. The highest count of TC and FC is observed at Kalinadi at upstream of Gulaothi town in Bulandsahar, Hindon at Binauli town, Gomti at Jaunpur downstream and Kalinadi at Downstream of Muzaffarnagar in Uttar Pradesh.

### *Chambal, Khan, Kshipra, Parvati, Betwa, Sind, Tons, Sone Johila, Sankh, Mandakini and Dohad*

It is observed that the water quality of these tributary stereams is conforming to water quality criteria with respect to pH and conductivity at all the locations except Chambal at Nagda downstream in Madhya Pradesh, where the high conductivity of 8800 μmohs/cm is found. The DO varies from 1.0 to 10.8 mg/l. The low values of DO are observed in Chambal at Nagda downstream in Madhya Pradesh and Chambal at Kota downstream. The BOD ranges from 0.3-30 mg/l. The maximum value of 30 mg/l of BOD is observed at Khan at Kabit Khedi near Indore. Other locations having high BOD are Tons at Madhavgarh, Chambal at Nagda downstream and Mandakini at Chitrakoot. The Fecal coliform value ranges from 9-2,20,000 MPN/100 ml whereas the Total Coliform value ranges from 7-145x105 MPN/100 ml. The highest values of Total and Faecal Coliforms count is observed in Chambal at Etawah before confluence to river Yamuna and Sone at kodwar in Bihar.

The water quality of the tributary streams Damodar and Rupnarayan with respect to pH, Conductivity and D.O are meeting the water quality criteria. The DO varies from 3.5 to 9.9 mg/l. The lowest and highest values of DO are observed in Damodar at Haldia downstream, Barakar at Asansol in West Bengal. The BOD ranges from 0.4-6.0 mg/l. The highest value of BOD is observed at Haldia downstream. The Fecal coliform (FC) value ranges from 200 to 11x105 MPN/100 ml, whereas the Total Coliform (TC) value ranges from 800 to 45x105 MPN/ 100 ml. The nitrite ($NO_2$-) values ranges from 0.001-0.688 mg/l. The highest value of nitrite is observed at Damodar near Majher Mana village in West Bengal. Nitrate ($NO_3^-$) values ranges from 0.142-1.611 mg/l. The highest concentration of nitrate is also observed at Damodar near Majher Mana village in West Bengal.

## RIVERS IN BRAHMAPUTRA BASIN

The Brahmaputra basin extends over an area of nearly 5,80,000 sq km and traverses a distance of about 2900 km through Tibet (China), India and Bangladesh. In India, the basin lies in the states of Arunachal Pradesh, Assam, Nagaland, Meghalaya and West Bengal. The river rises in the Great glacier in the northern-most chain of the Himalayas in the Kailash range at an elevation of about 5,510 m. It enters India across the Sadiya frontiers tract, west of Sadiya town into the Assam valley. Here it is joined by two more tributaries viz. the Dibang or Sikang and the Lohit, from here onwards the river is known as the Brahmaputra. The river then descends down into the Assam valley from east to west for a distance of about 720 km with its channels meandering from side to side and forming several islands, one of these islands, Majuli covers an area of 1,250 sq. Km. during its course the river receives many more tributaries both from the north and the south while some of them are trans-Himalayan rivers with considerable discharges.

The Brahmaputra has the highest discharge of all the rivers, in India, because of heavy annual average rainfall in the catchment area. The river has eight significant tributaries in India, three from the north are the Manas, the Kameng (or the Jia Bharali) and the Subansiri and three from the east are the Dibang or Sikang, the lohit and the Buri Dihing and two from the north West are the Tista and the Jaldhaka.

The basin area of Brahmaputra is covering the States of Assam, Nagaland, Meghalaya and West Bengal. The important urban centres in these States are Shillong (Meghalaya), Guwahati, Jorhat Dilbrugarh, Siliguri, Alipurduar, Dhubri,

Nagaon, Tezpur, Tinsukia (Assam), Dimapur (Nagaland), Kohima (Sikkim), Darjeeling, Dabgram Jalpaiguri Koch-Bihar (West Bengal)

The State Pollution Control Boards of Assam, Nagaland and Sikkim at 31 locations are doing the water quality monitoring of the river Brahmaputra and its several tributaries in the basin. The tributary streams covered under the monitoring programme are Dhansiri, Teesta, Subansiri, Burhidihing, Digboi, Disang, Jhanji, Bhogdoi, Mora Bharali, Borak, Bharalu, Deepar Bill, Dickchu, Maney Khola and Ranichu.

The Water quality of river Brahmaputra indicates that pH, DO and Conductivity are satisfying the water quality criteria for various uses. The BOD value ranges from 1-4mg/l. The highest value of 4mg/l of BOD is observed at Dibrugarh in Assam. The COD value ranges from 6-11mg/l. The count of Fecal Coliforms ranges from 300 to 24000 MPN/100 ml whereas Total Coliforms ranges from 360-240000 MPN/100 ml. The TC and FC are not meeting the water quality criteria at all the locations under monitoring programme..

The water quality of river Dhansiri is conforming to water quality criteria with respect to pH, DO and Conductivity. The DO varies from 7.1 to 20.0mg/l. The BOD ranges from 1-12mg/l. The maximum value of 12 mg/l of BOD is observed at Full Nagarjan, Town Boundary Bridge(Diphu Road) and Bridge near Purana Bazar. The other locations having high level of BOD are at Nutan Basti (10 mg/l) and at near Check Gate (Dimapur Khutkhuti Road) (5 mg/l) in Nagaland. The Fecal coliform value ranges from 930-3600 MPN/100 ml whereas the Total Coliform value ranges from 730-110000 MPN/100 ml.The Total and Faecal Coliforms count is considerably high and does not meet the criteria at Golaghat in Assam.

The water quality of river Teesta with respect to pH varies from 6.0 to 7.0 whereas conductivity is in the range of 260-320 umhos/cm.DO observed from 16 to 28 mg/l and BOD range from 5 to 14 mg/l.The maximum concentration of BOD observed at Melli downstream followed by the confluence with river Ranichu/industrial effluent discharge and at Singtam.The Total

Coliform count and Faecal Coliform count varies from 120-2400 MPN/100 ml and 11-1100 MPN/ml respectively.

The water quality of other tributary streams Subansiri, Burhidihing, Disang, Jhanji, Bhogdoi, Mora Bharali, Borak, is meeting the desired criteria for pH,DO,BOD and Conductivity, however the Total Coliform and Faecal Coliform are observed higher than the criteria in these rivers. River(s) Digboi, Bharalu, Deepar Bill, Dickchu, Maney Khola and Ranichu are having higher values of BOD,Total Coliform and Faecal Coliform in comparison to criteria limits. The highest value of BOD is observed in river(s) Bharalu (28 mg/l) followed by Ranichu (10 mg/l),Maney Khola (8 mg/l),Dickhu (7 mg/l), Deepar Bill (6mg/l) and Digboi (6mg/l). The highest count of Total Coliform and Faecal Coliform is observed in river Bharulu (TC & FC-240000), Digboi(TC & FC-240000) and Bhogdoi(TC & FC-110000) The TC and FC are not meeting the water quality criteria in river(s) Bharalu,Digboi and Bhogdoi at all the locations under monitoring programme.

The Water quality of river Brahmaputra indicates that pH and Conductivity are satisfying the water quality criteria for various uses. DO is observed in the range of 1.2-11.5 mg/l. The BOD value ranges from 0.4-3.5mg/l. The highest value of 3.5mg/l of BOD is observed at Dibrugarh and Kherghat in Assam. The COD value ranges from 4.8-27.4mg/l. The count of Fecal Coliforms ranges from 300 to 240000 MPN/100 ml whereas Total Coliforms ranges from 360-240000 MPN/100 ml. The TC are not meeting the water quality criteria at all the locations under monitoring programme.

The water quality of river Dhansiri is conforming to water quality criteria with respect to pH, DO and Conductivity. The DO varies from 2.5 to 17.3 mg/l. The BOD ranges from 0.5-10.6 mg/l. The maximum value of 10.6 mg/l of BOD is observed at Full Nagarjan, Town Boundary Bridge(Diphu Road) (6.5 mg/l), Bridge Purana Bazar (6.2 mg/l), Nutan Basti and near Check Gate, Dimapur, Khutkhuti Road. The Fecal coliform value ranges from 360-240000 MPN/100 ml whereas the Total Coliform value ranges from 1500-240000 MPN/100 ml.

The water quality of river Teesta with respect to pH varies from 5.9 to 7.0 whereas conductivity is in the range of 30-320 μmhos/cm.DO observed from 14 to 26 mg/l and BOD range from 1 to 12 mg/l. The maximum concentration of BOD observed at Melli downstream and after the confluence with river Ranichu/ industrial effluent discharge. The Total Coliform count and Faecal Coliform count varies from 40-300 MPN/100 ml and 30-340 MPN/ml respectively.

The water quality of other tributary streams Subansiri, Burhidihing, Disang, Jhanji, Bhogdoi, Mora Bharali, Borak, is meeting the desired criteria for pH,DO,BOD and Conductivity however the Total Coliform and Faecal Coliform are observed higher than the criteria in these rivers. Rivers Digboi, Bharalu, Deepar Bill, Dickchu, Maney Khola and Ranichu are having higher values of BOD in comparison to criteria limits. The highest value of BOD is observed in river(s) Bharalu (76 mg/l) followed by Ranichu (10 mg/l),Maney Khola (8 mg/l),Dickhu (6.5 mg/l), Deepar Bill (4 mg/l) and Digboi (3.4 mg/l). The highest count of Total Coliform and Faecal Coliform is observed in the rivers Bharulu and Bhogdoi.

## RIVERS IN MAHI BASIN

The Mahi basin extends over an area of 34,842 sq. km. The interstate river Mahi is 583 km long, originating in Madhya Pradesh, passing through Rajasthan and Gujarat and draining into the Gulf of Khambhat. The Mahi flows northwards initially entering into Banswara district and then turning southward flowing through Udaipur and Dungarpur districts before entering into Gujarat. In Gujarat, it flows through Panchmahal, Kheda, Vadodara and Bharuch districts before draining into the Gulf. The principal tributaries of the river are the Som from the right and the Anas and the Panam from the left. The important urban centres in the watershed of Mahi are Godhra, Vadodara, Dohad and Dadhoi in Gujarat; Ratlam, Jaora in Madhya Pradesh; and Banswara in Rajasthan.

Vadodara is a metropolitan city as well as a centre for industrial activity. In Vadodara majority of industrial units are pharmaceutical and petrochemicals, besides units of caustic soda; distillery, fertilizer, dyes and pesticides also exist. The wastewater generated by IPCL, GSFC, Gujarat refinery, GIDC, Indian Dye stuff (P) Ltd. are being discharged into the Gulf of Khambhat through the Vadodara effluent channel. Although the large Vadodara industrial complex has extended considerably to the west of the small Dhadhar creek and discharges large quantity of effluent into the tidal segment of the river Mahi, the Dhadhar has its own independent catchment area (outside Mahi Basin) inclusive of its tiny tributary Viswamitri which is extremely polluted by the effluent generated from Vadodara.

The water quality monitoring of the river Mahi and several tributaries are being done in the basin by the State Pollution Control Boards of Gujarat and Rajasthan at 9 locations. The monitoring locations are on main stream of river Mahi (7) and tributaries-Anas (1) and Panam (1).

The water quality of river Mahi with respect to pH, DO, BOD, Total Coliforms and Faecal Coliforms is meeting the desired criteria. The water quality observed at five location of Mahi river indicates that pH ranges from 7.1-9.2. The maximum value of Conductivity 5720 umhos/cm is observed at Vasad that is due to the impact of sea water in estuarine region. The DO lies in the range of 0.2 to 8.5mg/l. The minimum value of DO (0.2 mg/l) is observed at Sevalia in Gujarat. The minimum value of BOD is observed as 3 mg/l. The total Coliforms ranges from 3-2400 MPN/100 ml whereas the Fecal coliforms ranges from 3-75 MPN/100 ml. The water quality of tributaries streams Panam and Anas are confirming to the criteria for all the parameters.

The water quality of river Mahi with respect to pH, Conductivity, DO, BOD, Total Coliforms and Faecal Coliforms is meeting the desired criteria. The water quality observed at seven location of Mahi river indicates that pH ranges from 7.0-8.8. The maximum value of Conductivity 750 μmhos/cm is observed at Mahi downstream confluence with river Chap in Rajasthan.

The DO lies in the range of 2.9 to 10.1mg/l. The minimum value of DO (2.9 mg/l) is observed at Mahi at Sevalia in Gujarat.

BOD observed in the range of 0.5 to 3.5 mg/l. The total Coliforms ranges from 4-2400 MPN/100 ml whereas the Fecal coliforms range from 2-28 MPN/100 ml. The water quality of tributaries streams Panam and Anas are confirming to the criteria for all the parameters.

## RIVERS IN SABARMATI BASIN

The Sabarmati basin extends over an area of 21,674 sq km. Located in Western India, the basin covers areas in the States of Rajasthan and Gujarat. It rises in the Aravalli hills. The total length of the river from the head to its outfall into the sea is 371 km. The principal tributaries of the river are the Sei, the Wankal, the Harnay, the Hathmati, and the Vatrak and the Meshwa.

The river Sabarmati and its tributaries are all rain-fed. The rainfall being fairly low in the basin, its water wealth potential is one of the two lowest in India. The lower part of the basin has become a haven for industries and GIDC has encouraged a new gene of small and medium industries many of them being engineering and chemical units generating significant water pollution. The textile industry continues to dominate the industrial scene in Ahmedabad. In the recent times about 100 km long 30 km wide Gandhinagar-Vadodara belt is a prosperous and fast developing urban industrial area.

The river is one of the most polluted rivers in the country although it is the life line of the State of Gujarat. intensive agricultural practices coupled with intensive withdrawal of water for cropping had left the river absolutely dry after it entered the Ahmedabad city limits. The river is in a very serious state and deserves urgent attention. About 85% of the large and 87% of medium scale units of the basin are located in Ahmedabad. Besides this there are thousands of small scale industries (SSI) units engaged in diversified products mostly concentrated in various industrial states like Naroda, Odhar, Vatva, Pilas, Chandola etc. All these industries are discharging their waste waters downstream (d/s) of Sabarmati Ashram whereas M/s AECO, thermal power plant is discharging upstream (u/s) of Sabarmati Ashram.

The river Sabarmati u/s of Ahmedabad city to Sabarmati Ashram and from Sabarmati Ashram to Vautha have been identified as polluted stretches. The immense urban and industrial growth combined with growing demand of irrigation water have taken their toll as observed by the deteriorating water quality recorded particularly from Ahmedabad city to Vautha. The total length of the stretch from Ahmedabad city to Vautha is of 52 km and in the polluted river stretch: the main contributing outfalls are the Maninagar (mixed effluent) and river Khari (industrial).

The basin area of Sabarmati is covering the States of Rajasthan, Madhya Pradesh and Gujarat. The important urban centres in these Gujarat, Gandhi, Nagar, Junagadh, Ahmadabad, Surendranagar, Gandhidham, Anand, Dholka, Himatnagar, Kalol, Unjha, Viramgam and Visnagar.

The water quality monitoring of the river Sabarmati and its three tributaries are being done in the basin by the State Pollution Control Boards of Gujarat. The monitoring locations are on main stream of river Sabarmati and tributaries-Meshwa, Shedi and Khari.

The water quality of mainstream of Sabarmati with respect to pH ranges from 2.9-8.6. The lowest value of pH is observed at sabarmati after confluence with Meshwa at vautha, which indicates that the river water is highly acidic due to industrial wastewater discharges. The value of conductivity ranges from 269-13530 micromho/cm.

The DO value varies from 0.6-7.9 mg/l. The lowest value of DO is observed at railway bridge Ahemdabad due to the discharge of wastewater from the municipal and industrial sources in Ahmedabad region. The BOD ranges from 1-475mg/l. The maximum value of BOD is observed at vautha. The Total Coliform count in the river ranges from 210-2800000 MPN/100 ml whereas the Faecal Coliform count varies from 28-2800000MPN/100 ml.

The water quality of tributary streams Shedi and Khari with respect to pH varies from 2.0-8.1. The lowest value of pH is observed in river Khari at Lali village near Ahemadabad.BOD varies from 33-2320 mg/l and the highest value (2320mg/l) is in Khari river observed at Lali village near Ahemdabad.

The Total Coliform count varies from 3-24000000 MPN/100 ml whereas the Faecal Coliforms count range from 3-24000000 MPN/100 ml. Dissolved Oxygen (21.8 mg/l) observed at kheda is indicator of highly eutrophicated water in river Shedi.

### Status of River Sabarmati

The water quality of mainstream of Sabarmati with respect to pH ranges from 5.6-9.1. The lowest value of pH is observed at V.N. Bridge, Ahmedabad, the acidicity of river water is attributed to industrial wastewater discharges. The value of conductivity ranges from 278-7270 micromho/cm. The DO value varies from 1.2-7.8 mg/l. The lowest value of DO is observed at Vautha, after confluence with Meshwa. The BOD ranges from 0.6-275 mg/l. The maximum value of BOD is observed at V.N.Bridge. The Total Coliform count in the river ranges from 9-11x106 MPN/100 ml whereas the Faecal Coliform count varies from 4-46x105 MPN/100 ml.

The water quality of tributary streams Shedi and Khari with respect to pH varies from 7.3-9.1. The lowest value of pH is observed in river Khari at Lali village near Ahemadabad. The conductivity varies from 408 to 31400 micromho/cm. BOD varies from 3.1-1867 mg/l and the highest value(1867 mg/l) is also observed at Lali village near Ahemdabad. The Total Coliform count varies from 75-24x106 MPN/100 ml whereas the Faecal Coliforms count range from 20-24x106 MPN/100 ml. Dissolved Oxygen (17.5 mg/l) observed at kheda is indicator of highly eutrophicated water in the river Shedi.

## RIVERS IN NARMADA BASIN

The Narmada basin extends over an area of 98,796 sq km. Lying in the northern extremity of the Deccan plateau, the basin covers large areas in the Madhya Pradesh and Gujarat and a comparatively smaller area in Maharashtra. The Narmada Basin is bounded on the north by the Vindhya, on the east by the Maikala range, on the south by the Satpura and on the west by the Arabian Sea.

Narmada is the largest west-flowing river of the Indian peninsula. Narmada rises from Amarkantak, in the Shahdol district of Madhya Pradesh. The total length of the river from the head to its outfall into the Gulf of Khambhat is 1,312 km. Although entirely rain fed, the Narmada has a fairly heavy discharge because of moderately heavy annual average rainfall in the basin, particularly in the upper catchment area.

Urbanisation unlike in other basins has been going on in a slow pace in this basin mainly due to the river passing through hilly terrain that has made it inaccessible in most places. The major urbanisation centres are Jabalpur, Dewas and Khandwa besides Bharuch in Gujarat State.

The industrial development in the Narmada basin is lower as compared to other river basins. The industrialized districts of the Narmada basin are Dhar, Jabalpur and Bharuch consisting of clusters of pharmaceuticals, pesticides, dyes & distilleries, leather & fertilizer units whereas in Jabalpur, Khandwa and Hoshangabad the main industrial activity are the paper mills. In most of the other districts the industries are almost non-existent.

The basin area of Narmada is covering the States of Madhya Pradesh, Gujarat and Maharashtra. The important urban centres in these States are Bharuch and Ankleshwar in Gujarat; Murwara (Katni), Jabalpur, Khandwa, Betul Hoshangabad, Itarsi and Khargone in Madhya Pradesh.

The water quality monitoring of the river Narmada and its tributary stream Chota Tawa is being done in the basin by the State Pollution Control Boards of Madhya Pradesh and Gujarat.

The water quality of mainstream of Narmada with respect to pH ranges from 6.9-9.3. The conductivity ranges from 102-1341 micromho/cm. The DO varies from 5.8-9.8 mg/l. The BOD ranges from1-4 mg/l that indicate about the relatively clean stretch of entire length of the river. The Total Coliform count in the river ranges from 9-2400 MPN/100 ml whereas the Faecal Coliform count varies from 2-64 MPN/100 ml which are the lowest numbers in the major rivers being monitored under National Programme.

The Water Quality of tributary stream chota tawa with respect to DO varies from 7.7-7.8mg/l and Conductivity range fom 142-151 micromhos/cm. The number of Total Coliforms are observed in the range of 80-110 MPN/100 ml. The BOD is observed as 1 mg/l. The water quality observations indicates that all the parameters are meeting the water quality criteria.

The water quality of mainstream of Narmada with respect to pH ranges from 7.1-8.5. The conductivity ranges from 95-441 micromho/cm. The DO varies from 4.5-9.5 mg/l. The BOD ranges from 0.4-3.3 mg/l that indicate about the relatively clean stretch of entire length of the river. The Total Coliform count in the river ranges from 4-1600 MPN/100 ml whereas the Faecal Coliform count varies from 1-20 MPN/100 ml, indicates relatively low level of pollution from human waste.

The Water Quality of the tributary chota tawa with respect to DO is observed as 6.9 mg/l and Conductivity as 119 micromhos/cm. The number of Total Coliforms observed as 50 MPN/100 ml. The water quality observations indicate that all the parameters are meeting the water quality criteria.

## RIVERS IN TAPI BASIN

The Tapi basin extends over an area of 65,145 sq km. Situated in the Deccan plateau, the basin covers large areas in the States of Madhya Pradesh, Maharashtra and Gujarat.

The Tapi basin is bounded on the north by the Satpura range, on the east by the Mahadeo hills, on the south by the Ajanta range and Satmala hills and on the west by the Arabian Sea. The total length of the river from the head to its outfall into the sea is 724 km of which 228 km is in Madhya Pradesh. 228 km in Maharashtra, 214 km in Gujarat and the remaining 54 km form the common boundary between Madhya Pradesh and Maharashtra.

The Tapi receives several tributaries on both its banks. The Bhokar, the Suki, the Mor, the Harki, the Guli, the Aner, the Arunavati, the Gomai, the Gomati and the Valer join it from the right and the Puma, the Bhogvati, the Vaghur, the Girna, the Bori, the Panjhra, the Amarvati, the Shiva, the Rengavati and the Nesu join from the left. The river basin is moderately rain fed and flows through intensively farmed black cotton-soil area.

The urban population has been observed to be higher in the tail reaches of the river compared to the Upper reaches of the basin, although the proportion of the geographical areas covered to these two reaches are in reverse order. The most populous town in Tapi basin is Surat followed by Amravati and Dhule in Maharashtra.

Major part of the upper Tapi basin is predominantly agricultural but in the lower basin area industrialisation has fairly developed in M.P. the industries are centred only in one district-East Nimar (Khandwa) while in Maharashtra Jalgaon is the most industrialised area. Distillery units contribute the largest share in Maharashtra where as textile occupies the predominant activity in Gujarat followed by food & beverages and chemical industries.

The Tapi receives several tributaries on both its banks. The Bhokar, the Suki, the Mor, the Harki, the Guli, the Aner, the Arunavati, the Gomai, the Gomati and the Valer join it from the right and the Puma, the Bhogvati, the Vaghur, the Girna, the Bori, the Panjhra, the Amarvati, the Shiva, the Rengavati and the Nesu join from the left. The river basin is moderately rain fed and flows through intensively farmed black cotton-soil area. The basin area of Tapi is covering the States of Madhya Pradesh, Gujarat and Maharashtra. The important urban centres in these States are Burhanpur and Sarni in Madhya Pradesh; Akola, Malegaon, Bhusawal, Jalagon, Amaravati, Dhule, AchalpurAkot Khamgaon Malkapur in Maharashtra; and Surat in Gujarat.

The water quality monitoring of the river Tapi and tributary stream Girna is being done in the basin by the State Pollution Control Boards of Gujarat, Madhya Pradesh and Maharastra.

The water quality of mainstream of Tapi with respect to pH ranges from 7.0-9.0. The conductivity varies from 76-700 micromho/cm. The level of DO range from 4.8-8.8 mg/l. The

BOD varies from1-10 mg/l and the higher values are observed at Uphad village, Ajnad village and at Bhusawal upstream. The Total Coliform count in the river ranges from 60-2100 MPN/100 ml whereas the Faecal Coliform count varies from 2-210 MPN/100 ml.

The Water Quality of tributary stream Girna with respect to pH varies from 7.3-8.6 and DO range from 4.2-7.0mg/l. The Conductivity is observed to vary from 131-500 micromhos/ cm.BOD is in the range of 5-9 mg/l which indicate that the river is moderately polluted at Malegaon and Jalgaon.The number of Total Coliforms are observed in the range of 150-550 MPN/ 100 ml and Faecal Coliform count varies from 5-14 MPN/100 ml indicates relatively less polluted with respect to municipal sewage.

**Monitoring in Tapi Basin**

The water quality of mainstream of Tapi with respect to pH ranges from 3.1-9.2. The conductivity varies from 119-1130 micromho/cm. The levels of DO range from 3.1-10.4 mg/l. The BOD varies from1-10 mg/l and the higher value is observed at Uphad village. The Total Coliform count in the river ranges from 30-930 MPN/100 ml whereas the Faecal Coliform count varies from 2-230 MPN/100 ml.

The Water Quality of tributary stream Girna with respect to pH varies from 7.2-8.4 and DO range from 5.6-7.5 mg/l. The Conductivity is observed to vary from 230-450 micromhos/cm. BOD is in the range of 5.0-6.6 mg/l, which indicate that the river is moderately polluted at Malegaon and Jalgaon with respect to BOD. The number of Total Coliforms are observed in the range of 175-350 MPN/100 ml and Faecal Coliform count varies from 4-11 MPN/100 ml indicates relatively less polluted with respect to bacterial contamination.

The river Tapi from Nepanagar to Burhanpur is a polluted stretch in the water scarce area of Madhya Pradesh. The river has very little flow during the lean periods. The significant withdrawal of water at Nepanagar upstream has resulted in the reduction of flow of the river. The river is grossly polluted by addition of domestic and industrial wastewater from the

Nepanagar paper mills their residential colony at Nepanagar downstream besides the sewage discharged at Burhanpur downstream. Although the Nepanager paper mills, have well designed effluent treatment plant for treatment of its effluent, however the treated effluent does not meet the prescribed consent limits. The major cause of water quality deterioration is depletion of dissolved oxygen, colour due to lignin and high coliform count.

## RIVERS IN MAHANADI BASIN

The Mahanadi basin extends over an area of 141 thousands sq km. Lying in the north east of the Deccan plateau, the basin covers large areas in the States of Madhya Pradesh and Orissa, and only small areas in Bihar and Maharashtra. The upper basin is a saucer-shaped depression known as the Chhatisgarh. The Mahanadi rises in a pool, 6 km from Pharsiya village near Nagri town in Raipur district of Madhya Pradesh, and falls into the Bay of Bengal, near False point about 16 km below the confluence of the Chitarala and the Mahanadi.The total length of the river from the head to its outfall into the sea is 851 km of which 357 km are in Madhya Pradesh and the balance of 494 km are in Orissa. The Seonath, the Jonk, the Hasdeo, the Mand, the Ib, the Ong and the Tel are the principal tributaries of the Mahanadi river.

The water quality study reveals that the water of Mahanadi is comparatively less polluted compared to the other similar rivers in the country. However, certain stretches like the downstream portion of river Ib at Brajrajnagar, downstream of Sambalpur and Cuttack have comparatively higher degree of pollution.

The pollution of Ib river is easily attributable to the discharges from a large paper industry situated in Brajrajnagar. in the majority of the other locations the BOD and the total coliform are the two parameters that are mainly responsible for lowering the water quality. While at places like Takarapara this could be due to run-off from the areas adjoining the river banks that are generally used by the village people for defection.

At the urban centres, the high BOD and coliform levels are obviously due to the discharges into the river from domestic sources either directly or indirectly. None of the towns small or large, on the banks of Mahanadi have any regular sewerage system or sewage treatment plants and the domestic wastes find their way mostly through small nullah or storm water drains which join the downstream of the Ib river at Brajrajnagar causing serious depletion of oxygen level along the whole stretch which cause serious threat to the aquatic lives.

Korba has been identified as a critically polluted area in this river basin. The industrial as well as domestic wastewater are being discharged into the River Hasdeo directly as well as through river Ahiran and Dengur Nala. The major source of pollution in the river is due to Thermal Power Plants, Bharat Aluminium Company, Captive power plant of BALCO, IBP (explosive unit) and coal mining operations. The action plan formulated suggest that the capacity of ash ponds of thermal ponds of BALCO have to be augmented.

The river has often been referred to as the 'Sorrow of Orissa'. The inhabited inner basin Chattisgarh plain suffered frequent droughts whereas the fertile deltaic area has been wrecked by repeated floods.

The basin area of the Mahanadi has a large number of industrial complexes in the Orissa portion of the basin the major industries are paper. textiles and thermal power plants at Choudwar, fertiliser and breweries at Paradeep, Sugar industries of Nayagarh, Badamba, Cement industry at Bargarh, paper industry of Brajrajnagar, coal mining areas of Rampur and lb valley, and an aluminium smelter at Hirakud.

Most of these industries are located on the banks of the river Mahanadi or its tributaries and distributaries, which are used to carry the industrial effluents and wastewater from these industries. From the point of view of significant environmental impacts, the important medium scale industries are the chemical, textile, paper, cement, and leather tanning which consume large quantities of water. Iron and steel industry at Bhilai, cement industries at Durg and Raipur, textile industry of Rajnandagaon, aluminium and thermal power plants at

Korba are the major polluting industries in the State of M.P. that falls in the river basin. All these major units are located on the river banks of Seonath, Kharoon and Hasdeo. The medium scale industries include chemical and distilleries of Durg,cement industries of Raipur, Iron and steel of Urla, paper industries of Bilaspur and many other agro based industries.

All the industries are discharging their wastewater either directly or indirectly to river Mahanadi as well as its tributaries. The vast mineral and human resources of the basin besides power generation infrastructure has resulted in a growth of a large variety of industries. The industries using the river bodies as the ultimate sink need to establish effluent treatment plants so that the designated best use of the river is sustained.

The basin area of Mahanadi is covering the States of Chhattisgarh, Madhya Pradesh, Orissa and Jharkhand. The important urban centres in these States are Rajnandgaon Madhya Pradesh Korba Bilaspur Durg Raipur Dhamtari Madhya Pradesh Raigarh Rajharajharandalli in Madhya Pradesh & Chhattisgarh.

Cuttack Bhubaneshwar Puri Sambalpur Jatani Balangir Orissa Bargarh Bhawanipatna, Brajarajnagar Jharsuguda in Orissa.

The water quality monitoring of the river Mahanadi and its several tributaries are being done in the basin by the State Pollution Control Boards of Chhatissgarh, Madhya Pradesh and Orissa at 29 locations.

The water quality of mainstream of Mahanadi with respect to pH ranges from 7.3-8.9. The value of conductivity ranges from 114 at Hirakund Reservoir to 15940 micromho/cm at Paradeep downstream. The DO value varies from 1.3-10.4 mg/l. The BOD ranges from 1-8 mg/l. The highest value of Total Coliform (30,000 MPN/100 ml) and Faecal Coliform (17,000 MPN/100 ml) is observed at Cuttack downstream due to discharge of untreated sewage from Cuttack city and at Sambhalpur downstream.

The Water Quality of tributary stream Seonath with respect to DO varies from 5.9-8.0mg/l and Conductivity range from

151-379 micromhos/cm. The number of Total Coliforms is observed in the range of 9-2400 MPN/100 ml. The BOD is observed in the range of 1-2.9 mg/l. The water quality observations indicates that all the parameters are meeting the water quality criteria except river Kharoon a tributary of Seonath is a relatively clean river as the BOD is observed below 2 mg/l and maximum number of Total Coliform as 93 MPN/100 ml.

The tributary stream Hasdeo is flowing through Korba and Champa townships however the maximum BOD concentration of BOD is observed 3 mg/l and Total Coliform number does not exceed 220 MPN/100 ml indicates that due to enough dilution in river impact of wastewater discharged from Korba does not affect its quality.Another tributary stream Ib maintains adequate level of DO in the range of 6.8-9.8 mg/l and BOD is observed in the range of 1-4 mg/l.The Total and Faecal Coliform numbers are varying from 40-16000 and 40-3000 MPN/100 ml respectively. The level of DO in other three tributaries Kuakhai, Kathjodi and Birupa is in the range of 6.1-9.9 and BOD level varies from 2-6 mg/l.The Total and Faecal Coliform are varying from 90-35000 and 80-22000 MPN/100 ml in these tributaries. Kuakhai D/S of Bhubaneshwar and Kathanodi D/S of Cuttack are not meeting the criteria limit in respect of BOD and Total Coliform.

The water quality of mainstream of Mahanadi with respect to pH ranges from 6.5-8.6. The value of conductivity ranges from 77 μmoh/cm at Tikarpada to 83600 μmoh/cm at Paradeep downstream. The high conductivity at Paradeep can be attributed to high salinity of water due to estuarine region. The DO value varies from 4.7-10.1 mg/l. The BOD ranges from 0.3-5.6 mg/l and the highest value was observed D/S of paradeep. The highest value of Faecal Coliform count (28,000 MPN/100 ml) is observed at Sambalpur downstream and at Paradeep downstream; whereas the Total Coliform count (35,000 MPN/100 ml) is observed at Sambalpur downstream, Paradeep downstream and at Cuttack downstream due to discharge of untreated sewage. The concentrations of Nitrite ($NO_2^-$) range from 0.001-4.9 mg/l. The high nitrite concentrations (mg/l) of

4.9, 3.41 and 3.0 are observed at Cuttack downstream, Sambalpur downstream and Cuttack upstream respectively. Concentrations of Nitrate (NO3-) ranges from 0.001-2.584 mg/l, while the highest concentration of nitrate (2.584mg/l) is recorded at Paradeep downstream.

The Water Quality of tributary stream Seonath with respect to DO varies from 6.3-8.2 mg/l and Conductivity range from 120-425 micromhos/cm. The number of Total Coliforms is observed in the range of 7-2400 MPN/100 ml. The BOD is observed as in the range of 0.8-2.2 mg/l. Ammonical Nitrogen (NH4-N) concentration ranges between 0.091-0.446 mg/l. The water quality observations indicate that all the parameters are meeting the water quality criteria. River Kharoon, a tributary of Seonath is a relatively clean river as the BOD is observed below 2 mg/l and maximum number of Total Coliform count as 80 MPN/100 ml.

The tributary stream Hasdeo is flowing through Korba and Champa townships however, the maximum BOD concentration (3.3 mg/l) is observed at upstream of Korba and Total Coliform number does not exceed 350 MPN/100 ml indicates that due to enough dilution in river, impact of wastewater discharged from Korba does not affect its quality. Another tributary stream Ib maintains adequate level of DO in the range of 6.0-14.2 mg/l and BOD is observed in the range of 0.3-3.5 mg/l. The Total and Faecal Coliform numbers are varying from 230-22000 and 130-7900 MPN/100 ml respectively.

The three tributaries of Mahanadi Kuakhai, Kathajodi and Birupa are meeting the water quality criteria with respect to pH, conductivity and Dissolved Oxygen (D.O). The level of DO is in the range of 4.5-10.6 mg/l and the BOD levels vary from 0.7-5.1 mg/l. The highest level of BOD is observed in Kuakhai at Bhubaneshwar D/S and in Kathajodi at Cuttak downstream. The Total and Faecal Coliform are varying from 500-92000 MPN/100 ml and 230-24000 MPN/100 ml in these tributaries. The concentrations of Nitrite ($NO_2$-) range from 0.001-3.9 mg/l. The high nitrite concentration is observed at Choudwar in Birupa tributary. The concentration of Nitrate ($NO_3$-) ranges from 0.001-1.724 mg/l while the highest concentration of nitrate (3.9 mg/l) is recorded in Kuakhai tributary at Bhubaneswar downstream.

## RIVERS IN BRAHMANI AND BAITARNI BASIN

The Brahmani-Baitarani basin extends over an area of 51,822 sq km. Lying in the northeast of the Deccan Plateau, the basin covers large areas in the States of Orissa and Jharkhand and a small area in Madhya Pradesh. The Chhotanagpur Plateau on the west and south bound the basin on the north by the ridge separating it from the Mahanadi basin, and on the east by the Bay of Bengal. The Brahmani sub-basin covers an area of 39,033 sq km while the Baitarani sub-basin covers an area of 12,789 sq km.

The Brahmani known as the South Koel, in the upper reaches, rises near Nagri village in the Ranchi district of Jharkhand State. The total length of the river from the head to its outfall into the Bay of Bengal is 799 km of which 258 km is in Jharkhand and 541 km is in Orissa. The Baitarni river rises in the hill ranges of Keonjhar district of Orissa at an elevation of about 900 meters and has a length of about 355 km. Both the rivers outfall in the Bay of Bengal, forming a common delta. The important tributaries of Brahmani are, the Karo, the Sankh and the Tirka and those of Baitarni are the Salandi and the Matai.

The industrial complex of Angul Talcher has been identified as a critically polluted area in the Brahmani basin. The wasteweaters generated form the industries Viz, NALCO, TTPS, FCI, Orichem and mining operations are primarily responsible for deterioration of water quality of Nandira river which is a tributary stream of Brahmani river. Detailed survey of this stretch has been carried out and the action plans have been formulated to improve the water quality of this stretch.

The basin area of Brahmani and Baitarni is covering the States of Jharkhand, and Orissa.The important urban centres in these States are Raurkela in Orissa; and Gumia in Jharkhand

The water quality monitoring of the river Brahmani, Baitarni and tributaries are being done in the basin by the

State Pollution Control Boards of Jharkhand and Orissa at 20 locations. There are eleven (11) monitoring locations on the main stream of river Brahmani, five on tributary Baitarni, one each on tributaries Karo and Sankh; and two on tributary stream Koel.

The water quality of mainstream of Brahmani with respect to pH and DO are meeting the desired criteria. BOD is exceeding the criteria limit at downstream of Pamposh (4-6 mg/l), Rourkela (3-4 mg/l) and Kamalanga (3-4 mg/l) due to wastewater discharges from the industrial and residential complexes of Rourkela and Talcher. The Total Coliform numbers are observed higher than the criteria at downstream of Pamposh (930-90000 MPN/100 ml), Rourkela (750-22000 MPN/100 ml), Kamalanga (2800-9000 MPN/100 ml), Bhuban(700-11000 MPN/100 ml) and Dharamashala (600-11000 MPN/100 ml).

The corresponding number of Faecal Coliform is also observed high on the same locations in the river. The water quality of tributary streams Sankh, Koel and Karo is meeting the criteria with respect to pH, DO, BOD and Total Coliform.However Faecal Coliform are found upto 700 MPN/100 ml in Sankh and Koel; and upto 330 MPN/100 ml in river Karo indicates that the tribuataries are receiving wastewater or the contribution is from open defecation. Conductivity ranges from 81 to 376 micromhos/cm in river Brahmani that is suitable for irrigation as well as drinking purpose after treatment and disinfection.

The water quality of major tributary streams Baitarni observed at 5 locations is meeting the criteria for pH and DO however BOD is exceeding the criteria at Chandbali (3-5 mg/l) and Dhamra (3-7mg/l). The Total coliform varies from 900-22000 MPN/100 ml whereas fecal coliform varies from 110-11000 MPN/100 ml. The Total coliform is not meeting the criteria at Anandpur, Jajpur , Chandbali and Dhamra. The conductivity value varies from 54 to 78400 micro mho/cm. The very high value of conductivity is observed at Dhamra which is in the estuarine zone of the river.

The water quality of mainstream of Brahmani with respect to pH, DO and conductivity are meeting the desired criteria.

The BOD varies from 0.2 to 6.0 mg/l. The highest value of BOD is observed at downstream of Panposh in Orissa, due to wastewater discharges from the industrial and residential complexes of Rourkela and Talcher.

The Fecal Coliform (FC) count ranges from 60 to 14x103 MPN/100 ml whereas the Total Coliform (TC) count ranges from 90 to 24x103 MPN/100 ml. The highest values of FC and TC are observed at downstream of Panposh in Orissa. The nitrite (NO2-) ranges from 0.001-2.355 mg/l. The highest value of nitrite is observed at Rourkela downstream in Orissa. Nitrate (NO3-) values ranges from 0.012-7.056 mg/l. The high concentration of nitrate, 7.056 mg/l, 6.43 mg/l and 5.733 mg/l are observed at upstream of Panposh, downstream of Panposh and at Rengali in Orissa respectively.

The water quality of major tributary streams Baitarni observed at 5 locations is meeting the water quality criteria for pH and DO and conductivity however, The high values of conductivity are observed at Chand Bali (8540 μmoh/cm) and at Dhamra (54802 μmoh/cm) due to estuarine region of the river. BOD values are observed in the range of 0.3-3.5 mg/l and the high BOD is observed at Dhamra. The Fecal Coliform (FC) count ranges from 230 to 9x103 MPN/100 ml whereas the Total Coliform (TC) count ranges from 330 to 16x103 MPN/100 ml. It is observed that the highest values of FC and TC are observed at Dhamra in Orissa. The nitrite (NO2-) values ranges from 0.001-4.932 mg/l. The highest concentrations of nitrite are observed at Jajpur (4.932 mg/l) and at Dhamra (4.479 mg/l) in Orissa. Nitrate ($NO_3$-) values ranges from 0.002-0.48 mg/l. The highest concentration of nitrate, 0.48 mg/l is observed at Dhamra in Orissa.

## RIVERS IN SUBARNAREKHA BASIN

The Subarnarekha rises near Nagri village in the Ranchi district. Of its total length 269 km are in Jharkhand and 64 km in West Bengal and 62 in Orissa. The river drains a total area of 19,296 sq km. The Subarnarekha is the smallest of the basins and is falling short only marginally to be called a 'major basin'. It has virtually no significant tributary; the tiny Kharkai has gained a name only because of its support to the Jamshedpur steel city.

The river Subarnarekha passes through an important industrial belt of Bihar. The industries like Heavy Engineering Corporation, Usha Martin Industries, MECON, SAIL (P&D) in Ranchi, Indian Aluminium Industries at Mari, Tata Steel, TELCO, Indian Tube Company, Tin Plate (of India), Tata Pigments in Jamshedpur, and Hindustan Copper Ltd. and Uranium Corporation of India in Ghatshila, are existing in the basin.

The river is basically a rainfed peninsular river with the wet months being June to September. The river in its upper and middle reaches remains more or less as a stagnant pool, often highly charged with pollutants, particularly during dry periods. The largest concentration of population is located in the Singbhum and Ranchi districts of Bihar. The river and its tributaries are the main sources of urban water supply with the ground water resources still under utilized. Nearly 60 percent of the water supplies eventually find their way to surface water systems. Some of the important towns are also significant industrial centres. As per the river basin survey report the urban wastewater in the Subarnarekha basin has a biochemical oxygen demand (BOD) as high as 211 mg/1. None of the towns except partly for Jamshedpur and Tatanagar railway colony have wastewater treatment facility worth mentioning.

The Subarnarekha being a mineral rich area, it is natural that mining activity would always be an important element in the pollution control programme. The possibility of contamination of surface and ground water derived from the ore dumps and radioactive waste materials in the uranium mines at Jaduguda is very great. The organic pollution load in the urban area is largely domestic and as per the river basin survey report nearly 69% of the total organic load (BOD) was contributed by the domestic effluents and the remaining originated from industrial effluents.

River Subarnarekha from Hatia to Bahragora in the Bihar State has been identified as polluted river stretch under the proposed National River Action Plan. Intensive study of the polluted stretch has been carried out and it has been observed that the water quality of Subarnarekha river has deteriorated mainly due to discharge of untreated, domestic and industrial effluent. The level of Dissolved Oxygen in the river from Hatia Dam to Baharagora is observed in the range of 1.0 mg/l with lowest value at D/S of Mango town. Similarly biochemical oxygen demand (BOD) was found in the range of 0.2 mg/l to 70 mg/l with the highest value at D/S of Mano town. The total coliform count was observed in the ranges of 140 MPN/100 ml to 2.7x105 MPN/100 ml with a highest value at Bahragora. The basin area of Subarnerekha is covering the States of Jharkhand and Orissa. The important urban centres in these states are Jamshedpur, Chaibasa and Ranchi in Jharkhand; and Bhadrak in Orissa.

The water quality monitoring of the river Subarnarekha are being done in the basin by the State Pollution Control Boards of Jharkhand and Orissa at 5 locations. The monitoring locations are on mainstream of river Subarnerekha.

The water quality observed at five locations on Subarnarekha river indicates that pH and DO are meeting the desired water quality criteria at almost all locations. DO was observed 3.4 mg/l at Jamshedpur on one occasion and does not meet the criteria of 4 mg/l whereas the BOD is higher than the criteria at Jamshedpur (12 mg/l) in Jharkhand. The BOD value observed between 1 to 12 mg/l. The Total Coliform number varies from 150-1800 MPN/100 ml whereas the Faecal Coliform number ranges from 70-540 MPN/100 ml. The conductivity ranges from 113 to 355 micromho/cm. The above ranges indicate that expect BOD at Jamshedpur, all parameters are meeting the desired water quality criteria.

The water quality of Subarnarekha river with respect to pH, D.O and Conductivity during the year indicates that it is meeting the desired water quality criteria in Orissa. DO is observed in the range of 6.4-8.4 mg/l. The highest BOD value is observed (2 mg/l) at Rajghat. The highest Total Coliform (7900 MPN/100 ml) and Fecal Coliform (3300 MPN/100 ml) number observed at Rajghat indicate wastewater discharges in the river. The highest concentration of Nitrite ($NO_2$-) is observed as 0.086 mg/l and the maximum concentration of Nitrate ($NO_3^-$) is observed as 0.896 mg/l.

## RIVERS IN GODAVARI BASIN

The Godavari basin extends over an area of 3,12,812 sq km which is nearly 10 percent of the total geographical area of the country. The basin lies in the Deccan plateau, and covers large areas in the States of Andhra Pradesh, Madhya Pradesh, Chattisgarh and Maharashtra, in addition to smaller areas in Karnataka and Orissa.

The Godavari basin is bounded on the north by the Satmala Hills, the Ajanta Range and the Mahadeo Hills, on the south and east by the Eastern Ghats and on the west by the Western Ghats. The Godavari is the largest river of the Penninsular India, inspite of its massive catchment area, the discharge is not very impressive because of moderate annual average rainfall in the basin. Its four important tributaries are the Manjira, the Pranhita, the Indravati and the Sabari. The wastewater generation from domestic (both rural and urban) and the industrial sector are the main sources of pollution in the river basin.

Amongst the five states Orissa State is least industrialized followed by M.P. and Karnataka, with Maharashtra having the high urban industrial pockets. Most of the industrial activities are centred mainly at Aurangabad & Nasik in Maharashtra, East & West Godavari Distt. in Andhra Pradesh Sugar and distillery units are large in number in Maharashtra followed by pharmaceuticals, leather, pulp and paper and pesticide units. Whereas in A.P. sugar, distillery units are large in number followed by Pulp & Paper, fertiliser industries. The above mentioned industries are massive water consuming by nature and the deterioration in water quality in the river cannot be ruled out particularly from Nashik to Nanded in Maharashtra and at Baster, in Chattisgarh and Burganpad in Andhra Pradesh.

The basin area of Godavari is covering the States of Maharashtra, Madhya Pradesh, Chhastisgarh, Jharkhand, Andhra Pradesh, Karnataka and Orissa. The important urban centers in these states are Nagpur, Ambejogai, Ballarpur, Bhandara, Buldhana, Chalisgaon, Hinganghat, Hingoli, Manmad Nandurbar Osmandabad Parli Pusad Shrirampur Udgir Latur Kamptee Ahmadnagar Parbhani Aurangabad Wardha Bid Nashik Chandrapur Jalna Nanded Yavatmal, Amalner and Gondiya in Maharashtra; Jagdalpur in Chhatisgarh, Chiklikalan Parasia ,Chindwara Seoni Balaghat in Madhya Pradesh, Rajahmundry Nizamabad Ramagundam Eluru Warangal Khammam Kothagudem Karimnagar Bhimavaram Kakinada Adilabad , Bellampalle Bodhan Jagtial Kagaznagar Mancherial Mandamarri Narsapur Nirmal Palacole Palwancha Sangareddy Siddipet Siricilla Tadepalligudem and Tanuku in Andhra Pradesh; Bidar in Karnataka; and Jeypur in Orissa

The water quality monitoring of the river Godavari are being done in the basin by the State Pollution Control Boards of Maharashtra, Andhra Pradesh, Madhya Pradesh and Orissa at 20 locations. The monitoring locations are on main stream of river Godavari (11) and tributaries Manjeera(2), Maner(2), Nira(1), Wainganga(3), and Wardha (1).

The water quality of river Godavari on eleven locations indicates that the DO value ranges from 3.2-10.9 mg/l. The minimum value of 3.2 mg/l of DO is observed at Nasik D/S in Maharashtra.

The BOD value ranges from 1-78 mg/l and the highest value is observed at Nanded in Maharashtra. The Fecal Coliforms ranges from 3-3640 MPN/100 ml whereas the Total Coliform ranges from 8 to 5260 MPN/100 ml. At Rajahmundry downstream, maximum number of Total and Faecal Coliform are observed due to the proximity of large city.

The Water Quality of tributaries steams Manjeera, Maner,Wardha, Weinganga and Nira indicates that expect BOD other parameters like pH,DO,TC and FC are meeting the desired water quality criteria. The DO ranges from 9.0-11.6mg/l.BOD ranges from 1-12 mg/l. The maximum value of BOD is observed on weinganga tributary at ashti and on river Nira at Pulgaon Cotton Mills,Wardha.The other rivers observed with higher level of BOD are Maner at Somnapalli, (11 mg/l) Wardha at

Rajura Bridge and Wainganga at Balaghat (6.0 mg/l). The Total Coliform number ranges from 11-2400 MPN/100 ml whereas the Faecal Coliform are observed from 3-410 MPN/100 ml.

The river Godavari from downstream of Nashik to Nanded and Nanded city limits in Maharashtra and upstream of Bhadrachalam at Mancheral and Ramgundam in A.P. have been identified as the polluted river stretches to be taken up under the proposed National River Action Plan. The major sources of pollution in the polluted stretches are from domestic and industrial wastewater generated from the Nashik and Nanded cities in Maharashtra and Mancherial, Ramgundam and Bhadrachalam cities in Andhra Pradesh.

Depletion of dissolved oxygen has been reported due to addition of high organic load into the river besides bacteriological pollution has also been reported. To maintain the desired water quality uses of the Godavari river in these stretches, the municipalities need to treat their wastewater and the industries to install effluent treatment plants (ETP) before discharging into the rivers for sustaining the desired level of water quality.

The water quality of river Godavari on eleven locations indicates that the DO value ranges from 3.2-9.3 mg/l. The minimum value of 3.2 mg/l of DO is observed at Panchavati at Ramkund. The BOD values ranges from 1.7-53 mg/l and the highest value is observed at Panchavati at Ramkund. The Fecal Coliforms ranges from 4-1400 MPN/100 ml whereas the Total Coliform ranges from 70-68200 MPN/100 ml. At Rajahmundry downstream, maximum number of Total and Faecal Coliform are observed due to the proximity of large city.

The Water Quality of tributaries steams Manjeera, Maner, Wardha, Weinganga and Nira indicates that expect BOD other parameters like pH, DO, TC and FC are meeting the desired water quality criteria. The DO ranges from 4.2-8.7 mg/l. BOD ranges from 1-9 mg/l. The higher values of BOD are observed on weinganga tributary at ashti and on river Nira at Pulgaon Cotton Mills, Wardha. The other locations with higher levels of BOD are river Maner at Warangal upstream in Andhra Pradesh, Wardha at Rajura Bridge and Manjeera river near Ganapathi Sugars, Medak District, Andhra Pradesh. The Total

Coliform number ranges from 11-8x104 MPN/100 ml whereas the Faecal Coliform are observed from 4-18400 MPN/100 ml.

## RIVERS IN KRISHNA BASIN

The Krishna basin extends over an area of 2,58,948 sq km which is nearly 8% of the total geographical area of the country. Lying in the Deccan plateau, it covers large areas in the States of Maharashtra, Karnataka and Andhra Pradesh. All the major tributaries draining the base of the triangle fall into the river in the upper two-thirds of its length.The Krishna rises in the Western Ghats at an altitude of 1,337 meter just north of Mahabaleshwar, about 64 km from the Arabian Sea and flows from west to east through the States of Maharashtra, Karnataka and Andhra Pradesh to join the Bay of Bengal. The total length of the river from the source to its outfall into the sea is about 1,400 km. Together with its tributaries, the river drains about 708 km of the Western Ghats which is its chief source of supply. The Krishna is the third longest river within India, yet it has a rather poor water wealth because of fairly low rainfall in the basin. The river has two large tributaries-the Bhima and the Tungabhadra and four smaller tributaries-the Ghataprabha, the Malprabha the Musi and the Muneru. The river basin survey report communicates that the most populous cities in the basin are Hyderabad Aggomeration in A.P. Pune aggomeration in Maharashtra and Bhadravati complex in Karnataka.Bhadravati in Karnataka and Patancheru-Bolaram in Andhra Pradesh are the critically polluted areas identified in the basin area of Krishna.

For Bhadravati the major source of water pollution is the wastewater generated from M/s Mysore Paper Mills Ltd., M/s Visveswariya Iron and Steel Ltd., besides the untreated sewge of the town, which is being discharged into Bhadra. It is suggested that sewage treatment plant may be provided for the sewage of the town and ETPs of the existing industries need modifications to comply with prescribed standards for restoration of water quality of the Bhadra river.In the Patancheru-Bolaram area in A.P. the effluent generated by M/s Voltas Ltd., Standard Agencies Ltd., Reliance Cellulose, NSL,

Dr. Reddys laboratories (units I & II), and A.P. metallurgy Engg. and M/s Taurus Chemicals (P) Ltd., Bolaram are the main sources of water pollution in the rivers Manpera and Nakkvagu. These industries are polluting ground water also.

The basin area of Krishna is covering the States of Maharashtra, Andhra Pradesh, and Karnataka. The important urban centres in Andhra Pradesh are Guntakal, Guntur, Hyderabad, Kurnool, Gudivada, Tenali, Machilipatnam, Vijayawada, Adoni, Mahaboob-Nagar, Bapatla, Chilakaluripet, Gudur, Kavali, Miryalguda, Nalgonda, Suryapet, Yemmiganur, Chikmagalur, Gangawati, Gokak, Harihar, Nipani, Rabkavi-Banhatti, Ranibennur, Shahabad; in Karnataka are Gadag-betagiri, Raichur, Hubli-Dharwad, Shimoga, Bijapur, Bellary, Gulbarga, Bhadravati, Hosepet, Davangere, Belgaum, Chitradurga, Bagalkot; and in Maharashtra are Karad, Pandharpur, Panvel, Satara, Kolhapur, Solapur, Pune, Ichalkaranji, Sangli and Barshi.

The water quality monitoring of the river Krishna are being done in the basin by the State Pollution Control Boards of Maharashtra, Karnataka and Andhra Pradesh at 46 locations. The monitoring locations are on main stream of river Krishna (17) and tributaries Bhadra (3), Bhima (9), Ghataprabha (2), Malprabha (3), Muneru (1), Musi (2), Nira (1), Paleru (1), Tunga (1), Tungabhadra (5) and Panchganga (1).

The water quality of Krishna river on 17 locations indicates that pH and DO are broadly meeting the water quality criteria. DO varies from 2.9 to 10.9 mg/l. The minimum value of 2.9 mg/l of DO is observed at Hamsaladeevi.

The BOD ranges from 1 to 10 mg/l. The maximum value of 10 mg/l of BOD is observed at Krishna Bridge, Karad and at Sangli in Maharashtra. The Faecal Coliform ranges from 3-10000 MPN/100 ml whereas the Total Coliforms ranges from 17-33300 MPN/100 ml. The maximum value of TC is observed at downstream of Devasagar Bridge in Karnataka and other locations not meeting the criteria are at downstream of Narayanpura Dam, Tintini Bridge, Thangadi and Gadwal Bridge.

The water quality of tributary streams Bhima, Panchaganga, Ghatprabha, Malprabha, Nira,Tungbhadhra, Tunga, Bhadra, Musi, Pallaru and Munreu indicates that pH ranges from 5.5 to 9.8. The lowest value of pH is observed at downstream of KIOCL road bridge near Holehonnur. The conductivity value ranges from 24 to 3880 micromho/cm. The maximum value of 3880 micromho/cm is observed in river Bhima at Narsinghpur, Maharashtra. DO varies from 0.5 to 11.5mg/l. The minimum value of DO is observed in Bhima at Pune downstream of Bundgarden in Maharashtra. The BOD value ranges from 1-58 mg/l. The maximum value of BOD is observed in Bhima at Pune downstream of Bundgarden. The Faecal coliforms ranges from 3-10000 MPN/100 ml whereas the Total Coliform number ranges from 13 to 230000 MPN/100 ml.

The water quality of Krishna river on 16 locations indicates that pH and DO are meeting the water quality criteria except at Hamsala Deevi in Guntur district of Andhra Pradesh. DO varies from 0.7 to 12.6 mg/l. The minimum value of 0.7 mg/l of DO is observed at Hamsaladeevi. The BOD concentrations range from 0.5 to 17 mg/l. The maximum value of 17 mg/l of BOD is observed at Krishna Bridge Karad in Maharashtra. The Faecal Coliform ranges from 2-2x104 MPN/100 ml whereas the Total Coliforms ranges from 6-7x105 MPN/100 ml. The maximum number of FC & TC are observed in river Krishna at Wadapally after confluence with river Musi in Andhra Pradesh. The water quality of tributary streams Bhima, Panchaganga, Ghatprabha, Malprabha, Nira,Tungbhadhra, Tunga, Bhadra, Musi, Pallaru and Munreu indicates that pH ranges from 6.1 to 9.8. The conductivity ranges from 25 to 2750 micromho/cm. The maximum value of 2750 micromho/cm is observed in river Musi down stream at Hyderabad. DO varies from 1.3 to 10.5 mg/l. The minimum value of DO is observed in Musi upstream at Hyderabad in Andhra Pradesh. The BOD value ranges from 0.1-84 mg/l. The maximum value of BOD (84 mg/l) is observed in Bhima at Pune downstream of Bundgarden.

The other locations having high BOD on Bhima are Pune upstreadm (80 mg/l), Bhima at Pargaon after confluence with Mula and Mutha (18 mg/l), Bhim after confluence with river

Daund and at Takli. River Panchganga at Ichalkaranji (6.6 mg/l), river Nira at Sarole Bridge (13.0 mg/l), river Tunga D/S of Shimoga Town (5.7 mg/l), Bhadra at Maleshwaram D/S of KIOCL (7.0 mg/l), Bhadra at D/S of Bhadravati and river Musi at upstream of Hyderabad (8.0 mg/l) and D/S of Hyderabad (35.0 mg/l) are potentially polluted locations having higher BOD levels. The Faecal coliforms range from 3-4000 MPN/100 ml whereas the Total Coliform number ranges from 5-44x103 MPN/100 ml. The maximum number of Total Coliform (44x103 MPN/100 ml) is observed at Bhima at Gangapur village in Karnataka. The major contributor to pollution from community source, in Maharashtra is from Pune City. The largest industrial pollution loads in the Maharashtra part of the basin comes from the Pimpri Chinchwada New Corporation part of Pune Urban Agglomeration. In Karnataka, the Harihar Polyfibres Ltd., at Harihar in Dharwad district discharge their wastewaters into the river Tungabhadra. The wastewater is generally treated but still the residual BOD present in the treated effluents add significant quantities of organic loads into Tungabhadra. Community wastes from Harihar town are also discharged into the river without any treatment. Part of the Davangere wastewater, is also discharged into the river in the same reach. The Bhadra River in Karnataka is also affected badly due to discharge of industrial effluents from M/s Mysore Paper Mills, Visveswariah Iron and Steel Limited. in Andhra Pradesh, the major pollution is from the industrial complex at Rangareddy and a number of distilleries situated at Vijaywada on the bank of Krishna.

In the Krishna Basin five polluted river stretches have been identified for improving water quality under the proposed National River Action Plan for restoration of water quality to the desired level. These stretches are on the main stem of the river Krishna; (a) from Karad to Sangli (b) Dhom Dam to Narsarobadi in Maharashtra; (c) upto Nagarjuna Sagar dam and from the Dam to upstream of Repella in Andhra Pradesh; (d) on river Nira, tributary stream in Maharashtra. The detail survey of the two stretches namely 'Karad to Sangli, and "Tirthahalli to confluence with Bhadra" on river Tunga have been carried out and the Action Plans are being prepared to control the pollution caused by wastewaters from the domestic as well as industrial sectors for restoration of water quality in river Krishna and its tributaries.

## RIVERS IN PENNERU BASIN

The Penneru basin extends over an area of 55,213 sq km. Located in Peninsular India, it covers areas in the States of Karnataka and Andhra Pradesh. The total length of the river from the head to its outfall into the sea is 597 km of which about 61 km are in Karnataka and the balance of 536 km are in Andhra Pradesh. The principal tributaries of the river are, the Jayamangali, the Kunderu and the Sagilery from the left and the Chitravati, the Papagni and the Cheyyeru from the right. The Penneru river has the lowest average flow, due to low annual average rainfall. The meagre water wealth of the basin has been utilized only for limited irrigational use, and additional support had to be obtained from the adjoining R.Krishna through the Kurnool-Cuddapah (K.C.) and Tungabhadra canals. The Penneru and its tributaries do not have enough flow to support direct abstraction for larger towns so; infiltration-wells are used for most of the riverside towns. Only Nandyal town abstracts from the K.C. canal.

Major industries situated on the banks of the Penneru river are Circar Paper Mills, Kovoor Straw Board , Nellore Straw Board and Sugar industry. The pollution abatement measures like sewage treatment plants for treating municipal wastewater and effluent treatment plants for industries should be established so that indiscriminate discharge of raw effluent directly into the river body shall not interfere with the designated best uses of the river Penneru. The basin area of Penneru is covering the States of Karnataka and Andhra Pradesh, The important urban centres in Andhra Pradesh are Proddatur, Hindupur, Anantapur, Cuddapah, Nellore, Nandyal, Dharmavarm, Kadiri, Madanapalle, Rayachoti and Tadipatri.

### Monitoring in Penneru Basin

The water quality monitoring of the river Penneru are being done in the basin by the State Pollution Control Board of Andhra Pradesh at 4 locations. The monitoring locations are on main stream of river Penneru (4). The water quality observed at four locations on Pennar river indicates that pH, DO,BOD and Total Coliform are meeting the desired water quality criteria at all locations.DO observed in the range of 6.0-9.3 mg/l whereas the BOD varies from 1-3 mg/l. The Total Coliform number varies from 460-1100 MPN/100 ml. The conductivity in the river water range from 364-978 micromhos/cm.

### Status of River Penneru during the Year 2003

The water quality observed at four locations on Pennar river indicates that pH, DO,BOD and Total Coliform are meeting the desired water quality criteria at all locations. DO observed in the range of 5.7-8.4 mg/l whereas the BOD varies from 1-6.3 mg/l. The Total Coliform number varies from 58-1100 MPN/100 ml. The conductivity of river water ranges from 387-987 micromhos/cm.

## RIVERS IN CAUVERY BASIN

The Cauvery Basin extends over an area of 87,900 sq km in the States of Kerala, Karnataka and Tamil Nadu. The total length of the river from the head to its outfall into the sea is 800 km of which about 320 km are in Karnataka 416 km in Tamil Nadu and the remaining length of 64 km forms the common boundary between the States of Karnataka and Tamil Nadu.

The important tributaries which join the Cauvery within the Karnataka State are the Harangi , the Hemavati, the Shimsha and the Arkavati on the north (left bank) and the and the Lakshmantirtha, the Kabani or Kapila and the Suvarnavati on the south (right bank). In the south (right bank), they are the Bhavani, the Noyil and the Amaravati.

The delta of Kaveri is so matured that the main river Kaveri has virtually lost its link with the sea, while Coleroon, the main distributaries, bears the brunt of the burden of flow. Like other rivers of South India, the Kaveri too has a rather limited water wealth because of moderate to low rainfall in the basin.

The basin area of Cauvery is covering the States of Karnataka and Tamil Nadu, The important urban centres in these states are Tumkur, Mandya, Mangalore, Mysore, Hassan, Bangalore, Channapatna, Dod, Ballapur, Ramanagaram, in Karnataka;Karaikal in Pondichery; Valparai, Tamilnadu, Pollachi, Coimbatore, Erode, Thanjavur, Karur, Tiruchirappalli, Salem, Kumbakonam, Bhavani, Chidambaram,Coonoor, Devershola, Mannargudi, Mayiladuthurai, Mettuppalaiyam Nagappattinam, Pattukkottai, Pudukkottai, Tiruchengodu, Udhagamandalam, Udumalaippettai, Villupum in Tamil Nadu.

Industrial activity is also high in this basin, particularly in the Bangalore area (Karnataka) and the towns Mettur and Coimbatore in the Tamil Nadu State, followed by the districts of Mysore and Mandya in Karnataka and Periyar and Salem in Tamil Nadu.

The water quality monitoring of the river Cauvery is being done in the basin by the State Pollution Control Board Karnataka, Tamil Nadu and Kerala at 35 locations. The monitoring locations are on main stream of river Cauvery (20) and on tributaries are-Arkavati (1), Amravati (1), Bhawani (5), Kabini (4), Laxmantirtha (1), Shimsa (2), Hemavati (1). The Water Quality of cauvery river at twenty locations indicates that DO is meeting the desired water quality criteria except at Bhavani, Pallipalyam, Erode, Velore, Mohanur, Tiruchirapalli D/S, Trichy and Pitchavaram. DO is in the range of 0.1-12.6 mg/l. The minimum value of 0.1 mg/l of DO is observed at Pallipalayam. Faecal and Total Coliform values are observed more than the criteria at D/S of Tiruchirapalli. The Total Coliform bacteria are in the range of 39-160000 MPN/100 ml whereas the fecal coliforms bacteria varies from 2-28000 MPN/100 ml.

The highest value of Fecal and Total Coliforms are obsrved at Tiruchirapalli D/S. The BOD value ranges from 1-27 mg/l in river Cauvery with a highest value at Tiruchirapalli downstream. Other location having high level BOD in the river are at Pitchavaram, Trichy, Pallipalyam, Kushal Nagar and Erode. Conductivity in the river varies from 31-53100 micromhos/cm.

The water quality of tributary steams Hemavati, Shimsa, Arkavati, Lakshmantirtha, Kabbani, Bhavani and Amravati indicates that DO is not meeting the water quality criteria at 2 locations i.e Bhavani at Sirumugai and at Bhavani Sagar. BOD Value ranges from 1-8 mg/l with a highest value in river Arkavati at Kanakpura downstream.The Fecal Coliform ranges from 3-6600 MPN/100 ml whereas the total coliform ranges from 110-200000MPN/100 ml. The maximum numbers of Coliform are observed in Arkavati river at downstream of Kanakapura town in Karnataka.

## Monitoring in Cauvery Basin

The Water Quality of cauvery river at twenty locations indicates. DO is in the range of 2.1-13.5 mg/l. The minimum value of 2.1 mg/l of DO is observed at Pallipalayam. Total Coliform values are observed more than the criteria at most of the locations. The Total Coliform bacteria are in the range of 4-22000 MPN/100 ml whereas the fecal coliforms bacteria vary from 2-4000 MPN/100 ml. High values of Total Coliforms are obsrved at KRS Dam, downstream of Karekuara Village, Srirangapattana and at Sathyagalam Bridge, where as the highest values of faecal coliforms are reported at Erode near Chirapalayam and at Mohanur near Pattipalayam. The BOD value ranges from 0.2-10 mg/l in river Cauvery with a highest value (10mg/l) at Pitchavaram. Conductivity in the river varies from 42-57200 micromhos/cm. The high values of Conductivity are observed in the estuarine reaches at Coleroon (57200 micromhos/cm) & at Pichavaram (33800 micromhos/cm).

The water quality of tributary steams Hemavati, Shimsa, Arkavati, Lakshmantirtha, Kabbani, Bhavani and Amravati indicates that, DO is meeting the water quality criteria at all the locations. BOD Value ranges from 0.2-8 mg/l with a highest value (8mg/l) in river Bhavani at Sirumugai. The Fecal Coliform ranges from 3-4000 MPN/100 ml whereas the total coliform ranges from 110-14000 MPN/100 ml. The maximum numbers of Coliform are observed in Bhawani followed by Yediyar, Hemawati at D/S of Holenarsipur, Arkawati at D/S of Kanakpura, Lakshamantirtha at D/S of Honsur, Amravathi at Mudhuthukalam and Bhavani at Bhavanisagar.

## 2

# WATER RESERVOIRS

Lakes in India spread over an area of about 7.2 lakh hactares. There are very few lakes in India, and among them most are quite shallow and none of any considerable size. In the hilly regions, there are abundance of lakes. Lakes are an integral part of a drainage basin and landlocked body of water with a horizontal surface water level.

There are 64 monitoring locations on lakes, ponds and tanks. The Lakes being monitored are Hussainsagar(1), Saroornagar(1), Himayatsagar(1), Pulicate(1), Kankoria(1), Chandola(1), Ajwah(1), Sursagar(1), Brahamsarovar(1), Sukhna(1), Govindsagar(1), Pongdam(1), Renuka(1), Wuller(1), Dal(1), Ulsoor(1), Hebbala Valley(1),.Oruvathikotta(1), Sasthamcotta(1), Ashthamudi(1), Paravur(1), Vembanad(1), Periyar(1), Kodumgallor(1), Kayamkula(1), Punnamadakayal(1), Pookotekayal(1), Upper Lake(1), Lower Lake(1), Multai Lake(1), Loktak(4), Umiam(1), Ward(1), Thadlaskena(1), Osteri(1), Bahour(1), Harike(2), Pichola(1), Udaisagar(1), Ramgarh-Rajasthan(1), Pushkar(1), Fatehsagar(1), Kalyana(1), Nakki(1), Udhagamadalam(1), Kodaikanal(1), Yercaud(1), Lakshminarayan Baridigh(1), Rudrasagar(1), Ramgarh-Uttar Pradesh (1), Naini (1) and Rabindrasarovar (1).The tanks and ponds being monitoring are Dharamsagar(1), Bibinagar(1), Kistrapetrareddy(1), Gandigudem(1),Goysagar(1) and the ponds are Elangabeel System(1) and Lakshadweep Pond near Juma Masjid (1). The number of monitoring locations on each lake is given in parenthesis.

## LAKES, PONDS AND TANKS

Lakes, Tanks and Ponds in Andhra Pradesh, Karnataka, Kerala, Pondicherry, Tamilnadu and Union Territory of Lakshadweep.

The water quality monitoring of Lakes,Tanks and Pond in Andhra Pradesh, Karnataka, Kerala, Pondicherry,Tamilnadu and union Territory of Lakshadweep is carried out by the respective State Pollution Control Boards and PWD in Lakshadweep. The ranges of water quality observed in these rivers with respect to pH, Conductivity, DO, BOD, COD, Total Coliform(TC) and Faecal Coliform(FC) are presented as minimum, maximum and mean value to assess the extent of water quality variation throughout the year. DO varies from 1.3 mg/l to 13.0 mg/l. Lakes and Tanks having very low DO and does not meet the water quality criteria limits are Gandhigudem, Heballa Valley, Kistrareddypet, Pulicate, Udhagamanalem, Saroornagar, Vembanad. BOD observed in the range of 1 mg/l to 240 mg/l. Lakes and Tanks have high concentration of organic matter and does not comply to the standard limits for BOD are Hussain Sagar lake (36mg/l), Dharamsagar tank (8mg/l), Kistarareddypet tank (240mg/l), Saroornagar lake(25mg/l), Pulicate lake(10mg/l), Gandhigudem tank(64mg/l), Heballa Valley lake(16mg/l), Kayamkula lake(4mg/l), Osteri lake(7mg/l), Bahour lake(45mg/l),Udhagamandalam lake(6mg/l) and Kodaikanal lake(6mg/l). The highest number of Total Coliform are observed in Hussain Sagar lake (22600 MPN/100 ml) followed by Periyar lake(16600 MPN/100 ml) and Saroornagar lake (13000 MPN/100 ml) which are not complying to the criteria limit.

## GUJARAT AND RAJASTHAN

The water quality monitoring of Lakes,Tanks and Pond in Gujarat and Rajasthan is carried out by the respective State Pollution Control Boards. The ranges of water quality observed in these rivers with respect to pH, Conductivity, DO, BOD, COD, Total Coliform(TC) and Faecal Coliform(FC) are presented as minimum, maximum and mean value to assess the extent of water quality variation throughout the year. DO varies from

2.6 mg/l to 10.8 mg/l. Lakes and Tanks having very low DO and does not meet the water quality criteria limits are Kankoria Lake (2.6 mg/l),Pichola Lake (2.8),Pushkar lake (2.7 mg/l) and Fateh Sagar Lake(3.8 mg/l). BOD observed in the range of less than 1 mg/l to 36 mg/l. Lakes and Tanks having high BOD does not comply to the standard limits for BOD are Kankoria lake (36 mg/l),Sursagar lake (21 mg/l),Lower lake Bhopal (5 mg/l),Udaisagar lake (6 mg/l) and Pushkar lake (8 mg/l) The highest number of Total Coliform are observed in Kankoria lake (110000 MPN/100 ml).) which is not complying to the criteria limit.

## HARYANA, CHANDIGARH, HIMACHAL PRADESH, PUNJAB, UTTAR PRADESH AND WEST BENGAL

The water quality monitoring of Lakes, Tanks and Pond in Haryana, Chandigarh, Himachal Pradesh, Punjab, Uttar Pradesh and West Bengal is carried out by the respective State Pollution Control Boards. The ranges of water quality observed in these rivers with respect to pH, Conductivity, DO, BOD, COD, Total Coliform(TC) and Faecal Coliform(FC) are presented as minimum, maximum and mean value to assess the extent of water quality variation throughout the year. DO varies from 5.5 mg/l to 13.0 mg/l which indicates that all the lakes monitored are meeting the required level of water quality criteria. BOD observed in the range of 1 mg/l to 4 mg/l. Lakes and Tanks observed more than criteria are Renuka lake,Ramgarh lake and Rabindra Sarobar. The highest number of Total Coliform are observed in Rabindra Sarobar lake (85000 MPN/100 ml). All other lakes monitored in these States are meeting the standard limit.

## ASSAM, MANIPUR, MEGHALAYA AND TRIPURA

The water quality monitoring of Lakes,Tanks and Pond in Assam, Manipur, Meghalaya and Tripura is carried out by the respective State Pollution Control Boards. The ranges of water quality observed in these rivers with respect to pH, Conductivity, DO, BOD, COD, Total Coliform(TC) and Faecal Coliform(FC) are presented as minimum, maximum and mean value to assess the extent of water quality variation throughout the year. DO varies from 1.6 mg/l to 10.1 mg/l.DO observed lower than the desired criteria are Elangabeel System,Loktak lake at Sendra and Loktak lake at Karang Island. All other locations on lakes monitored are meeting the required level of water quality criteria. BOD observed in the range of 1 mg/l to 98 mg/l. Lakes and Tanks observed more than criteria are Elangabeel System (98 mg/l), Goy Sagar Tank (5 mg/l), Loktak lake at Sendra (4mg/l),Umiam lake at Barapani (13mg/l),Ward Lake at Shillong (13 mg/l), Thadlaskena lake (9mg/l) and Laxminarayan Bari Place Lake (10 mg/l) The highest number of Total Coliform are observed in Goy Sagar Tank (46000 MPN/100 ml) and Elangabeel System Ponds (46000 MPN/100 ml). All other lakes monitored in these States are meeting the standard limit.

## Lakes, Tanks and Ponds

Lakes,Tanks and Ponds in Andhra Pradesh, Karnataka, Kerala, Tamilnadu and Union Territory of Lakshadweep.

The water quality monitoring of Lakes, Tanks and Pond in Andhra Pradesh, Karnataka, Kerala, Tamilnadu and union Territory of Lakshadweep is carried out by the respective State Pollution Control Boards and PWD in Lakshadweep. The ranges of water quality observed in these rivers with respect to pH, Conductivity, DO, BOD, COD, Total Coliform(TC) and Faecal Coliform(FC) are presented as minimum, maximum and mean value to assess the extent of water quality variation throughout the year. DO varies from 0.6 mg/l to 10.4 mg/l.

Lakes and Tanks having very low DO and does not meet the water quality criteria limits are Ashthamudi lake, Paravur, Kayamkula, Gandhigudem, Heballa Valley, Kistrareddypet, Saroornagar and Vembanad. BOD observed in the range of 0.7 mg/l to 140 mg/l. Lakes and Tanks have high concentration of organic matter and does not comply to the standard limits for BOD are Hussain Sagar lake (5.7 mg/l), Dharamsagar tank (4.6 mg/l), Bibinagar tank (24.8 mg/l), Kistarareddypet tank(140mg/l), Saroornagar lake(23 mg/l), Pulicate lake (6.1 mg/l), Gandhigudem tank(64 mg/l), Heballa Valley lake (12 mg/l), Kayamkula lake(3.5 mg/l), Kodungalloor (3.9 mg/l), Udhagamandalam lake(15.5 mg/l) and Kodaikanal lake (5.7 mg/l). The highest number of Total Coliform are observed in Udagamandalam Lake (1,70,000 MPN/100 ml) followed by Kistarareddypet tank (48,000 MPN/100 ml), Bibinagar lake (42,000 MPN/100 ml), Gandhigudum (28,000 MPN/100 ml), Yercaud Lake (16,000 MPN/100 ml) and Perriyar Lake (6,200 MPN/100 ml), which are not complying to the criteria limit.

### Lakes,Tanks and Ponds in Gujarat, Madhya Pradesh and Rajasthan

The water quality monitoring of Lakes, Tanks and Pond in Gujarat, Madhya Pradesh and Rajasthan is carried out by the respective State Pollution Control Boards. The ranges of water quality observed in these rivers with respect to pH, Conductivity, DO, BOD, COD, Total Coliform(TC) and Faecal Coliform(FC) are presented as minimum, maximum and mean value to assess the extent of water quality variation throughout the year. DO varies from 2.9 mg/l to 17.8 mg/l. Lakes and Tanks having very low DO and does not meet the water quality criteria limits are Chandola Lake (2.9 mg/l) and Ramgarh Lake (2.2 mg/l). BOD observed in the range of less than 0.6 mg/l to 127 mg/l. Lakes and Tanks having high BOD does not comply to the standard limits for BOD are Kankoria lake (127 mg/l), Chandola lake (28 mg/l), Sursagar Lake (3.8 mg/l), Upper Lake Bhopal (3.7 mg/l), Lower lake Bhopal (5.4 mg/l), Pichola Lake (4.1 mg/l), Udaisagar lake (7.8 mg/l), Ramgarh Lake (4.5 mg/l), Pushkar lake (6.4 mg/l), Fatehsagar Lake (4.6 mg/l), Kayalana (4.6 mg/l) and Nakki (4.3 mg/l). The highest number of Total Coliform are observed in Kankoria lake (2,40,000 MPN/100 ml) and Chandola (46,000 MPN/100 ml) which are not complying to the criteria limit.

### Lakes, Tanks and Ponds in Haryana, Chandigarh, Himachal Pradesh, Punjab, Uttar Pradesh and West Bengal

The water quality monitoring of Lakes, Tanks and Pond in Haryana, Chandigarh, Himachal Pradesh, Punjab, Uttar Pradesh and West Bengal is carried out by the respective State Pollution Control Boards. The ranges of water quality observed in these rivers with respect to pH, Conductivity, DO, BOD, COD, Total Coliform (TC) and Faecal Coliform(FC) are presented as minimum, maximum and mean value to assess the extent of water quality variation throughout the year. DO varies from 1.4 mg/l to 12.4 mg/l. Except Naini Lake, all the lakes monitored are meeting the required level of water quality criteria. BOD observed in the range of 0.1 mg/l to 7.5 mg/l. Lakes and Tanks having BOD more than criteria limit are Renuka lake, Ramgarh, Harike Lake, Naini Lake and Rabindra Sarobar Lake. The highest number of Total Coliform (14,00,000 MPN/100 ml) and Fecal Coliform (8,50,000 MPN/100 ml) are observed in Rabindra Sarobar lake, whereas all other lakes monitored in these States are meeting the standard limit.

### Lakes, Tanks and Ponds in Assam, Manipur, Meghalaya and Tripura.

The water quality monitoring of Lakes, Tanks and Pond in Assam, Manipur, Meghalaya and Tripura is carried out by the respective State Pollution Control Boards. The ranges of water quality observed in these rivers with respect to pH, Conductivity, DO, BOD, COD, Total Coliform(TC) and Faecal Coliform(FC) are presented as minimum, maximum and mean value to assess the extent of water quality variation throughout the year. DO varies from 0.9 mg/l to 10.0 mg/l. DO observed lower than the desired criteria are Elangabeel System and Loktak lake at Bishnupur whereas all other locations on lakes monitored are meeting the required level of water quality criteria. BOD observed in the range of 0.5 mg/l to 80 mg/l. Lakes and Tanks observed more than criteria are Elangabeel System (80 mg/l), Loktak lake at Thana(4.5mg/l), Bishnupur(7.9mg/l), Sendra (4.3mg/l) and Karang Island(5.3mg/l); Umiam lake at Barapani (12.5 mg/l), Ward Lake at Shillong (13 mg/l), Thadlaskena lake (6.5 mg/l) and Laxminarayan Bari Place Lake (5.7 mg/l). The highest number of Total Coliform are observed in Goy Sagar Tank (1,10,000 MPN/100 ml) and Elangabeel System Ponds (2,40,000 MPN/100 ml) whereas all other lakes monitored in these States are meeting the standard limit.

## QUALITY OF THE GROUNDWATER

The groundwater occurance and availability is largely governed by the state of cementation and compaction of the formation which control the pore volume. The geological formations encountered in the country may be broadly divided into three categries-the unconsolidated,the semi-consolidated and the consolidated.

| State | No. of wells |
|---|---|
| Andhra pradesh | 24 |
| Assam | 10 |
| Chhatissgarh | 4 |
| Dadra and nagar haveli | 1 |
| Daman (zov) | 1 |
| Gujarat | 3 |
| Himachal pradesh | 8 |
| Kerala | 15 |
| Lakshdweep | 15 |
| Madhya pradesh | 5 |
| Meghalaya | 5 |
| Orissa | 15 |
| Pondicherry | 7 |
| Rajasthan | 18 |
| Tamil nadu | 2 |
| Tripura | 7 |
| Uttar pradesh | 25 |
| Uttranchal | 1 |
| West Bengal | 15 |
| Total | 181 |

In India a sizable proportion of population is dependant on ground water for drinking and other household utilities besides its use in irrigation at large.Due to limited cost effective treatment options for polluted ground water, the affected resource is generally lost for drinking and other utilities.

To assess the problem of groundwater quality deterioration, network of groundwater quality monitoring is extended to 181 locations. The Statewise number of groundwater monitoring locations are 24 in Andhra Pradesh, 10 in Assam, 4 in Chhatissgarh,1 in Dadra and Nagar Haveli, 1 in Daman , 3 in Gujarat, 8 in Himachal Pradesh, 15 in Kerala,15 in Lakshadweep, 5 in Madhya Pradesh, 5 in Meghalaya,15 in Orissa, 7 in Pondicherry, 18 in Rajasthan ,2 in Tamil Nadu, 7 in Tripura,25 in Uttar Pradesh, 1 in Uttaranchal and 15 in West Bengal.

The ranges of water quality observed in groundwater with respect to pH, Conductivity, BOD, COD, Total Coliform(TC) and Faecal Coliform(FC) are presented as minimum, maximum and mean value to assess the extent of water quality variation throughout the year.

**Andhra Pradesh**

The water quality monitoring of ground water in Andhra Pradesh is carried out by Andhra Pradesh Pollution Control Boards. pH of groundwater was in the range of 6.8-9.1 and meet the water quality criteria. Conductivity varies from 226 to 9291 μmhos/cm.

Except few locations conductivity is meeting the criteria limit for drinking as well as irrigation purposes. Very high level of conductivity is observed in Vishakhapatnam (9291 Open well near Rama Temple, Ward No.2, Mindi) and in Kakinada (open well near Partap Nagar Bridge). BOD and Total Coliform are meeting the desired criteria at all the locations except in the wells mentioned for having high conductivity.

**Assam, Meghalaya and Tripura**

The water quality monitoring of ground water in Assam, Meghalaya and Tripura is carried out by respective State Pollution Control Boards. pH of groundwater observed in the range of 5.9-8.4 and meet the water quality criteria.

Conductivity varies from 104-1420 μmhos/cm. Conductivity is meeting the criteria limit for drinking as well as irrigation purposes. BOD is meeting the desired criteria at all the locations. Total Coliform are not meeting the desired criteria at monitoring locations in Silcher, Barpeta, Bongaigaon and Guwahati.

## Gujarat and Madhya Pradesh

The water quality monitoring of ground water in Gujarat and Madhya Pradesh is carried out by respective State Pollution Control Boards. pH of groundwater observed in the range of 6.9-8.1 and meet the water quality criteria. Conductivity varies from 370-33330 μmhos/cm. Conductivity is observed high in the well at Narol (33330 μmhos/cm). BOD and Total Coliform are meeting the desired criteria at all the locations.

## Himachal Pradesh

The water quality monitoring of ground water in Himachal Pradesh is carried out by respective State Pollution Control Boards. pH of groundwater observed in the range of 7.1-8.6 and meet the water quality criteria. Conductivity varies from 153-1428 μmhos/cm. BOD is found in the range of 1-4 mg/l and the location at Kala Amb is exceeding the criteria limit.Total Coliform are meeting the desired criteria at all the locations.

## Kerala

The water quality monitoring of ground water in Kerala is carried out by respective State Pollution Control Boards. pH of groundwater observed in the range of 3.8-8.5 and does not meet the water quality criteria at few locations such as Kundra in Kollam,Punkunnam in Trissur, Kalamassery in Ernakulam,Punalur and Kannur. Conductivity varies from 57-3800 μmhos/cm. Conductivity is observed high in the well at Alwaye (3800 μmhos/cm). BOD and Total Coliform are meeting the desired criteria at all the locations.

## Lakshadweep

The water quality monitoring of ground water in Lakshadweep is carried out by PWD. pH of groundwater observed in the range of 7.6-8.3 and meet the water quality criteria. Conductivity varies from 616-6620 μmhos/cm. Conductivity is observed high in the well at Circuit House (6620 μmhos/cm),at Old Police Barrack (6090 μmhos/cm) ,near Ottavathilpalli (3900 μmhos/cm), near MPSAF Quarters (3720 μmhos/cm) and at Govt Press (2790 μmhos/cm). BOD observed more than the criteria at J.B.School,Kadat Palli, opposite

S.B.School, near Ottavathilpalli and adjacent to Chakikilum in Kavaratti.Total Coliform are exceeding the desired criteria at Chekkillam, at Govt Press and at Old Police Barrack.

**Orissa**

The water quality monitoring of ground water in Orissa is carried out by respective State Pollution Control Board. pH of groundwater observed in the range of 5.0-8.6 and does not meet the water quality criteria at Capital Hospital area in Bhubaneshwar. Conductivity varies from 102-946 μmhos/cm and meeting the criteria for various uses. Maximum BOD was 1.0 mg/l and Total Coliform was 20 MPN/100 ml.

**Pondicherry and Tamilnadu**

The water quality monitoring of ground water in Pondicherry and Tamilnadu is carried out by Pollution Control Committee and State Pollution Control Board. pH of groundwater observed in the range of 6.6-8.8 and meet the water quality criteria. Conductivity varies from 199-37500 μmhos/cm. Conductivity is observed high in the well in Chunmbar river (37500 μmhos/cm). BOD observed in the range of 1-50 mg/l and location having BOD more than the criteria are Well in Chunmbar river and Collector well at Thirupuvanam for Madurai Water Supply Scheme. Total Coliform are meeting the desired criteria at all the locations.

**Rajasthan**

The water quality monitoring of ground water in Rajasthan is carried out by State Pollution Control Board. pH of groundwater observed in the range of 6.8-8.5 and meet the water quality criteria. BOD observed in the range of 1-7 mg/l and location having BOD more than the criteria are Handpump near Kansua Nallah in Kota and Well in Pali Town (Bhopal Singh). Total Coliform are meeting the desired criteria at all the locations.

**Uttar Pradesh**

The water quality monitoring of ground water in Uttar Pradesh is carried out by State Pollution Control Board. pH of groundwater observed in the range of 7.0-8.0 and meet the water quality criteria. Conductivity varies from 350-1300 μmhos/cm and meeting the criteria for beneficial uses. BOD observed in the range of 1-3 mg/l and the locations are meeting the criteria. Total Coliform are meeting the desired criteria at all the locations.

### West Bengal

State Pollution Control Board carries out the water quality monitoring of ground water in West Bengal. pH of groundwater observed in the range of 2.1-7.9 and meet the water quality criteria. Conductivity varies from 411-2140 μmhos/cm and observed high at Hindustan Liver Factory and IOC Refinery in Haldia. Other locations having high conductivity are Tangra, Topsia, Dhapa and Garia in Calcutta. BOD observed in the range of 1-7 mg/l and the locations are meeting the criteria. Total Coliform is meeting the desired criteria at all the locations.

## Ground Water Quality

### *Andhra Pradesh*

The water quality monitoring of ground water in Andhra Pradesh is carried out by Andhra Pradesh Pollution Control Boards. pH of groundwater was in the range of 6.6-8.7 and meet the water quality criteria. Conductivity varies from 129 to 4270 μmhos/cm except few locations, conductivity is meeting the criteria limit for drinking as well as irrigation purposes. Very high level of conductivity is observed in Vishakhapatnam (4270 μmhos/cm) near open well near Rama Temple, Ward No.2, Mindi and in Ramagundam(2350 μmhos/cm) (near ash ponds of NTPC, Kundanpally); in Bollaram Panchayat Office (3820 μmhos/cm) and in Pashamaylam(3380 μmhos/cm) (near Chaitanya Chlorides).

BOD does not meet the criteria in well at Vijayawada, well near ash pond of NTPC, Kundanpally, in Bibi nagar Primary School, Rudravelly, in Kurnool near Tungabhadra river and in Nandyal. Total Coliform are meeting the desired criteria at all the locations. The concentration of Nitrate ($NO_3$-) is observed in the range of 0.5-13.0 mg/l.

### *Assam, Meghalaya and Tripura*

The water quality monitoring of ground water in Assam, Meghalaya and Tripura is carried out by respective State Pollution Control Boards. pH of groundwater is observed in the range of 4.9-10.4 and meets the water quality criteria. Conductivity varies from 38-1326 μmhos/cm. Conductivity is meeting the criteria limit for drinking as well as irrigation purposes. BOD is not meeting the desired criteria at Karbianglong (27.0 mg/l) and in Bonaigoan (7.4 mg/l) in Assam,. Total Coliform are not meeting the desired criteria at monitoring locations in Sibsagar(2,40,000 MPN/100 ml) and Guwahati (9300 MPN/100 ml). The concentration of Nitrate (NO3-) and Ammonical Nitrogen (NH4-N) is observed in the range of 0.020-2.05 mg/l and 0.020-0.5 mg/l respectively.

### *Gujarat and Madhya Pradesh*

The water quality monitoring of groundwater in Gujarat and Madhya Pradesh is carried out by respective State Pollution Control Boards. pH of groundwater is observed in the range of 6.9-8.1 and meet the water quality criteria. Conductivity varies from 370-3920 μmhos/cm. Conductivity is observed high in the well at Narol (3920 μmhos/cm). BOD and Total Coliform are meeting the desired criteria at all the locations.

### *Himachal Pradesh*

The water quality monitoring of ground water in Himachal Pradesh is carried out by respective State Pollution Control Boards. pH of groundwater observed in the range of 7.2-8.8 and meet the water quality criteria. Conductivity varies from 450-1648 μmhos/cm. BOD is found in the range of 0.1-5.6 mg/l and the locations at Barotiwala (5.6mg/l), at Kala Amb(5.5mg/l) and at Paonta Sahib(4.5mg/l) are exceeding the criteria limit. Total Coliform are meeting the desired criteria at all the locations.

### *Kerala*

The water quality monitoring of ground water in Kerala is carried out by respective State Pollution Control Boards. pH of groundwater observed in the range of 4.3-7.8 and does not meet the water quality criteria at few locations such as Kundra in Kollam, Punkunnam in Trissur, Kalamassery in Ernakulam and Kannur. Conductivity varies from 42-550 μmhos/cm. BOD and Total Coliform are meeting the desired criteria at all the locations.

### *Lakshadweep and Tamilnadu*

The water quality monitoring of ground water in Lakshadweep is carried out by PWD. pH of groundwater observed in the range of 6.4-8.5 and meet the water quality criteria. Conductivity varies from 550-6000 μmhos/cm. Conductivity is observed high in Kadat Palli (2760 μmhos/cm) the well at Circuit House (3000 μmhos/cm), at Old Police Barrack (5200 μmhos/cm), near Ottavathilpalli (6000 μmhos/cm), near MPSAF Quarters (5800 μmhos/cm), Well near helipad (5500 μmhos/cm) and at Govt Press (4700 μmhos/cm).

BOD observed more than the criteria at Collector well in Thirupuvanin for Madurai water supply scheme (6.0 mg/l). Total Coliform is meeting the desired criteria at all the locations.

### *Orissa*

The water quality monitoring of ground water in Orissa is carried out by respective State Pollution Control Board. pH of groundwater observed in the range of 4.3-8.2 and does not meet the water quality criteria at Capital Hospital area in Bhubaneshwar.

Conductivity varies from 79-3840 μmhos/cm and meeting the criteria for various uses. Maximum BOD was 1.6 mg/l and Total Coliform was 84 MPN/100 ml. The concentrations of Nitrate is observed in the range of 0.082-36.44 mg/l, the highest value is observed at Jagatpur Induatrial area in Cuttack.

### *Rajasthan*

The water quality monitoring of ground water in Rajasthan is carried out by State Pollution Control Board. pH of groundwater observed in the range of 7.0-8.0 and meet the water quality criteria. The conductivity varies from 111-23000 μmhos/cm, the high values are observed in well of Bhopal Singh in Pali (23000 μmhos/cm), well upstream 1km. From Jodhpur town (22000 μmhos/cm) and hand pump of Vidhani Village,

Goner road in Jaipur (3000 µmhos/cm). BOD observed in the range of 0.1-6.1 mg/l and location having BOD more than the criteria observed at Well U/s 1 Km. From Jodhpur town(6.1 mg/l). Total Coliform are meeting the desired criteria at all the locations.

### *Uttar Pradesh*

The ground water quality monitoring in Uttar Pradesh is carried out by State Pollution Control Board. pH of groundwater observed in the range of 5.7-8.4. Conductivity varies from 63-1840 µmhos/cm and meeting the criteria for beneficial uses. BOD observed in the range of 1.2-9.2 mg/l and the locations not meeting the criteria are, at Sardar Nagar and at Captainganj. Total Coliform are meeting the desired criteria..

### *West Bengal*

State Pollution Control Board carries out the water quality monitoring of ground water in West Bengal. pH of groundwater observed in the range of 7.1-8.0 and meet the water quality criteria. Conductivity varies from 586-2070 µmhos/cm. BOD observed in the range of 0.1-6.8 mg/l and the locations does not meet the criteria are, near IOC refinery, Haldia and Barasat Municipality in North 24 Parganas. Total Coliform is meeting the desired criteria at all the locations.

## RECENT SCENARIO

Access to enough water of sufficient quality is fundamental for all human, animal, and plant life as well as for most economic activity. At the global level, plenty of water is available. But to meet the demand, water has to be supplied where and when it is needed. These spatial, temporal, and qualitative characteristics pose the greatest challenge to meeting the rising demand in all sectors. Water withdrawals are only part of the picture. Almost all uses put something back into the water that degrades it for other users. Water quality and competition between users are therefore critical issues for the future of water use. There is no single "magic bullet" to solve these complex and interrelated problems. Increases in water supplies, and especially storage, are needed, but so is demand management, including not only economic instruments but also education and other efforts to change behavior. Appropriate technologies and institutions must both play a role.

## Trends in Water Use

Throughout history, farmers and nations have depended on irrigation to produce sufficient, stable food supplies. Today, an estimated 40 percent of agricultural products and 60 percent of the world's grain are grown on irrigated land. Irrigation accounts for around 70 percent of water withdrawals world-wide and over 90 percent in low-income developing countries. But water constraints may make expanding irrigation to feed an additional 1.5 billion people by 2025 impossible. Access to clean water for drinking, cooking, bathing, and other household needs is fundamental, but over 1 billion people still lack safe domestic water supplies, and 2.4 billion lack adequate sanitation. Compared to other uses, the volume of water required for basic domestic needs is not great; municipal and industrial demands are growing much faster. By 2025, urban populations are expected to grow by over 2 billion, posing additional challenges for municipal water supply. While water quantity is not a major constraint on domestic use, chemical and biological contamination threatens the quality of water for human consumption.

Water is the source of life and livelihoods. Water also sustains natural ecosystems. Excessive human water withdrawals and pollution have disrupted many vital habitats and species, leading to calls to reduce water withdrawals and reserve water for nature. Yet most economic activities require water. Factories need water for processing, cooling, and waste disposal. In the last 50 years, agricultural water consumption doubled, but industrial consumption increased six-fold worldwide, and even more rapid increases in industrial use are expected. The competition for water among domestic use, agriculture, industry, and nature is leading to scarcity even in areas that seemed water-abundant. Two ways of dealing with scarcity are to increase supply and limit demand. We examine each of these in turn.

## Options to Increase Water Supply

Many countries have sufficient water to meet demands for all uses. However, much of the rainfall and river flows are highly seasonal, so there is excess at some times and not enough at others. Domestic and industrial uses require water every day, and demands may be even higher in the dry season. Agriculture can accommodate seasonal flows of water, but irrigated production in the dry season is often the most productive and profitable type of farming.

Storage is the key constraint to providing water in dry periods, when demands are highest and supplies lowest. Dams, groundwater aquifers, and small-scale water harvesting provide water storage. Dams have received the greatest investment, especially in the last 50 years. However, dams have become increasingly expensive in financial, environmental, and political terms. As the best sites are used up, the environmental costs of submerging forests and wildlife and the loss of land and livelihoods for those who are flooded out have given rise to organized political opposition.

Groundwater is a major source of stored water for irrigation as well as for rural and urban domestic use. Heavy withdrawal has led to falling water tables in many areas, limiting the potential for expanding groundwater use without more recharge of aquifers. Furthermore, arsenic, fluoride, salinity, and other aquifer contaminants have become serious problems for those relying on groundwater.

As the limitations of larger-scale storage in reservoirs and aquifers have become apparent, there has been renewed interest in smaller-scale water harvesting. Although small, water-harvesting structures can collect considerable volumes of water for storage above ground or in soil profiles. However, water harvesting can be expensive per unit of water, and is unlikely to be able to meet rapidly growing water demands.

Other options to increase supply include interbasin transfers and nonconventional sources. Interbasin transfers bring water from areas of abundance to those of scarcity, but they share many of the financial and environmental problems of dams.

Desalination is expensive and energy-intensive, and hence has limited application at present. Other types of recycled wastewater can be used for some purposes. Urban waste-water is used for peri-urban irrigation in many areas, but the financial costs of treating sewage and the health costs of using water with fecal contamination and heavy metals call for caution in relying too heavily on such recycling.

Overcoming water scarcity requires using all options to increase available water supply and storage capacity, but supply options face serious financial and environmental constraints. We need to look to managing demand as the other half of addressing scarcity problems.

### Options to Manage Water Demand

Economic measures such as pricing and water markets often receive the most attention in demand management. Water pricing is promoted as a means to recover the costs of building and operating water control structures. Water prices can also create incentives to conserve water, provided users can be charged based on how much they use. However, measuring and billing are often technically difficult and costly. There may also be public opposition to charging for water. Water markets can create economic incentives to conserve water, but the infrastructure and institutions to transfer water from one user to another must be in place.

Rationing is a prevalent demand-management measure and can be an equitable way of meeting basic needs because it does not depend on ability to pay, but it may be unpopular and difficult to administer. Rotational irrigation deliveries, limited hours of domestic water supply, or limits on water volumes for industry are examples of rationing.

Other forms of regulation can help reduce demand. Mandating water-saving toilets, flow regulators in plumbing, efficiency requirements for particular industries, and technological measures such as stopping leaks in municipal water supply systems or shifting to sprinkler or drip irrigation can also save water. Education, social marketing, and public awareness campaigns to change behavior deserve much greater attention in water demand management. Awareness of water problems can motivate water conservation, while education can lead to effective changes in water-use practices. Such campaigns can also make pricing, rationing, or regulatory measures more acceptable to the public and more effective. Finally, measures to reduce water pollution such as regulations on industrial effluents, reductions in agrochemical use, or sewage treatment plants also alleviate water scarcity.

## Technology and Institutions

New technologies can increase supplies through low-cost desalination, wastewater treatment, water-lifting devices, or even long-distance transport. Technologies can also reduce water demand and increase productivity through water-saving industrial processes, household plumbing, irrigation devices, or new crops and varieties.

However, past experience has shown that science alone will not solve water problems. Much technology already exists but is not used because organizations and water users do not have the finances, knowledge, or incentives to use them. The right institutions are also required. Instead of separate government agencies for irrigation, water supply, sanitation, and environment, effective water management organizations will have to include new combinations of public sector, private sector, and civil society.

Basin management organizations can coordinate uses and allocate water among different sectors and regions. Effective basin management can result in more efficient and equitable water use and reduce conflict over water, especially in water basins that cross two or more countries.

Allocating water, whether through basin organizations or water markets, requires attention to many types of water rights. Rather than the government trying to establish rigid water rights, it should provide forums for negotiation between different users and claimants and work to strengthen the rights of the poor and disadvantaged groups.

Governments alone cannot and should not be expected to provide sufficient quantities of clean water for all uses. Users' participation in management is crucial for irrigation as well as domestic water supply systems and can contribute to more effective river basin organizations. Creating proper incentives and effective organizations for all users-women and men, poor and rich, from different sectors-to participate is complex and can be costly and time-consuming, but the returns in terms of improved water management, reduced conflict, and long-run sustainability of systems make this a vital investment.

Rapid increases in water use and degradation of water quality are putting extreme pressures on this vital resource. There are a number of strategies for dealing with these challenges outlined in the following briefs, but there is no single solution to overcoming water scarcity and quality constraints. Concerted efforts are needed to increase supplies as well as balance the demands of agriculture, domestic use, industry, and the environment through economic measures, regulation, and campaigns to motivate and equip users to conserve. Technological and institutional approaches must combine to accomplish these goals. Achieving such a coordinated approach to water is challenging, but essential for feeding the world, reducing poverty, and protecting the earth.

## WATER AND FOOD PRODUCTION

Water for agriculture is critical for food security. However, water for irrigation may be threatened by rapidly increasing nonagricultural uses in industry, households, and the environment. New investments in irrigation and water supply systems and improved water management can meet part of the demand.

But in many arid or semiarid areas-and seasonally in wetter areas-water is no longer abundant. The high economic and environmental costs of developing new water resources limit supply expansion. Therefore, even new supplies may be insufficient. Whether water will be available for irrigation so that agricultural production can provide for national and global food security remains an urgent question for the world.

This brief examines the relationship between water and food production over the next 30 years using IFPRI's

IMPACTWATER model. This global model simulates the relationships among water availability and demand, food supply and demand, international food prices, and trade at the regional and global levels (Rosegrant and Cai 2000 describes the methodology and data sources).

The baseline scenario incorporates our best estimates of the policy, investment, technological, and behavioral parameters driving the food and water sectors. We then look at how faster growth in municipal and industrial (M&I) demand and slower investments in irrigation and water supply infrastructure would affect food production.

## Water Increasingly Scarce for Irrigation

Water withdrawal and consumption in 1995 and 2025 are shown in the table below. Withdrawal refers to water removed from a source, some of which may be returned to it and reused. Consumptive use is the water withdrawn from a source and actually consumed or lost to seepage, contamination, or a "sink" where it cannot economically be reused. Under the baseline scenario, total global water withdrawals for agricultural, domestic, and industrial use are projected to increase 23 percent from 1995 to 2025. Projected withdrawals increase 28 percent in developing countries.

Global consumptive use of water will increase by 16 percent, the vast majority in developing countries, where consumptive use across all sectors will increase by 18 percent.

Non-irrigation water demand will increase by 62 percent worldwide, 96 percent in developing countries, and 22 percent in developed countries.

Consumptive use of water for irrigation worldwide will grow only 3.9 percent, which is significantly lower than the 12 percent increase in the rate of water use to meet full demand for irrigated crops.

Of critical importance, the slow growth in irrigation water supply, especially in developing countries, will be due to water supply constraints and high non-irrigation demand, which will increase water scarcity for irrigation.

## Food Production, Demand and Trade

Under the baseline scenario, world food prices will decline, but more slowly than in the past two decades. Wheat prices are projected to decline by 8 percent between the base year and 202125, maize prices by 7 percent, and rice prices by 17 percent. This compares to a decline of 3040 percent in these commodity prices between 1985 and 1995. The importance of developing countries in global food markets will increase substantially: 86 percent of the projected increase in global cereal consumption and nearly 90 percent of the increase in global meat demand between 1995 and 202125 will come from developing countries. Total cereal demand is projected to grow 43 percent by 760 million metric tons (mt).

Substituting food imports for irrigated agricultural production paid for by urban and commercial growth (so-called imports of "virtual water") is a possible strategy for reducing agricultural water use. However, even under the baseline scenario, developing countries' reliance on food imports will increase dramatically. With the slowing of crop yield growth, import demand in developing countries is projected to increase from 108 million mt in 1995 to 238 million mt in 202125. Irrigated and rainfed production will each account for about half of the increase in cereal production between 1995 and 202125. Irrigation plays a more dominant role in cereal production in developing countries, where nearly 60 percent of future cereal production will come from irrigated areas, accounting for four-fifths of the growth in global irrigated cereal production.

## WATER AND CROP YIELDS

With area harvested projected to grow slowly, crop yield growth is essential to future food production. However, cereal yield growth in most countries will slow. The global yield growth rate for all cereals is expected to decline from 1.5 percent per year during 198295 to 1.0 percent per year during 19952025; and in developing countries, average crop yield growth will decline from 1.9 percent per year to 1.2 percent. Increasing water scarcity will be a primary cause of the slowdown in projected irrigated cereal yield growth in developing countries. The relative crop yield for cereals in irrigated areas in developing countries is projected to decline from 0.86 in 1995 to 0.74 in 2025. Relative crop yield is the ratio of the projected crop yield to the maximum economically attainable yields at specified crop and input prices under conditions of zero water stress. The fall in the relative crop yield index is a significant drag on future yield growth. For developing countries, the drop represents an annual cereal production loss of 139 million mt, which is higher than China's total rice production in 1995.

## Alternative Scenarios

The baseline scenario, characterized by declining water supply reliability and relative crop yields, indicates the potential vulnerability of agricultural production to a worsening in water scarcity. What would happen if there were significant increases in non-irrigation water demand or declines in water investment and policy reform compared to the baseline? Under the high non-irrigation water (HNIRW) demand scenario that postulates faster growth in M&I demand, non-irrigation consumption will reach 681 km3 in 202125, 33 percent of total water consumption (versus 25 percent under baseline).

Under the second alternative scenario, which assumes low investment in infrastructure (LINV), the net increase of global reservoir storage for irrigation and water supply rises by only 396 $km^3$ between 1995 and 2025 compared to an increase of 690 $km^3$ under the baseline. Global average basin irrigation efficiency increases only to 0.57 versus 0.61 under the baseline, corresponding to a water consumption savings of 23 $km^3$ under the LINV scenario compared to 115 km3 under the baseline. The net increase in withdrawal capacity between 1995 and 2025 is only 301 $km^3$ under the LINV scenario versus 844 $km^3$ under the baseline. The scenarios that project significant negative impacts on irrigation water consumption and irrigation investment result in declines in cereal production and large increases in cereal prices.

By 2025, irrigated cereal production will be 58 million mt less under HNIRW, and 103 million mt less under LINV than under the baseline. Rice prices are projected to be 30 percent higher than the baseline in 202125 under LINV and 15 percent higher under HNIRW. Maize prices are 22 percent higher under LINV and 27 percent higher under HNIRW, and wheat prices 22 percent higher under LINV and 19 percent higher under HNIRW. High non-irrigation water use and low investment also results in increased variability in international prices, which can pose adjustment problems for farmers. Moreover, the fall in irrigated area and production creates additional pressure on the relatively fragile rainfed land base. Due to rising prices, rainfed cereal area will increase by an annual average of 7 million hectares under the LINV scenario in 20212025.

At the local and regional levels, price increases of this magnitude would cause a significant decline in the real income of poor consumers. Malnutrition would increase because many of the poorest people in low-income developing countries spend more than half their income on food.

## Conclusions

Investments and policy reforms in water and irrigation management will be significant determinants of future food production, demand, prices, and trade. Rapidly growing municipal and industrial water demand in developing countries will increase water scarcity for agriculture, and with a continued slowdown in water investments, could be a serious threat to future growth in food production. Food production, demand, trade, and prices will be affected. Three broad strategies can address the challenge of increasing water scarcity:

(1) Attack the problem from outside the water sector-for example, through crop breeding for more rapid yield growth;

(2) Increase the supply of water for food production through investments in irrigation, dams, or urban water supply; and

(3) Conserve water and improve the efficiency of water use through water management and policy reform. Appropriate water and food strategies must be

countryspecific and will combine elements of each of these approaches.

A decline in water available for irrigation without compensating investments and improvements in water management and water use efficiency-in both irrigated and rainfed areas-will reduce production growth and sharply increase international cereal prices, causing negative impacts on low-income developing countries and consumers.

## EMERGING WATER QUALITY PROBLEMS IN DEVELOPING COUNTRIES

Safe water in sufficient quantities is fundamental to human health. The most important water-associated health problem is diarrhea, accounting for 3 to 5 million deaths per year, especially among children. Availability of safe drinking water, combined with sanitary facilities for disposal of feces and improved hygiene standards, could prevent diarrheal disease to a great extent in developing countries. Much emphasis has been placed on reducing biological contamination, but contamination from naturally occurring chemicals in groundwater and from industrial and agricultural waste is also becoming a serious problem in developing countries. Conventional strategies that treat the drinking-water supply separately from water used for other purposes have limitations. Many emerging water-quality problems-and potential solutions-come from the interactions among uses, especially between domestic use and irrigation.

### Contamination of Rural Water Supplies

Policy documents on integrated management of water resources give highest priority to the drinking-water supply in water-allocation decisions. Rural drinking water may not seem to be a problem because water used for domestic purposes is only a small fraction of a country's total fresh water consumption. In Pakistan, water withdrawn for domestic purposes was estimated at 26 cubic meters per person in 1990, compared to 1,226 cubic meters of water per person for irrigation. The notion prevails that a small diversion from the irrigation sector could fulfill the demands of a growing population for domestic water. However, reallocation of water among sectors can be difficult, and a truly integrated water-management approach is constrained by traditional sectoral thinking and by priorities set by professionals in various disciplines.

Public health officials are mainly concerned with increasing deterioration of water quality due to industrial, agricultural, and urban waste and to insufficient investments in domestic water supply infrastructure. This global concern for water quality reflects the high standards imposed on drinking-water quality by institutions and professionals in the Western world, where the quality of drinking water ranks above all and where the direct use of surface water from irrigation systems for drinking seems unacceptable.

On the other hand, those who manage water for agricultural production believe their main responsibility is to provide water to meet crop-water requirements. Although few irrigation managers see supplying water for domestic use as their mandate, many rural residents draw their domestic water supply, directly or indirectly, from irrigation systems. Without acknowledging this reality, efforts to make irrigation systems more efficient might adversely affect the availability of irrigation water for nonagricultural uses. For example, lining canals with concrete to reduce seepage losses can cause shallow drinking-water wells to dry up.

The main strategy for improving rural drinking water has been to install low-cost hand pumps that draw groundwater uncontaminated by disease-causing microbes. In Bangladesh alone, more than 4 million tubewells have been installed over the past 20 years to provide safe drinking water to 95 percent of the population. This has reduced the incidence of diarrhea.

Only recently have the high concentrations of arsenic in many of the tubewells become apparent. What seemed like a public-health success story became one of the biggest environmental health crises of the 20th century-chronic poisoning of more than 20 million people exposed to high arsenic concentrations in their drinking water. A similar crisis is developing in India, where an estimated 66 million people drink groundwater with too high a fluoride content. While arsenic is toxic and carcinogenic, fluoride is an essential element for development and protection of teeth and bones. In excess, however, fluoride leads to serious dental and skeletal deformities and other health problems. Installing filters or other devices at millions of tubewells to remove arsenic and fluoride is an almost impossible task. Therefore, alternative sources of drinking water must be found in affected areas.

In some regions, the availability of shallow groundwater for drinking is an increasing problem because of overexploitation for agricultural and industrial purposes. In some of the major breadbaskets of Asia, such as the Punjab in India and the North China Plain, water tables are falling 2 to 3 meters a year. Wealthier farmers can continue to drill deeper tubewells with larger, more expensive pumps. But poor farmers are not able to do so. All stakeholders see falling groundwater levels as a threat to food security. Groundwater depletion also causes the shallow drinking-water wells of poor communities to run dry, a problem that has received less attention. Deepening these wells is costly and beyond the resources of the poor. Too little is known about how pumping groundwater for irrigation might affect the levels of arsenic and fluoride in drinking water. However, it is clear that overpumping in coastal areas causes saltwater to invade freshwater aquifers, making the water unsuitable for drinking.

The often poor water quality in tubewells and the reduced availability of water in shallow dug wells make it necessary to look at other sources of drinking water. Harvesting rainwater is being explored, but it might not be feasible in very poor arid and semiarid countries. Is reverting to the use of surface water an option when this water is increasingly polluted by human fecal material?

### Recycling Urban Waste Water

Poor surface-water quality is due mainly to disposal of untreated wastewater from urban areas in rivers, canals, and lakes. An alternative is to reuse wastewater for agriculture, an ancient practice being revisited because of growing water scarcity. Wastewater can be seen as a resource with high potential for reuse in agriculture, which presents an opportunity for increasing food security in rapidly growing urban areas. Definite environmental and economic benefits accrue from reuse that

- Avoids direct pollution of rivers, canals, and other surface water;
- Conserves water;
- Conserves nutrients, thereby reducing the need for chemical fertilizer;
- Disposes of municipal wastewater in a low-cost, sanitary way; and
- Provides a reliable water supply to farmers.

However, a number of disadvantages cannot be ignored:

- Health risks for the irrigators and communities in prolonged contact with wastewater;
- Health risks for the consumers of produce irrigated with wastewater;
- Contamination of groundwater with nitrates;
- Build-up of heavy metals and other chemical pollutants in the soil;
- Creation of habitats for mosquitoes and other disease vectors; and
- Possible limiting of marketing options (particularly for export) of agricultural produce. To safeguard the health of irrigators and consumers, the World Health Organization (WHO) has formulated international guidelines on wastewater reuse in agriculture and aquaculture. The guidelines establish the number of fecal coliform bacteria and worm eggs allowed for unrestricted irrigation.

Using wastewater for irrigation has the effect of localizing the health risk because the exposed group remains relatively small. Adequate health measures could be targeted at this exposed group. If untreated wastewater is dumped into surface-water sources, much larger populations of downstream water users could be exposed to less certain health risks. This is especially relevant for arid and semiarid countries such as Pakistan and Mexico, where irrigation canals are often the only open water bodies. These irrigation canals receive untreated wastewater from large cities, which is used for washing, bathing, and even drinking.

The solution appears simple: treat the wastewater before use and disposal. Excellent treatment methods exist. But they are prohibitively expensive for most developing countries, which have the most need for this source of irrigation water. The reality today is that two-thirds of the urban wastewater generated in the world receives no treatment at all. The cost of providing wastewater treatment facilities for all cities is astronomical.

Even if the resources were available, improved water quality is not guaranteed. Many of the existing wastewater treatment plants are not functioning properly because local authorities often prefer high-technology solutions to more appropriate, lower-cost alternatives. Most conventional treatment methods remove the nutrients in wastewater, reducing economic benefits to farmers.

Restricting the type of crops being cultivated with untreated wastewater to tree or nonfood crops that pass less contamination into the food chain is another option, but difficult to enforce in many developing countries. Crop restriction also reduces economic benefits from the use of wastewater, since the vegetables most susceptible to contamination are also the most profitable.

In the foreseeable future, many towns in developing countries will continue or expand the irrigation of high-value vegetable crops with untreated wastewater. Governments may wish to regulate reuse but are unable to offer practical solutions to the users. It is urgent, therefore, to develop a framework for evaluating different options and trade-offs so that governments and communities can make better-informed decisions.

Contamination of groundwater with arsenic and fluoride and increasing pollution of surface water with waste from urban areas are major water-quality problems. Since the same water serves multiple uses and users, solutions should be found within the framework of sustainable water management and in optimal recycling of water. This requires that policymakers, governments, donors, international organizations, and the research community appreciate the close links between water used for food production and water used for drinking. The growing worldwide scarcity of good-quality fresh water makes it essential to bridge the gap between the different sectors involved in water-resource management.

## WATER AND RURAL LIVELIHOODS

Livelihoods are the means people use to support themselves, to survive, and to prosper. Livelihoods are an outcome of how and why people organize to transform the environment to meet their needs through technology, labor, power, knowledge, and social relations. Livelihoods are also shaped by the broader economic and political systems within which they operate.

Water is the essential element in rural livelihoods because of the food security and income options it generates in rainfed and irrigated crop production, industry, domestic processing, aquaculture, livestock, recreation, navigation and transport, and electricity supply. Safe water and sanitation also shape health through potable water supply, safe food preparation, hygiene, better nutrition, and relaxation. Environmental security depends on peoples' actions to control salinity, drainage, and water pollution; manage droughts and floods; and manage land and water to guard those resources.

Unless there is new action to recognize both the roles water plays in rural livelihoods and people's capacity to manage their water sustainably and with social justice, water scarcity threatens to change people's options in production, employment, and exchange, and the relations among these activities. in ways that will exclude the small producer. For example, in Zimbabwe, new smallholder irrigation systems are being developed and old ones are receiving new support that can improve water supply and livelihoods for more people. However, irrigators must also now renegotiate water rights in the face of growing competition for water and new water legislation to promote more integrated water resources management. While there is still scope for improving livelihoods in irrigation and aquaculture, emerging competition for water will drive water users to defend and negotiate their water rights when their livelihoods are threatened. Water scarcity increases the need for pro-poor development support.

## Improving Livelihoods with Pro-poor Water Programs

Improved access to water is a powerful tool to diversify livelihoods and reduce vulnerability for small producers (see Box). Low prices, fluctuating markets, adverse tenancy, and insufficient labor can all explain why small farmers must engage in diverse livelihood strategies; they cannot survive from agricultural activities alone, even with better water husbandry. As water users, small farmers value their water access for its contribution to income, household needs, and the social networks and entrepreneurship it supports. Many argue that new opportunities still exist to help small farmers gain better livelihoods despite water scarcity and to build a more vibrant local economy around them. Indeed, it is essential to prioritize small farmers' water access in the interests of reducing poverty, vulnerability, and social injustice.

### Access to Water

***Transforms Rural Livelihoods***

- Production options in farmlands and home gardens for food, cash crops, and livestock extend across the year; yields and output improve for home consumption and sale.
- Employment for families, with and without land, increases; more local people are employed in operation of water systems and in agroprocessing; and livelihood options in fishing, tourism, and recreation emerge.
- Health improves through access to safe domestic water supply and sanitation.

- Opportunities to exchange gifts of food and seed and to build social networks increase.
- Participation in water committees widens social networks and empowers people.
- Farmers spend additional income locally, improving markets for goods and services.
- When women control outputs, they spend more on family welfare.

Pro-poor programs work to build water assets, to widen different users' access to them, and to reduce the vulnerability of low-income cultivators and workers through water-related activities. These initiatives help, in particular, to reduce gender imbalances in access to and benefits from water use. They recognize the important roles women play in production and food security, and the competent roles they can play in water management. Pro-poor water and asset-based livelihood promotion has the following goals:

- Raise local value-per-drop of water. New technologies and production systems can promote the manufacture of high-value products locally. Programs can maximize employment through developing a range of productive enterprises and involving local people in construction and operation of systems. Planners can use water systems as "growth points" where services, markets, and employment are also stimulated. New methods are under development for assessing the value of water to small producers, including "water and well-being" indicators.
- Create and manage community-based water assets through small water points, water harvesting, or better soil and water management. Initiatives can also build disaster preparedness, use short-term relief measures that build water assets, and work to break the link between ill health and poor water management.
- Allocate water in a way that creates roles for and empowers excluded groups, with a special focus on

opportunities for women. Techniques to assess water use and value at the system and basin levels can aid decision-making about remaining water development options.

- Improve services through more accountability to water users in public and private water services, and through recognizing unregistered and excluded users, especially when they are poor.

These initiatives can work well in localized programs focused on specific water systems and watersheds. However, some water scarcity conditions and production transformations threaten to provoke struggle on a larger scale and require action of a different kind.

## Negotiating and Defending Livelihoods

When people build their livelihoods around water, they create relationships of cooperation and control in order to acquire and manage water systems, link with government and the private sector, broaden opportunities, and strengthen their negotiating power. How livelihoods survive under scarcity is related to how people understand water scarcity, organize social action to remedy it, and act to defend their rights.

"Livelihood thinking," which developed in the 1980s as an alternative to "production thinking," challenged beliefs about the neutrality of technology and the absolute ability of experts to promote optimal production systems. It also required a new professionalism to make resource management and technology serve small farmers. Livelihood thinking involves understanding water environments and technologies; understanding and working with the political processes through which local groups can question water assessment and allocation mechanisms, including "expert" solutions; and working directly with small farmers. This shift in orientation can foster local water-control initiatives that support users in negotiating their rights to water and livelihoods-within both water-basin and local water systems. Livelihood thinking builds key design skills, communication and management capacities, and principles for collaboration on new actions that promote:

- Diversity in ecology, livelihood strategies, and water institutions. This includes participatory design and agro-ecological planning that builds on the knowledge and management capacities of users; strategic targeting of niche markets and production; and working with alternative production and construction systems to help maximize biomass productivity, equity, local employment, and use of local materials.
- Fair and sustainable water delivery. To resolve water scarcity issues, livelihood thinking seeks to understand the opportunities and needs created by different water technologies and institutions, and the interactions between them, given available water supply.
- Water-management reform negotiations. Empowering local groups and evolving user-sensitive water assessment tools can help build new multi-stakeholder platforms and institutions between local and catchment levels.

Creative thinking coupled with effective negotiation have already brought about new livelihoods for people in peri-urban settlements, in irrigation systems with temporal scarcities, in watersheds with new water harvesting options, and in systems and basins where water trading takes place. The combination has also yielded new rights for those previously excluded from formal recognition and has helped people explore local options before pursuing major changes in allocations between sectors or users.

# 3

# ENVIRONMENT AND WATER

Water and ecosystems are inextricably linked. The ecosystems of our planet, and the plants and animals that live within them, need water for their survival. For instance, the Okavango Delta in Botswana, the largest Ramsar site (wetland) in the world at 35,000 square kilometers, directly provides a livelihood to 150,000 people and harbors a unique biodiversity with 2,500 plant species, 65 fish species, 20 large herbivores, and over 450 bird species.

Ecosystems, in turn, regulate the quantity and quality of water. Wetlands retain water in periods of high rainfall, slowly release it during dryer periods, and purify it of heavy metals and other contaminants. Forests recharge our groundwater, which can be used elsewhere for drinking or irrigation. The functions (goods and services) that natural and semi-natural ecosystems provide to humankind are often neglected in economic planning and decisionmaking. They include:

- Regulatory functions for essential ecological processes and life support systems, including air quality, climate, water supply, soils, waste treatment, and biological control of pests and pollination;
- Habitat functions for wild plants and animals (and native people) to maintain biological and genetic diversity, including refuges and nurseries for resident and migratory species;
- Production functions for food, fiber, shelter, fuel, fodder, fertilizer, medicines, genetic resources, and ornamental resources; and

- Information, aesthetic, and spiritual functions such as opportunities for reflection, relaxation, communion with nature, and cognitive development through aesthetically valued scenery, recreation and tourism, cultural and artistic inspiration, connection to history and heritage, and scientific education.

Not only do natural ecosystems help to prevent floods or provide shelter, millions of people also directly derive their food, water, and fuel from these areas. In the Hadejia Nguru Wetlands of Nigeria, the traditional use of the floodplain yields US$12 per cubic meter of water, compared to US$0.04 per cubic meter for a proposed irrigation scheme. Globally, natural ecosystems provide an estimated US$32 trillion to societies.

### The Decline of Nature and Water

People are overusing water and natural resources. Half of the world's wetlands have already been lost due to overabstraction of water and conversion into agricultural land.

With the loss of their ecosystems, more than 3,500 species are threatened worldwide, of which 25 percent are fish and amphibians. In 1999, 20 million hectares of forest were lost. Overuse and misuse of water harm the human population as well. When too much water is abstracted from rivers, one effect can be that seawater comes inland and makes arable land infertile. It can also damage coastal mangroves, which are vital spawning areas for shrimp and fish.

Human water management affects ecosystems, which in turn affect the livelihoods of the people that depend on them. Hydrological, ecological, and social processes are closely connected. People are an inalienable part of the ecosystem. Therefore, we must look at the big picture: the management of fresh water within an ecosystem.

### The Ecosystem Approach

An ecosystem approach looks beyond specific sectors, such as food production, hydropower, nature conservation, or sanitation, to find integrated solutions for the variety of demands we place on our freshwater resources. It establishes a management regime that mimics natural processes and productivity and considers all goods and services to be on equal footing with water delivery. It strives to maintain biodiversity and to conserve land and water resources and includes environmental monetary values in determining the cost-effectiveness of interventions and the sustainable allocation of resources.

Because users within a basin are interdependent, an integrated water management approach is essential. Upstream uses of water have an impact on downstream users, the management of the land affects the water resources, and vice versa. The ecosystem approach is holistic, taking all these aspects into account. Even though the ecosystem approach appears to emphasize hydrological and ecosystem processes, the real focus is on human processes. The different human uses and behaviors in a basin are interlinked; the actions of one can have an impact on another.

Large dams are a good example. In 1979, a dam was constructed in Waza-Logone (northern Cameroon) to supply water to a 70-square-kilometer irrigated rice scheme. But the resulting lack of water downstream of the dam changed the biodiversity of a 50,000 square kilometer area. Fish disappeared and grasses for livestock no longer grew. Downstream, people eventually moved out of the area because they could not feed their livestock. The benefits of the dam went to the owners of the irrigated lands. The communities downstream bore the costs. For the proper management of a basin, all people that change the quality or quantity of water (the stakeholders) have to be involved and have a say in water management. Fighting over the resource will not work. It is better to establish the different needs of all parties involved and find the optimum solution for everyone. Local communities, governments, technical institutions, private companies, and nongovernmental organizations have to work together on problem definition, planning, and management of the natural resource base. Such cooperation also allows for setting objectives at the local and basin levels for conservation, sustainable management, and poverty alleviation.

## Ecosystems for Water

The protection of ecosystems should be a premise of water management deliberations, as ecosystems are the source of water and life. Some ecosystems, such as cloud forests, springs, and certain wetlands, provide clean water directly. Other ecosystems produce goods upon which communities rely. For ecosystems to continue producing their goods and services, a minimum amount of water must be left for the ecosystems to function. Using all the water there is destroys ecosystems and the communities that depend on them.

With regard to dams, there have been many debates on the negative impacts on downstream communities and biodiversity and the minimum flood releases required to mitigate or prevent such impacts.

The recommendations of the World Commission on Dams need to be complemented by specific tools for optimizing dam design and management. More work needs to be done on the trade-offs between retaining water behind the dam for "reservoir-based livelihoods" (irrigation, hydropower) and releasing it downstream for "flood-based livelihoods." Based on this work, recommendations can be made for using multi-criteria analytical methods to make decisions on flood releases.

The consequence of the ecosystem approach would inevitably be to reduce the amount of water abstracted from ecosystems. The demand for water will have to decrease from irrigated agriculture, which is 70 percent of all the water used in the developing world, but also from industry and households (especially in the developed world). This requires both behavioral changes and technical improvements to increase water efficiency (drip agriculture, crops that require less water).

The same line of thought could lead to the restoration of ecosystems that have been degraded. As in the Hadejia Nguru Wetlands, traditional multipurpose use can be more beneficial than single-use, irrigated agriculture. Unfortunately, much of the economic value an ecosystem provides has been ignored in the past. At times, it can even be economically efficient to restore an ecosystem to deliver certain functions, especially if clean water becomes a scarce resource. Increasingly, we see that certain parties in basins are paying for specific services. A water company may pay farmers for not using certain insecticides that pollute the water, or a city may pay mountain communities for protecting the forest that is vital for its water supply. Attention to the financial aspects of water management needs to increase and should start with a proper valuation of the services ecosystems provide. At the moment, much of their value is taken for granted or underestimated. Their proper assessment would certainly lead to other choices for management. Political systems also need to make the participation of stakeholders in basin negotiations possible, and effective laws are required to regulate the processes involved.

### The Path Ahead

Water is a scarce resource. If we continue to overuse and pollute our water and destroy our natural ecosystems, we may fulfill the prediction that 30 percent of the world's population will not have enough water by 2025.

The coming decade will be important for the management of water. The question is how we will use the available water to provide food, safe environments, health, and livelihoods to a growing world population, in harmony with nature. We need to grow more food with less water, meet the growing needs in cities and industry, and so on. It is a question of daunting complexity, but one that has to be answered in the coming years.

The ecosystem approach to water management may provide answers to the social, economic, and ecological problems we face. Water security is based on protection of the ecosystems on which resources depend. Recognizing the vital role of healthy ecosystems in the water cycle and protecting them should form the basis of any water management decision.

## DAMS AND WATER STORAGE

Dams are at the center of many controversies related to the management of water resources and proposals to relieve water scarcity. Two strategic contributions to the Second World Water Forum held in The Hague in March 2000 provide insight. Van Hofwegen and Svendsen estimate that water supplies used in agriculture will have to be augmented by an additional 15 to 20 percent during the next 25 years-or a higher percentage if the assumptions regarding significant improvements in irrigation and agricultural productivity are not realized. In contrast, the IUCN (World Conservation Union) warns that over-abstraction will lead to depletion of groundwater, reduction in biodiversity, and loss of livelihoods that are dependent on a healthy ecosystem. It calls for a different approach to new infrastructure development that recognizes the value of ecosystems and re-examines the operation of existing projects. There has been a recent trend of declining dam construction. Financing for dam projects from multilateral and bilateral sources dropped from an estimated US$4.4 billion per year in the early 1980s to US$2.6 billion per year in the late 1990s.

## Searching for a Solution

Such contrasting positions, coupled with significant social consequences, underlie the intense debate on dams that ultimately led to the establishment of the World Commission on Dams (WCD) in May 1998. This was born out of a multi-stakeholder workshop organized by the World Bank and IUCN.

There are more than 45,000 large dams around the world, which, overall, have played a role in helping communities and economies manage water resources for food production, energy generation, flood alleviation, and domestic and industrial use. Current estimates suggest that some 30 to 40 percent of irrigated land worldwide now relies on dams and large dams are estimated to support 12 to 16 percent of global food production. Hydropower projects generate 19 percent of world electricity and account for over 50 percent of electricity generated in 63 countries. These are considerable contributions.

However, the projects in the Commission's knowledge base showed a high degree of variability in meeting predicted water and electricity services and related social benefits. A considerable portion fell short of projected physical and economic targets, while many continued to generate benefits beyond their projected economic life. Extensive impacts on ecosystems were evident including the loss of habitats, species, and aquatic biodiversity. In many cases, the measures explicitly designed to mitigate such impacts proved ineffective.

Those who bear the social and environmental costs and risks of large dams-especially the poor, the vulnerable, and future generations-are often those that receive neither the water and electricity services nor the social and economic benefits from them. An estimated 40 to 80 million people have been displaced by dam projects. Although some compensation was invariably provided, the Commission found that the full range of social impacts was frequently neither accounted for nor addressed.

In particular, the impacts on the lives, livelihoods, and health of the affected communities upstream and downstream of the projects were not considered, and distribution of benefits was extremely inequitable. This gave rise to growing opposition to dams by affected communities worldwide. While dams have delivered many benefits, in too many cases the price paid to secure those benefits has been too high and could have been avoided. Applying a "balance-sheet" approach to assess the costs and benefits of large dams is seen as unacceptable, given existing commitments to human rights and sustainable development.

In proposing a way forward beyond the prevailing conflicts, the Commission provides a new framework for decisionmaking based on recognizing the rights of and assessing the risks to all stakeholders. Clarifying the rights context for a proposed project is an essential step in identifying those with legitimate claims and entitlements. The notion of risks is an important dimension to understanding how, and to what extent, a project may have an impact on such rights. The rights-and-risks approach introduces a departure from a balance-sheet approach, where the loss to those adversely affected has been traded off against the gain to the intended beneficiaries. It encompasses the concepts that those adversely affected should participate in the planning process and have a share in project benefits.

Seven strategic priorities and corresponding policy principles for water and energy resource development are proposed that build on the rights-and-risks approach. They can be summarized as follows:

1. Gaining public acceptance by recognizing rights, addressing risks, and safeguarding the entitlements of all affected people, particularly indigenous and tribal peoples, women, and other vulnerable groups. Decisionmaking processes should enable informed participation by all groups.
2. Undertaking comprehensive options assessment based on clearly defined needs for water, food, and energy, and giving social and environmental aspects the same significance as economic and financial factors.
3. Addressing existing dams to optimize benefits by changing water use priorities, physical and land use in the river basin, and by developing technological changes in environmental, safety, economic, and technical regulations. Outstanding social issues and environmental mitigation and restoration measures should be addressed.
4. Sustaining rivers and livelihoods through understanding, protecting, and restoring ecosystems at river-basin level, avoiding negative impacts, prioritizing good site selection and project design, and releasing tailor-made environmental flows to help maintain downstream ecosystems and the communities that depend on them.
5. Recognizing entitlements and sharing benefits through joint negotiations with adversely affected people that result in mutually agreed-upon and legally enforceable resettlement, mitigation, and development provisions that improve livelihoods and quality of life.
6. Ensuring compliance with commitments made by governments, developers, regulators, and operators in the planning, implementation, and operation of dams. Regulatory and compliance frameworks use incentives

and sanctions to ensure effectiveness where flexibility is needed to accommodate changing circumstances.

7. Sharing rivers for peace, development and security, especially with regard to transboundary rivers, so that the use and management of resources increasingly becomes the subject of agreement between states to promote mutual self-interest for regional cooperation and peaceful collaboration. The focus shifts to sharing benefits. External financing agencies support the principles of good faith negotiations between riparian states.

The Commission offers practical advice for implementing these priorities: a set of criteria for five key decision points in the planning and project cycles along with 26 advisory guidelines based on examples of good practice from around the world. Some examples of the advisory guidelines include: using multi-criteria analysis in options assessment to raise the significance of social and environmental concerns; conducting a distribution analysis to determine how costs and benefits of any option are shared; and developing mechanisms that provide incentives to promote greater compliance with commitments.

In the long run, the Commission's report offers the opportunity to reduce conflict, delays, and overall costs to the dam operator, the government, and to society in general.

## Where do We go From Here?

When all 12 Commissioners from such varying backgrounds signed the WCD report, they sent a clear signal that it was possible for the international community to move beyond the conflict of the dams debate. With the launch of the report, the Commission completed its mandate and disbanded. The Commission recognized that its report was not the final word. Rather, it was the start of a process.

Governments, financiers, affected-peoples' groups, NGOs, professional organizations, and the private sector reviewed the recommendations and have begun to take the process forward in a series of local multistakeholder initiatives. Given the contested nature of the debate, the wide range of reactions-from support to criticism-is not surprising. While a consensus has not been reached on all aspects of the WCD report, there is general agreement on the Commission's core values and strategic priorities. The challenge now lies in implementing them.

A Dams and Development Unit, hosted by the United Nations Environment Programme (UNEP), was established to continue the Commission's dissemination activities, promote dialogue, provide networking opportunities for those interested in learning from others' experiences and, where requested, to assist countries to work with the recommendations of the report.

The upcoming World Summit on Sustainable Development (Rio +10) in Johannesburg, South Africa in 2002 will involve much discussion on sustainable water management, integrating land and water management, and promoting participatory approaches. The policies of many international organizations are being adapted to accommodate these concerns and to make them operational. There remains a significant gap between policy and practice. The dams debate embodies the tensions between providing water for increasing needs, alleviating poverty, and protecting the environment. The WCD report can help bridge the gap between policy and practice provided it is used in a responsible way. The challenge of constructive engagement, modeled on the Commission's own process, should be embraced by all involved.

## POTENTIAL AND CONSTRAINTS

Groundwater problems emerging in many parts of the world reduce drought-buffer supplies, threaten environmental values, and increase risks for many of the world's poorest people. Programs to improve public understanding and basic scientific information regarding the resource base and to encourage the evolution of groundwater management systems are essential. Furthermore, because many countries will need years to develop systems for managing groundwater, policies should encourage users to adapt to water scarcity conditions rather than attempt to solve water problems per se.

## Nature and Scope of Groundwater Problems

The Green Revolution, which led to dramatic increases in food production, especially in Asia, has also been called the "tubewell revolution" because part of what drove it was groundwater development on an unprecedented scale. The number of mechanized wells in India grew from a few thousand at the time of independence in 1947 to tens of millions today. As a buffer against drought and precipitation variability, groundwater plays a critical role in food and livelihood security. Increased access to groundwater has reduced risks substantially, enabling many farmers to move out of poverty. All such benefits, however, may have come at a high cost. In recent summers, flows from the world's second-largest spring, the headwaters of the Al Khabour River in Syria, have declined from a long-term average of 50 cubic meters per second to only a few cubic meters per second. Similar stories are emerging in many regions. Groundwater-level declines of 13 meters per year are commonly reported for monitored wells in arid and semi-arid regions. In extreme situations, such as Sana'a in Yemen, shallow aquifers are almost depleted.

Efforts to tap new groundwater supplies in Sana'a have been unsuccessful despite the drilling of wells that exceed two kilometers in depth. In the Middle East and North Africa, it is no longer uncommon to encounter wells drilled to depths that have historically only been seen in the oil industry. Even in humid regions such as Bangladesh, water-level fluctuations may be increasing, and water is scarce during the dry season. Furthermore, scarcity and quality concerns are linked. Groundwater pumping often mobilizes water that is saline or contains natural contaminants such as arsenic or fluoride. When combined with increasing pollutant loads from agriculture, industry, and municipal sewage, this pumping can irreversibly contaminate aquifers. The threats to groundwater resources are clear, but their extent is far less so. Worldwide, most groundwater monitoring networks are relatively new and collect a limited array of data on water levels and basic water quality parameters. Detailed data on water quality and pollutants are rarely available except in relation to specific local concerns.

Data are also often unavailable on critical components of the water balance-such as groundwater extraction, evapotranspiration from native vegetation, and deep inflows to aquifers. Furthermore, data on water-level changes can be misleading. Aquifers can take tens to hundreds of years to equilibrate when disturbed. As a result, short-term waterlevel declines do not necessarily indicate overdraft.

Nonetheless, water-level changes and fluctuations are the most important factors influencing access to groundwater for the environment and for human uses. For small farmers along the Ganges, the deep saturated basin beneath their fields is irrelevant. What they care about is whether or not water is available within the tens-of-meters range from which they can afford to pump. When levels decline below or fluctuate outside that range, farmers lose access to irrigation and households may lose access to drinking water.

Fluctuations are equally important from an environmental perspective. Stream flows and wetlands often depend on high groundwater levels. Even modest seasonal declines can affect surface water bodies severely.

Water quality is also affected when changing levels mobilize low-quality water or cause waterlogging and associated salinization problems.

From the perspective of current usage, this dynamic-the interaction between groundwater levels, underground flow patterns, surface water bodies, and the economics of groundwater access-is far more important than the overall balance between extraction and recharge within an aquifer. Moreover, this dynamic is highly variable, heavily dependent on local conditions, and often missed in the data sets collected by groundwater departments.

## Options for Managing Groundwater

The lack of information and understanding regarding groundwater dynamics presents a major challenge for those developing effective management systems. The challenge is as much social as technical. Without both data and a shared understanding of the problems, the social consensus needed to implement decisions is difficult to generate-and groundwater management decisions are often difficult.

Standard approaches to reducing groundwater overdraft, for example, often require metering of all wells, establishment of formal water rights, and regulatory and economic mechanisms to bring extraction down to sustainable levels. While progress toward this goal has been made in a few water-scarce countries such as Jordan and Israel, the situation is more complex in locations (such as India) with tens of millions of wells and conditions that vary greatly even at local levels. Even where management is most advanced, it is socially and politically difficult to reduce groundwater extraction to sustainable levels. Wells are generally private and highly dispersed.

Inventorying them and monitoring extraction are problematic. Furthermore, reducing use to sustainable levels in arid regions often requires substantial reductions in extraction, which can have tremendous economic and social impact. As a result, governments are not inclined to force reductions.

Groundwater experts often propose community management of groundwater as an alternative to state regulation.

Although global experience in this area is limited, experience with resources other than water indicates that several factors are critical to the success of community management-for example, clear boundaries on the resource and its user group, the ability to control free riders, and information on the use and condition of the resource. Such factors are difficult to establish in the case of groundwater.

Successful groundwater management has been achieved through intermediate-level institutions such as the quasigovernmental groundwater districts in the western United States and somewhat similar organizations in parts of France. Organizations of this type hold much promise. Their development, however, often takes decades, and to be effective they require data, technical capacity, and some degree of supporting social consensus.

Markets are also central to any framework for groundwater management. Water markets in the western United States are based on water rights systems that attempt to quantify the volume sustainably available in aquifers and allocate it among users.

Transactions involve contracts and often the formal transfer of the water right as well as the water itself. In developing countries formal water rights are rarely involved. Instead, informal transactions occur between well owners and adjacent farmers for irrigation or tanker companies that deliver the water to urban customers.

Prices for irrigation are low compared with tanker deliveries. In 1986 in Yemen, for example, the cost of extraction near Ta'iz was approximately US$0.005 per cubic meter. Rural irrigators paid US$0.020.05 per cubic meter; urban bulk users paid an average of US$2.60 per cubic meter for tanker supplies; and smaller customers paid as much as US$25.00 per cubic meter for purified groundwater. That pattern is typical: the urban poor generally pay the highest prices.

Two points merit attention. First, because formal rights are not involved, prices reflect short-term pumping capacity, not the longer-term sustainability of extraction rates. Second, even with rights systems, markets indicate the value individual users gain from extracting groundwater but not the economic, environmental, and sustainable use values that accrue when groundwater is left in place.

Aside from groundwater market prices, energy is the primary variable cost affecting groundwater extraction. In countries such as India, energy subsidies were used to encourage groundwater development during the Green Revolution.

Now, despite water-level declines and huge effects on state budgets, those subsidies have proved politically difficult to eliminate. As a result, agriculture now officially consumes more than 50 percent of total power production in some Indian states. Appropriately structured energy prices can provide users with a major incentive to use groundwater more efficiently. Still, given the high yields associated with groundwater and the numerous factors affecting the economics of agriculture, energy prices alone cannot be expected to reduce groundwater extraction to sustainable levels.

## Action in the Short and Long Term

How can emerging threats to the groundwater resource base be addressed? Most groundwater experts advocate the development of comprehensive integrated management systems. While important, such efforts require long-term data on aquifer conditions along with well-established institutional capacities that are unavailable in many regions. Therefore, integrated management initiatives rarely generate results over the short term. Alternative approaches-in particular those that encourage populations to adapt to conditions of water scarcity and to reduce pressure on the resource base-are essential. Existing coping strategies-such as the migration of populations out of agriculture and into urban areas along with the development of nonagricultural economic systems-represent a starting point for reducing pressure on areas where overdraft levels are high. Although they do not ensure sustainability of the resource base, such strategies can provide essential breathing space for the longer-term development of management institutions.

# 4

# WATER HARVESTING AND MANAGEMENT

The world's freshwater shortages result more from uneven distribution of water over time and space than from absolute scarcity. Even in some of the world's highestrainfall areas, rain falls in concentrated periods followed by prolonged dry spells, so users must capture rainwater when it is abundant to use later when it is scarce. Similarly, even in some of the driest areas, occasional intense rainfall generates runoff that can be captured and stored for subsequent use. For example, harvesting only 100 millimeters of rainfall over a one-hectare plot would yield 1 million liters of water. Ancient water-harvesting systems throughout the world took advantage of this principle to smooth intertemporal variations in water availability, making human settlement possible in a wide variety of ecosystems.

Local water harvesting declined with the development of large systems in which water is transported hundreds of miles through canals and pipes or pumped from great depths below the ground. However, growing scarcity and intersectoral competition for water, along with groundwater depletion and the problems facing major surface-water control systems, have raised interest in revitalizing water-harvesting systems that capture rainwater wherever it falls.

### Definition and Types of Waterharvesting Systems

Water harvesting refers to the small-scale concentration, collection, storage, and use of rainwater runoff for both domestic and agricultural use. This definition implies that the catchment area from which the water is drawn is larger than the command area, where it is collected and used. The ratio of catchment to command is inversely related to the amount and intensity of rainfall, the impermeability of soil, and the slope of the land on which it falls. Rainfall intensity is particularly important, since intense storms generate the most runoff.

A watershed is an area that drains to a common point. It may be managed for various objectives, depending on local needs, including capturing runoff, minimizing erosion, and reducing nonpoint source pollution. In management of small watersheds, capturing runoff for local use is conceptually equivalent to harvesting water. This brief encompasses all small-scale, local systems for capturing runoff from rainfall.

Water-harvesting systems either concentrate water into a storage reservoir or apply water directly to the soil in the cropped area. Both types of systems can vary in scale from a few square meters benefiting a single household to a few square kilometers serving a larger group of people.

**Reservoir Systems**

Systems that concentrate water into storage reservoirs can be used for a variety of purposes, including household, irrigation, or livestock consumption. Rooftop water-catchment systems provide domestic water in many places, especially dry areas with inadequate municipal supplies. A rooftop that is 50 square meters can supply an annual average of 50 liters per day with 500 millimeters annual rainfall. This supply can help reduce competition between agricultural and household demands and can free women from the chore of collecting water.

Harvesting water to collect it in village ponds is an ancient system in some places, including southern India. The principle behind this approach is to concentrate water spatially and temporally. In arid and semi-arid areas where rainfall is low and variable, harvesting rainwater allows users to conserve it until enough water is collected to reliably support a crop. The volume of water stored at the end of the rainy season determines how much area can be cultivated. Traditional water-harvesting systems store water in ponds and reservoirs and deliver it by gravity. With the spread of motorized pumps in recent decades, water can now be captured in some places using the same techniques but allowing collected water to percolate into groundwater aquifers. The systems are small in scale, drawing from gullies and microcatchments to recharge groundwater that supplies a number of local wells.

### Soil-moisture Storage Systems

In many traditional water-harvesting systems, runoff water is channeled directly to the cropped area during rainfall and stored in the soil. Where rainfall is unevenly distributed and soils have high water-holding capacity, this system may store water until the end of the rainy season, when a crop is grown under gradually receding moisture. Where soils are sandier and do not retain moisture for a long time, moisture may be channeled spatially to the location where crops or trees can take advantage of it. Farmers in West Africa commonly use such systems, cultivating their dryland crops behind a variety of small earthen barriers designed to capture moisture. These systems can remain productive several months into the dry season when the surrounding land is barren.

Water-harvesting systems vary a great deal in the ratio of catchment to cultivated area. In dry areas with less available water, this ratio can easily reach 20:1. In such water-harvesting systems, cultivation systems must be extensive and located in sparsely populated areas so that command and catchment areas do not interfere with each other. Where rainfall is higher, the ratio declines-sometimes to the point that the entire catchment area lies within a single plot.

### Adoption and Replicability

Constraints to developing improved water-harvesting systems and adapting existing ones for productive use relate to technical feasibility, financial viability, and social organization.

### Technical Feasibility

The key technical question for agricultural water-harvesting systems is whether capturing and storing enough water to raise crop yields is feasible. Much research has gone into measuring the water available to plants under different rainfall, soil, and slope conditions and into developing ways to increase runoff, reduce erosion, or improve storage.

In field conditions, technical feasibility depends in large part on local agroclimatic conditions. For example, in India the Indo-German Watershed Development Project works only in villages where the terrain is conducive to water harvesting-that is, there is a sloped, uncultivated catchment area and a good opportunity to build storage ponds.

**Financial Viability**

Even where water harvesting is technically feasible, it may not be cost-effective. A review of African water-harvesting systems found that many of them cost much more than US$1,000 per hectare to install, making adoption prohibitively expensive.

A typical problem in storing water is the need to line catchment or storage areas so that water can be stored until dry periods when it is actually needed. However, using a plastic or concrete lining can raise costs beyond the financial returns. An example of where lining is most likely to be cost-effective is in mountain regions where water enables farmers to grow counterseasonal crops that can be sold in the plains at high prices.

The main constraints to rooftop collection systems are the need for a tile or sheet metal roof that can capture runoff and a storage tank, both of which can be prohibitively expensive in very poor areas. In that case, village-level systems housed on public buildings may be more viable, along with smaller-scale household systems. The key issue with storage tanks is how to make them large enough to store plenty of water while also keeping costs down.

Given growing water scarcity and the high financial, social, and environmental costs of alternatives, governments may find subsidizing water-harvesting systems attractive, especially those for domestic supply. Some countries already subsidize rooftop collection systems.

## Social Organization

Water harvesting requires collective action in densely populated areas where more than one person uses catchment and command areas for multiple purposes. The key question in such cases is whether the benefits of water harvesting exceed the costs of coordination among users. Often this can be the most daunting constraint of all, especially where some resource uses are mutually incompatible and any intervention will impair at least one potential use, as in India. Successful water harvesting requires protecting upper reaches of small catchments against erosion that would re-duce water-storage capacity in the lower reaches. Typically, upper catchments are denuded, so protecting them requires limiting their use for grazing and fuel collection. This restriction imposes the greatest costs on landless people who depend the most on these areas and who do not stand to gain directly from water harvesting. Long-term success requires devising institutional approaches to ensure that landless people gain from the water-harvesting intervention.

Water harvesting is certain to grow in importance in coming years as policymakers and planners seek cost-effective solutions to water supplies. Many simple systems can easily be put in place to overcome water scarcity, particularly rooftop collection for domestic use. As water becomes increasingly scarce, treatment of storage ponds to reduce leakage may become more financially viable. On the other hand, systems that require cooperative management and strict limits on land use will probably not become any simpler as local economies and land-use systems become increasingly complex.

Water harvesting does not make large dams and groundwater extraction obsolete. Rather, each system has its own advantages and disadvantages, and all systems can complement each other. The major advantage of water harvesting is that it begins to address problems locally, relieving the pressure on large-scale, centralized systems. Integrating water harvesting with other systems, as well as improving the management of demand, will lead to reliable, costeffective water systems.

Water pricing policy has the potential to mitigate water scarcity. Because of its key role in managing water demand and augmenting water supply, water pricing is an important policy instrument for creating incentives to conserve and allocate water efficiently.

By providing financial justification for developing additional supplies from conventional and unconventional sources, pricing policy can make more water available to users. Unfortunately, the water pricing policies being pursued in most countries fail to perform these vital roles due to faulty approaches and inappropriate institutions, both of which have their roots in political economy.

The state provides many irrigation and domestic water supply systems at subsidized rates because doing so delivers public goods in the form of secure food supplies, public health, or legitimacy for the government. But low water charges and poor cost recovery lead to declining funds available for investment in water infrastructure, poor maintenance of existing systems, inefficient water allocation, and growing conflicts between those with and without access to water.

Economic and political pressures stemming from these problems have promoted a renewed debate on water pricing policy.

## Role of Water Pricing Policy

Financially, water pricing is the main mechanism for cost recovery. Economically, it signals the scarcity value and opportunity cost of water and guides allocation decisions within and across water subsectors. The financial function requires water rates to cover the cost of supplying water to users. The supply cost is usually calculated by adding the operation and maintenance costs and the capital costs of constructing the system. But full cost recovery also requires water rates to reflect the long-term marginal cost (the cost of supplying an additional unit of water including the social cost of externalities).

The economic and allocative role of water pricing requires water rates to capture the scarcity value (or the marginal productivity/ utility) and to equalize the opportunity costs (the value of water in its next best use) of the resource across uses. As water moves from least productive to most productive uses, places, and time points for efficient allocation, there will be a convergence of the scarcity value, opportunity cost, and longterm marginal cost of the resource.

Unfortunately, such a convergence is rarely seen in practice. Unrealized opportunities still exist and water rates can be designed to capture at least a part of these opportunity costs. For this to occur, technology to store, transport, and deliver water is required, as are institutions to govern the development, allocation, and utilization of the resource.

## Cost Recovery and Economic Incentives

The effectiveness of the financial and economic roles of water pricing policy depends on pricing methods, sectors, and countries. Water pricing may be either volumetric (based on the quantity of water used) or flat rate (based on area irrigated or households benefited). Volumetric pricing is conducive to creating incentives for efficient allocation and use, but the cost of establishing volumetric water delivery structures is often prohibitive, especially in large and spatially spread surface irrigation systems serving many smallholders.

As a result, areabased fixed rates are dominant in most irrigation systems. However, volumetric water rates are widely used in many urban water supply systems.

Water rates are generally higher in countries with severe water scarcity (such as Algeria, Sudan, and Israel) and institutionally developed water economies (such as Australia and Israel). The industrial and power sectors within a country usually pay the highest water rates and receive a higher, more costly level of service throughout the year, as do domestic users. Agriculture pays the least, but also receives the lowest level of service. Within each sector and country, there can also be a wide variation in costs as domestic users buying water from private vendors pay much more than those connected to municipal systems and farmers receiving irrigation from public canals pay far less than those receiving irrigation from private wells.

Full cost recovery is legitimate both in economic and equity terms only if the users gain all the benefits from investment. On this count, some argue that since food prices fall when irrigation increases food production, consumers benefit, and that higher water rates for full cost recovery could adversely affect farmers' incomes.

But this need not be the case because farmers benefit from irrigation partly from higher output and partly from increased land prices. In any case, the kind of full cost recovery being contemplated in many contexts does not cover even 10 percent of the additional income from irrigation, let alone the land value appreciation.

Water rates are still subsidized even in countries with a relatively mature water economy such as Australia, Israel, and the United States. This is rooted in the political economy of water, as powerful state and user interests often oppose charging the full cost of water.

As a result, the gap is vast between the observed water rates and the ideal economic prices of water, as reflected by its scarcity value and opportunity cost. This illustrates the real magnitude of the task of designing pricing policies effective enough to play, simultaneously, the financial and economic roles.

## The Institutional Dimension

The policy debate has increasingly focused on the broader economic and allocative roles of water pricing. There is growing recognition that a realistic water pricing policy that ensures full cost recovery can be politically feasible only when it is designed to perform well in its economic and allocative roles.

Also notable is the growing realization that institutional reforms to enhance the effectiveness of water pricing policy are indispensable. Pricing reform does not end with raising water rates. It also involves concurrent changes in pricing methods and approaches and the creation and strengthening of supportive institutions.

Volumetric pricing, though necessary, is not sufficient to ensure an effective economic role for water pricing. As long as the rates are below both supply cost and water productivity and there is no upper limit on individual water withdrawals, volumetric pricing per se can neither achieve full cost recovery nor solve the key incentive problem.

For this purpose, volumetric pricing needs to be accompanied by price levels that are consistent with prevailing economic and resource realities. A system of transferable water quotas (rights) specifying upper limits for individual water withdrawals needs to be established for water markets to emerge that can, in turn, provide a basis for determining economically consistent water rates.

Pricing reform can be effective and practical only with the necessary institutional and technical conditions that enable cost recovery and allocative roles for water pricing policy. These institutions include an independent water pricing agency and regulatory body, financially autonomous agencies to supply water, clearly defined water rights, and transfers of management to user organizations or the private sector.

Technical conditions include volumetric delivery, measurement structures, and infrastructure to move water over space, type of use, and time. These institutional and technical conditions can encourage the emergence of direct allocation mechanisms such as water markets and implement water pricing reforms.

It is true that the institutional and technical changes involve huge costs. But the present bureaucratic system of water administration is equally costly. International experience shows clearly that the promotion of intra-and intersectoral water allocation through markets in tradable water rights can have financial, efficiency, and equity gains far higher than the costs of transacting the reforms.

## Conclusion

Although water continues to be subsidized in most sectors and countries, there is growing recognition of water pricing as a key policy instrument for cost recovery and demand management. Given the seriousness of the informational, technical, and political constraints, the technical and institutional conditions needed for full cost recovery or for efficient allocation cannot be created overnight. A realistic strategy for water pricing reform involves, therefore, an incremental approach that sequences reform components appropriately, focuses first on cost recovery, and gradually broadens to address the economic and allocative role of water pricing.

Enhancing and sustaining the economic and welfare contributions of water resources depends ultimately on the ability to face the twin challenges of supply augmentation with the lowest ecological and social costs, and the development of institutional frameworks for an efficient use of existing and future supplies. The future of the market-based water economy in most countries rests on how quickly the institutional reforms are undertaken.

## MARKETS FOR TRADABLE WATER RIGHTS

Water markets have been advocated as a means of improving water resources management by increasing the efficiency of water use and allocation within and among sectors. Water markets are more flexible than command-and-control instruments in moving water to higher-valued uses in a manner agreeable to all parties, thus promoting economic growth and diminishing social tension from competition for scarce water resources. Sometimes water markets are also expected to mitigate environmentally detrimental effects from overexploitation of water resources. However, they can also have drawbacks, and decisions about the introduction of a water market in a specific setting need to be informed by a thorough institutional analysis of the local socioeconomic, cultural, and hydrological context.

### What is a Water Market?

In its most basic definition, a water market is an arrangement in which holders of water rights trade them with each other or to outside parties. However, there are differences between water markets, and design will depend on the prevailing hydrological regime, including whether trades involve surface water, groundwater, or both; the previous existence of informal water rights and trading; the types and numbers of water users and right holders, including whether all are irrigation farmers or from different water-use sectors; and the physical arrangements for moving water between users. However, appropriate institutional arrangements must be in place to ensure positive outcomes from water markets.

### Institutional Arrangements for Effective Functioning of Water Markets

The implementation of water markets requires both government involvement and active water-user participation. Institutional ingredients needed for other approaches to improving water-resources management-such as an administrative system that registers and enforces timely water deliveries, a transparent and accepted water measurement system, and a well-maintained delivery system-are all required for a functioning market. Therefore, the difference between the implementation of administrative systems and a market system may not be as large as expected. The principal difference is the need for the following:

- Definable and transferable water rights. Reallocation by trading means getting compensated. That is different from administrative reallocation, where right holders may not receive any compensation when water is reallocated to a different use. Under water markets, right holders will not only consider what the water can produce for themselves, but also the opportunity cost of the water (such as the value added by using the water in car manufacturing). Thus, the highest value of water use is taken into account, providing an incentive for more efficient use and reallocation of water to a higher-valued use.
- Internal institutional market arrangements. Buyers and sellers need to find each other and have confidence in the characteristics of the goods they want to exchange. In a well-functioning water market, this implies measuring the water available for trading, developing a simple mechanism to find prospective buyers and

sellers, and carrying out the transfer. If the official transfer is difficult, then informal trading will likely occur anyway. The disadvantage of informal trading is that water use is hard to track. This is the case in Mexico and India, where groundwater levels keep sinking despite water trading.

- A physical delivery system. Traded water is likely to move from one user to another. Depending on the hydrological conditions or previously constructed infrastructure, the cost of adequate infrastructure may be too high and outweigh the benefits from transfers, rendering the water price so high that no buyers can be found. The government may absorb the cost, but thorough analyses are needed to establish whether the introduction of a tradable system will produce sufficient societal benefits to warrant large investments.

**Handling Externalities**

Imagine a river where a right holder uses only 70 percent of her water so that the remaining 30 percent is available for her neighbors. If she decides to sell her full right to a buyer who will use all of this water, then the downstream neighbors will be deprived of the extra water, which they count on. They may go to court to prevent the sale, thereby causing high transaction costs, or courts may not be available and they will have to accept the loss. A mechanism is therefore needed to either negate third-party interests or to mitigate the impacts of water trading on the different stakeholders, including an effective conflict resolution system. Such a system could be linked to water courts or taken care of by the riverbasin management agencies where the market is located.

The most challenging institutional feature of a water market may thus be the definition and registration of water rights, together with the implementation of adequate information and transaction mechanisms that provide equal possibilities for all water users to participate in the market. These mechanisms would have to include access to price information and the registration, enforcement, and monitoring of rights.

## Introducing Water Markets in Developing Countries

Developing countries characteristically suffer from weak institutional frameworks, such as slow judicial systems, unclearly defined land rights, strong concentration of land ownership, and unenforced laws and environmental regulations. Before the introduction of water markets, the necessary legal and institutional requirements in each site should be compared with what already exists. An evaluation should be made to determine whether the laws and institutions could be changed with low political and social transaction costs to permit the introduction of a well-functioning water market.

Socioeconomic asymmetries need to be considered because of the different types of water users, who will vary in their educational background, culture, and economic power. When water rights were allocated and made tradable in Chile, electricity companies bought up a large number of them to be held for future use, to the detriment of smaller users who at the outset did not understand the implications of their selling the rights. Given that water is the basis for agricultural production, the sale of a water right may severely undermine smallholders' livelihoods. In response, the Chilean government has been discussing the prohibition of holding water rights for more than five years without beneficial use.

As in the case of land rights, poor farmers may use newly allocated water rights to pay off their debts, ending up without their entitlement in the long run. A phased approach to water trading may be the most appropriate, starting with the introduction of water rights, monitoring, and enforcement, and followed at a later stage by tradability. This would give water users-especially the more vulnerable segments of society-the time to realize the value of their new rights. Instituting a seasonal or annual leasing system could also permit right holders to experience market transactions without permanently endangering their livelihoods.

Another important issue is the impact of water reallocation on higher-valued uses and their impact on regional economies and the environment. International experience is inconclusive. In Mexico, small farmers with severe groundwater overdraft do not have the capital to invest in deeper wells, so they sell their water rights to large agribusinesses that do invest in wells. The small farmers win because, without the water market, they could neither invest and nor receive any compensation. Furthermore, the company creates local and regional jobs. On the other hand, by obtaining more water rights, the company also strongly contributes to the declining groundwater level, thus hurting more small farmers and the environment.

The need for integrating a functioning system of waterresources management with the water market approach is clear. Such a system would include water measurement, enforcement, sanctioning of infractions, and user participation in decisionmaking about regional water-resources management goals. The Chilean and Mexican examples also show that water markets-like other approaches-have social and environmental implications that cannot be disregarded if they are to enhance sustainable development and economic growth.

Water markets can help improve water allocation and use. To function, they need a set of institutional arrangements, which are partly the same as so-called "administrative watermanagement tools," namely riverbasin management, water measurement, enforcement, sanctioning, water availability information, and water-user participation. In addition, some parts of the institutional arrangements needed are incremental, such as tradable water use rights, and appropriate infrastructure and transaction mechanisms.

A gradual approach to introducing water markets may be the most appropriate, putting into place water measurement systems, defined (though not tradable) water rights , and water user participation. In many settings worldwide, these steps would be the basis for much-improved water-resources management and would permit the stakeholders to get adjusted to a new set of rules. Eventually, rights to water use could be made tradable, but should take into account and make appropriate provisions for vulnerable user groups and uses, including the environment.

While the benefits of water markets can be substantial, potential negative socioeconomic or environmental impacts need to be included in the analysis prior to taking any steps toward implementation. The gradual approach proposed here would not only permit a long-term evaluation of institutional change, but would also help include the different stakeholder groups in shaping the institutional arrangements for water resources management.

## RECOGNIZING WATER RIGHTS

The time when water could be freely used without being subject to legal rights and obligations is past. Because of population growth, industrial and agricultural development, and new water technologies, water has become increasingly scarce. As competition has become more acute, the tendency to appropriate water and exclude others from using it has increased. This has created pressures on the regulation and appropriation of water resources and rights for different purposes, such as drinking, agriculture, industry, and hydropower. It has also made the need for new regulation more urgent. Moreover, technical measures-such as building an irrigation system, dam, or river lining-may affect existing rights to water and create new rights without explicit legislation. In the near future, competition over water will only increase and the need for regulation will be more acute than ever.

Control over and use of water has been regulated in diverse ways that involve bundles of rights. These bundles assign legitimate authority and the obligations to control water and determine the priority of water use. They lay down who has the right to appropriate water, whether or not water can be transferred, and the relation between water rights and land rights.

Such bundles of rights range from the most exclusive forms of individual ownership, to communal rights at the local-community level, to public regulation at the national or state level, to agreements at the international level, or a combination of these. Usually, any set of regulations regarding a particular water resource involves both private and public rights and obligations. The specific character of water resources requires forms of organization that often transcend or cut across the ordinary administrative boundaries of local community, district, and state. A command area of an irrigation system may lie in more than one village; a river basin may run through several countries.

**State and Customary Law**

In many countries, the state claims sovereignty and ownership over all its water resources. However, especially in developing countries, state law is not the only source of regulation. Local regulations (or "customary" law) and religious regulations often assign rights and obligations that differ from and sometimes contradict state law. By definition, customary legal orders are based on different notions of who may control, regulate, and have access to water. The state does not always recognize non-state legal orders and their ideas about water rights as valid. Nevertheless, they continue to exist and exert their influence on water-resource management practices.

Recognition of customary and religious law has been a political issue since colonial times and recently has acquired new impetus with debates about efficient and equitable use of water. The debates lead to such questions as:

- Are some types of rights more conducive to efficient or sustainable use of water than others?
- What are the criteria for equitable distribution?
- Are state regulations more efficient and equitable than customary legal forms?

These issues have been subject to misunderstandings that result from untenable assumptions concerning the character and function of the various kinds of water rights. In dealing with these questions, policy must not only devise new sets of water rights and obligations based on realistic assumptions but also accommodate complex existing legal constellations in the field of water resources management.

In assessing the nature and function of customary legal rights, policymakers often make three mistakes. First, many assume that all norms and regulations that do not emanate from state institutions are customary and long established. In fact, many rules and regulations emerge locally as new responses to outside intervention by the state or other institutions. Second, policymakers assume that everybody acts according to these rules because they are deeply ingrained in local society. However, human behavior never fully corresponds to norms and regulations. Every property regime allows for variations in behavior, and each local community adapts its legal system and the structure of rights to changing social and economic conditions. Third, policymakers assume that all customary property is communal property. In fact, no property regime is fully communal; it is always a combination of communal and individual elements, and of public and private elements.

The focus of interest shifted from economic development to sustainable development in the late 1960s in the debate about appropriate management of "the commons." Communal property rights were blamed at that time for unsustainable resource use. More recently, the argument has been reversing. Communities, community-based rights, and communities' customary law are now being promoted as inherently conducive to sustainable resource use. The arguments are particularly powerful in relation to natural resources, such as water, forests, fisheries, and natural reserves. However, here again experience has shown that overexploitation and resource degradation can occur under state, individual, or communal ownership. The extent to which resources are managed sustainably depends on the ways in which wealth is distributed and on whether the users have alternative economic possibilities.

Customary law is also often considered to be more equitable than other legal regimes. However, there is little consensus on how equity is defined. Customary legal systems may show considerable inequalities based on class, gender, age, and caste. One important reason is the unequal distribution of land. Rights to water are usually closely connected to land rights. Springs are often owned by whoever owns the land on which the spring originates. People living along a river are entitled to draw water from the river. In cases of irrigation, the rights to irrigation water are usually distributed among those having land in the command area; or they belong to those who participate in building the system, again usually people that own the land to be irrigated. Where land is unequally distributed, water is also usually unequally distributed. Poor people tend to have land at a disadvantaged position within irrigation systems or even outside the command area of irrigation systems.

Water is also distributed unequally by gender. For their water rights, women often depend on men: fathers or brothers while unmarried, husbands after marriage. Thus, women are excluded from the right to make decisions in public arenas. Interests that tend to be more specific to women, such as accessibility to household and drinking water, are often disregarded. This is not so much a result of a conscious exclusion from water rights as such, but of more general gender differences that do not allow women to participate in the public domain, or that do not allow women to inherit or acquire property independently.

State water regulations may also show inequalities. Present state policies to create water markets, meant to increase efficiency, will certainly increase inequality unless very serious measures are taken to ensure that the poor have access to this market.

## Policy Implications

This brief should not be read as a plea for following customary law blindly in all respects. There may be very good reasons for wanting to change customary water rights, for example, to bring about more efficiency, sustainability, and gender equality, or to alleviate poverty. In addition, major changes in the scope of water redistribution cannot be achieved at the relatively small political and geographical scale on which customary legal systems operate.

Change should build upon a realistic and careful assessment of existing rights to water and other natural resources in all their complexity. Because rights to water are intimately linked to a wider set of social relationships, successful change requires a full analysis of existing inequalities within a society.

Any policy that simply ignores existing rights-whether defined in state law, in local legal systems, or in religious law-is bound to fail and to create more, rather than less, insecure rights. This is potentially harmful for the people that policymakers intend to protect. Policies based on false assumptions about the social working of law inevitably lead to disappointment. Replacing customary water rights with a new property regime designed from scratch is bound to meet with strong opposition from those threatened with loss of their existing rights. Changing water rights alone may only marginally redress inequity in access to water. Making changes in inheritance regulations or land redistribution may also be required.

Devising a new set of categories of rights to water will not suffice unless attention is also given to the actual distribution of water through these rights. This involves deciding on the distribution of available water resources among different uses and setting priorities. It also involves distribution decisions between different segments of the population within sectoral uses, and the legally valid means through which such redistribution is to be effected.

The legal complexity of this issue and its potential for social and political tension also demand a policy style that is open to hearing and negotiating with those holding rights to water under multiple legal orders. Perfect legal regulation is likely to be an illusion, and compromises will have to be made.

Finally, local and customary rights vary considerably in content and function from region to region. Policymakers are well advised not to cover them under uniform legislation that does not take these variations into account. New legislation should lay down a general framework and leave room for the elaboration of local variations in specific cultural, legal, and hydrological conditions.

## INTEGRATED MANAGEMENT OF WATER IN RIVER BASINS

Until the beginning of the 19th century, human water use was limited. Natural features and forces largely dictated river flow regimes, and natural biota were the primary water users. By the 20th century, a great remaking of river systems occurred as humans manipulated the natural hydrology to meet the domestic supply, sanitation, food, fiber, and industrial needs of growing populations and rising standards of living. Water resources in many river basins are fully committed to a variety of in-stream and remote purposes, degrading water quality, threatening river-dependent ecosystems, and intensifying competition and strife.

## What is Integrated River Basin Management?

Integrated river basin management (RBM) systems bring fragmented water uses and users together (see Box). RBM creates a framework that deals with an entire basin or sub-basin, such as the Colombia, the Indus, or the Limpopo, not just a single water use or administrative jurisdiction. A river basin can be defined by the watershed limits of a system of waters, both ground and surface, flowing to a common terminus. RBM integrates this system of waters within its broader natural environment and its social, economic, and political contexts. Basin units cut across administrative divisions used to manage water. This is their strength and their challenge.

Water in a river basin is both renewable and reusable. The hydrologic cycle renews the resource annually; water within a basin can be reused many times on its way from headwaters to the sea. Some are in-stream uses, such as hydropower generation, navigation, recreation, or ecological sustenance. Other uses, such as municipal water supply, industrial cooling, or irrigation, extract water but return much of it downstream. As a result, a blend of water that has been used and reused comprises the lower reaches of most major river systems. This multiplier effect allows withdrawals to exceed by many times the natural flow in a river and provides a number of management options for optimizing the utility of water in a basin, but creates significant measurement and quality management problems.

Because of the large variability in river flows across seasons and years, flood protection works and artificial storage are important elements of river basin systems. The degree of control afforded by reservoirs varies enormously. The reservoirs on the Colorado River in the U.S. can store four times the annual flow of the river, whereas the Mekong River in Southeast Asia is largely unregulated. There are many more management options and the value of water in the Colorado River basin is higher, since regulated flows generally have much greater utility for human uses than unregulated ones.

## Integrated Basin Management

Although the term "integrated" most commonly refers to integration across use sectors, such as agriculture and urban water supply, it can also encompass a num-ber of other divisions, including the following:

- Administrative jurisdictions;
- Ground and surface water;
- Upstream and downstream reaches;
- Environmental and human uses;
- Supply and demand management;
- Water quantity and quality;
- Land and water use; and
- Transboundary uses.

This value comes at a cost to natural ecosystems, which have evolved from and adapted to natural cycles of flood and recession. Manipulating reservoir releases to mimic key portions of these natural cycles has increased, but much remains to be learned in this area.

As river basins approach full utilization, systems of specifying, quantifying, and assigning rights to the water become more formalized. Those affected try to protect, defend, and perhaps augment their rights; interact with other right holders, claimants, and aspirants; and sometimes conflict with them. RBM must therefore establish the rules of the game and mechanisms to govern these interactions, so that they take place in a productive and efficient way. All interests and stakeholders in the water affairs of the basin must have suitable protection and adequate representation, including the natural environment and less powerful water users. The most important decisions in RBM are made on the basis of contemporary social values, not on technical grounds. Effective RBM requires both good process and good science.

**Types of Management Structures**

There are two archetypal organizational models for implementing RBM. The first is the authority model, in which a single unified organization is empowered to make decisions. The second is the coordinative model, in which existing administrative units work together to cover an entire river basin or subbasin. While new structures may be created, the bulk of routine work is done by existing organizations.

A strength of the authority model is that its operational span of control coincides with the boundaries of the basin. This internalizes upstream/downstream and other conflicts, making them easier to deal with. And it concentrates the decisionmaking authority needed to resolve disagreements. But there are disadvantages too. Since the authority will very likely deal only with water, water will be isolated from relevant policy sectors such as agriculture, the environment, and the economy. Authority is centralized rather than devolving to the lowest practicable level. And for international rivers, the authority model requires establishing a supranational authority, which is extremely difficult to do. Finally, governance of an RBM authority may not include broad-based stakeholder representation and accountability.

The coordinative model addresses some of these weaknesses. Because coordination involves voluntary agreement among participating jurisdictions, it provides a strong political base for action. Linkages between water and other types of policy remain, since states, nations, or other jurisdictions are jointly responsible for a range of policy sectors. Such a set-up also provides a natural base for decentralization of responsibilities. On the other hand, decisionmaking can be cumbersome, costs of coordination may be high, and political changes in participating jurisdictions can upset agreements.

These two models represent polar extremes. Specific cases often blend the two. In Australia's Murray-Darling Basin, a cooperative Ministerial Council comprising representatives of the four involved states and the federal government, sets policy while an authority-like commission supports and executes the council's decisions. In France, a river commission made up of local and national government representatives and users sets water policy, which an associated water agency implements. Publicly held companies manage the distribution infrastructure and make bulk water deliveries to user associations. In the United States, there is generally no formal apex council in a river basin, and policymaking authority is distributed among federal and state agencies and departments.

Committees and working groups link stakeholders to discussion and decisionmaking fora. Legislation and legally binding negotiated agreements are important instruments for establishing policy and practices, and the court system resolves disagreements and disputes. In the state of California, a water plan that is updated every five years provides a rolling framework for managing the state's water resources.

The most prominent examples of authorities are those whose primary mandate is to develop a river basin, such as the Tennessee Valley Authority (TVA) in the U.S., the Rio São Francisco Development Agency in Brazil, and the Mahaweli Development Authority in Sri Lanka. When their primary development tasks are finished, authorities often transition to a broader resource management role, with varying degrees of success.

### The Contextual Fit

Most of these examples are from higher-income countries. But can RBM models from wealthy countries like Australia and the United States work in other contexts? River basins across the world are reaching full allocation and experiencing many of the problems outlined earlier. The TVA model has successfully developed water resources in places like Sri Lanka, but its record as an RBM model is checkered. Sri Lanka is struggling to transform the Mahaweli Authority into a basin management agency. Applying the TVA model to the Damodar Valley Authority in India in the 1950s was a resounding failure. Current attempts to use the Murray-Darling model in Vietnam and China are encountering fundamental problems. Experience with RBM in developing countries and in developed countries may differ because in developing countries:

- Dense populations live in upper watershed catchments and require access to water along with downstream urban populations;
- Water use is widely dispersed rather than concentrated and easily controlled;
- Administrative capacity to monitor and enforce regulations and standards is limited;
- Governance mechanisms to assign rights and regulate and enforce agreements and contracts are nonexistent or weak;
- Technical capacity to measure and monitor basin hydrology is limited;
- Civil society does not possess the internal structure of groups and associations needed to represent various stakeholder interests;
- Pressures for transparency in public decisionmaking and regulation, including independent, investigative media, are not strong.

These differences preclude the wholesale importation of developed-country models. RBM strategies must be adapted to the particular context. Building institutional capacity in critical areas may have to proceed simultaneously with the development of RBM organizations. In such cases, it may be necessary to defer assigning particular functions to these organizations until sufficient capacity has been developed.

Achieving effective basin management requires a strong knowledge base, suitable governance mechanisms, administrative capacity, adequate stakeholder representation, transparency, and political will. This challenging set of requirements is matched by equally rewarding potential outcomes, such as more efficient use of each drop of water, enhanced reuse of water, mitigation of past environmental damage, and redirection of water to uses that society values most highly. The overarching imperative is to accomplish these ends in a way that treats all stakeholders, particularly weaker and poorer stakeholders, fairly and equitably.

## WATER, CONFLICT, AND COOPERATION

River basins and groundwater aquifers that cross international boundaries present increased challenges to effective water management because hydrologic needs are often overwhelmed by political considerations. While the potential for paralyzing disputes is especially high in these transnational basins, the record of violence is actually greater within a nation's boundaries. Moreover, history is rich with examples of how water has become a catalyst to dialogue and cooperation, even among especially contentious riparians.

### Water and Intranational Conflict

The scarcity of water for human and ecosystem uses leads to intense political pressures, often referred to as "water stress." As a consequence, competition for water resources has contributed to tensions around the globe between competing uses-urban vs. agricultural, environmental protection vs. industry-and users, from neighboring irrigators to neighboring nations. While water quantity has been the major issue of the 20th century, water quality has been neglected to the point of catastrophe. Water demands are increasing, groundwater levels are dropping, surface-water supplies are increasingly contaminated, and delivery and treatment infrastructure is aging. These tensions have spilled into violence on occasion, mostly at the intranational level, and generally among ethnic, religious, or tribal groups; water-use sectors; or states/ provinces. Examples of internal water conflicts range from interstate violence and death along the Cauvery River in India, to California farmers blowing up a pipeline meant for Los Angeles, to much of the violent history in the Americas between indigenous peoples and European settlers.

While these disputes can and do occur at the sub-national level, the human security issue is subtler and more pervasive than violent conflict. As water quality degrades-or as quantity diminishes-over time, tensions can spill across boundaries. The overall effect on the stability of a region can be unsettling.

## Background on International Waters

There are 261 watersheds and countless aquifers that cross the political boundaries of two or more countries. International basins cover 45.3 percent of the land surface of the Earth, affect about 40 percent of the world's population, and account for approximately 60 percent of global river flow. These basins have certain characteristics that make their management especially difficult, most notably the tendency for regional politics to exacerbate the already difficult task of understanding and managing complex natural systems.

Disparities between riparian nations-whether in economic development, infrastructural capacity, or political orientation further complicate international water resources management. As a consequence, development projects, treaties, and institutions are regularly seen as inefficient at best and, occasionally, as a source of new tension themselves.

## Development, Crisis and Conflict Resolution

A general pattern has emerged for international basins over time. Riparians of an international basin first implement water development projects unilaterally on water within their territory in an attempt to avoid the political intricacies of the shared resource. At some point, one of the riparians, generally the regional power (either upstream riparian or country with the most military, political, or economic strength), will implement a project that impacts at least one of its neighbors. The project might aim to continue meeting existing demand in the face of decreasing relative water availability, such as Egypt's plans for a high dam on the Nile or Indian diversions of the Ganges to protect the port of Calcutta; or to meet new needs reflecting new agricultural policy, such as Turkey's GAP project on the Euphrates. A project that impacts one's neighbors can, in the absence of relations or institutions conducive to conflict resolution, become a flashpoint, heightening tensions and regional instability, and requiring years or, more commonly, decades, to resolve.

It feels both counterintuitive and precarious that the global community can let water conflicts drag on to the extent they often do-the Indus treaty took 10 years of negotiations, the Ganges 30, and the Jordan 40-while water quality and quantity degrade to the point that the health of dependent populations and ecosystems is damaged or destroyed. A re-read of the history of international waters suggests that in the absence of agreement, neither human suffering and death nor the health of aquatic ecosystems is sufficient incentive to cooperate. This problem gets worse as the dispute gains in intensity. Some ecosystems, such as the lower Nile, the lower Jordan, and the tributaries of the Aral Sea, have been allowed to deteriorate because posturing states did not cooperate to protect them. They have effectively been written off to the vagaries of human intractability.

### Preventive Diplomacy and Institutional Capacity Building

There is some room for optimism, though, in the global community's record of resolving water-related disputes along international waterways. The record of cooperation has consistently prevailed over acute conflict related to international water resources. In fact, the last (and only) war fought specifically over water took place 4,500 years ago, between the city-states of Lagash and Umma along the Tigris River. Over the last 50 years, there have been only 37 acute disputes (those involving violence). During the same period, 157 treaties were negotiated and signed; only 507 events were conflict-related; 1,228 were resolved cooperatively. Moreover, almost two-thirds of all events are only verbal and, of those, more than two-thirds are reported as having no official sanction at all. The most vehement enemies around the world either have negotiated water-sharing agreements, or are in the process of doing so as of this writing. Violence over water seems neither strategically rational, nor hydrographically effective, nor economically viable. Shared interests along a waterway seem to consistently outweigh water's conflict-inducing characteristics.

Furthermore, once cooperative water regimes are established through treaty, they turn out to be impressively resilient over time, even between otherwise hostile riparians, and even while conflict is waged over other issues. For example, the Mekong Committee has functioned since 1957, exchanging data throughout the Vietnam War. Secret "picnic table" talks have been held between Israel and Jordan ever since the unsuccessful Johnston negotiations of 195355, even while these riparian nations were in a legal state of war. And the Indus River Commission not only survived two wars between India and Pakistan, but treaty-related payments also continued unabated throughout the hostilities.

These patterns suggest one valuable lesson: international waters are a resource whose characteristics tend to induce cooperation rather than incite violence, which is the exception. The greatest threat of the global water crisis, then, comes from the fact that people and ecosystems around the globe lack access to sufficient quantities of water at sufficient quality for their well-being.

## Lessons for the International Community

Despite the complexity of water disputes, the historical record shows that they do get resolved, and that the resulting water institutions can be tremendously resilient. The challenge for the international community is to get ahead of the "crisis curve," to help develop institutional capacity and a culture of cooperation in advance of costly, timeconsuming crises that in turn threaten lives, regional stability, and ecosystem health.

One productive approach to the development of transboundary waters has been to examine the benefits in a basin from a multi-resource perspective. This has required riparians to get past looking at water as a commodity to be divided and to develop instead an approach that equitably allocates not the water, but the benefits derived therefrom.

The most critical lessons learned from the global experience in international water resource issues are that:

- Water crossing international boundaries can cause tensions between nations that share the basin. While the tension is not likely to lead to warfare, early coordination between riparian states can help ameliorate the issue.

- Once international institutions are in place, they are tremendously resilient over time, even between otherwise hostile riparian nations, and even while conflict is waged over other issues.
- A gradual decrease in water quantity or quality, or both, is more likely than violent conflict. Over time, such water decreases can affect the internal stability of a nation or region, and act as an irritant among ethnic groups, water sectors, or states/provinces. The resulting instability may have effects in the international arena.
- The greatest threat of the global water crisis to human security comes from the fact that millions of people lack access to sufficient quantities of water of sufficient quality for their well-being.

## WATER PRICING: POTENTIAL AND PROBLEMS

Water pricing policy has the potential to mitigate water scarcity. Because of its key role in managing water demand and augmenting water supply, water pricing is an important policy instrument for creating incentives to conserve and allocate water efficiently. By providing financial justification for developing additional supplies from conventional and unconventional sources, pricing policy can make more water available to users. Unfortunately, the water pricing policies being pursued in most countries fail to perform these vital roles due to faulty approaches and inappropriate institutions, both of which have their roots in political economy.

The state provides many irrigation and domestic water supply systems at subsidized rates because doing so delivers public goods in the form of secure food supplies, public health, or legitimacy for the government. But low water charges and poor cost recovery lead to declining funds available for investment in water infrastructure, poor maintenance of existing systems, inefficient water allocation, and growing conflicts between those with and without access to water. Economic and political pressures stemming from these problems have promoted a renewed debate on water pricing policy.

## Role of Water Pricing Policy

Financially, water pricing is the main mechanism for cost recovery. Economically, it signals the scarcity value and opportunity cost of water and guides allocation decisions within and across water subsectors. The financial function requires water rates to cover the cost of supplying water to users. The supply cost is usually calculated by adding the operation and maintenance costs and the capital costs of constructing the system. But full cost recovery also requires water rates to reflect the long-term marginal cost (the cost of supplying an additional unit of water including the social cost of externalities).

The economic and allocative role of water pricing requires water rates to capture the scarcity value (or the marginal productivity/ utility) and to equalize the opportunity costs (the value of water in its next best use) of the resource across uses. As water moves from least productive to most productive uses, places, and time points for efficient allocation, there will be a convergence of the scarcity value, opportunity cost, and longterm marginal cost of the resource. Unfortunately, such a convergence is rarely seen in practice. Unrealized opportunities still exist and water rates can be designed to capture at least a part of these opportunity costs. For this to occur, technology to store, transport, and deliver water is required, as are institutions to govern the development, allocation, and utilization of the resource.

## Cost Recovery and Economic Incentives

The effectiveness of the financial and economic roles of water pricing policy depends on pricing methods, sectors, and countries. Water pricing may be either volumetric (based on the quantity of water used) or flat rate (based on area irrigated or households benefited). Volumetric pricing is conducive to creating incentives for efficient allocation and use, but the cost of establishing volumetric water delivery structures is often prohibitive, especially in large and spatially spread surface irrigation systems serving many smallholders. As a result, areabased fixed rates are dominant in most irrigation systems. However, volumetric water rates are widely used in many urban water supply systems.

Water rates are generally higher in countries with severe water scarcity (such as Algeria, Sudan, and Israel) and institutionally developed water economies (such as Australia and Israel). The industrial and power sectors within a country usually pay the highest water rates and receive a higher, more costly level of service throughout the year, as do domestic users. Agriculture pays the least, but also receives the lowest level of service. Within each sector and country, there can also be a wide variation in costs as domestic users buying water from private vendors pay much more than those connected to municipal systems and farmers receiving irrigation from public canals pay far less than those receiving irrigation from private wells.

Full cost recovery is legitimate both in economic and equity terms only if the users gain all the benefits from investment. On this count, some argue that since food prices fall when irrigation increases food production, consumers benefit, and that higher water rates for full cost recovery could adversely affect farmers' incomes.

But this need not be the case because farmers benefit from irrigation partly from higher output and partly from increased land prices. In any case, the kind of full cost recovery being contemplated in many contexts does not cover even 10 percent of the additional income from irrigation, let alone the land value appreciation.

Water rates are still subsidized even in countries with a relatively mature water economy such as Australia, Israel, and the United States. This is rooted in the political economy of water, as powerful state and user interests often oppose charging the full cost of water. As a result, the gap is vast between the observed water rates and the ideal economic prices of water, as reflected by its scarcity value and opportunity cost. This illustrates the real magnitude of the task of designing pricing policies effective enough to play, simultaneously, the financial and economic roles.

## The Institutional Dimension

The policy debate has increasingly focused on the broader economic and allocative roles of water pricing. There is growing recognition that a realistic water pricing policy that ensures full cost recovery can be politically feasible only when it is designed to perform well in its economic and allocative roles. Also notable is the growing realization that institutional reforms to enhance the effectiveness of water pricing policy are indispensable. Pricing reform does not end with raising water rates. It also involves concurrent changes in pricing methods and approaches and the creation and strengthening of supportive institutions.

Volumetric pricing, though necessary, is not sufficient to ensure an effective economic role for water pricing. As long as the rates are below both supply cost and water productivity and there is no upper limit on individual water withdrawals, volumetric pricing per se can neither achieve full cost recovery nor solve the key incentive problem. For this purpose, volumetric pricing needs to be accompanied by price levels that are consistent with prevailing economic and resource realities. A system of transferable water quotas (rights) specifying upper limits for individual water withdrawals needs to be established for water markets to emerge that can, in turn, provide a basis for determining economically consistent water rates.

Pricing reform can be effective and practical only with the necessary institutional and technical conditions that enable cost recovery and allocative roles for water pricing policy. These institutions include an independent water pricing agency and regulatory body, financially autonomous agencies to supply water, clearly defined water rights, and transfers of management to user organizations or the private sector. Technical conditions include volumetric delivery, measurement structures, and infrastructure to move water over space, type of use, and time. These institutional and technical conditions can encourage the emergence of direct allocation mechanisms such as water markets and implement water pricing reforms.

It is true that the institutional and technical changes involve huge costs. But the present bureaucratic system of water administration is equally costly. International experience shows clearly that the promotion of intra-and intersectoral water allocation through markets in tradable water rights can have financial, efficiency, and equity gains far higher than the costs of transacting the reforms.

## Conclusion

Although water continues to be subsidized in most sectors and countries, there is growing recognition of water pricing as a key policy instrument for cost recovery and demand management. Given the seriousness of the informational, technical, and political constraints, the technical and institutional conditions needed for full cost recovery or for efficient allocation cannot be created overnight. A realistic strategy for water pricing reform involves, therefore, an incremental approach that sequences reform components appropriately, focuses first on cost recovery, and gradually broadens to address the economic and allocative role of water pricing. Enhancing and sustaining the economic and welfare contributions of water resources depends ultimately on the ability to face the twin challenges of supply augmentation with the lowest ecological and social costs, and the development of institutional frameworks for an efficient use of existing and future supplies. The future of the market-based water economy in most countries rests on how quickly the institutional reforms are undertaken.

# 5

# WATER SUPPLY FOR HOME USES

The Earth was home to 6 billion people in 2000: 1.1 billion of them lacked safe water and 2.4 billion lacked adequate sanitation. As a consequence, water-and sanitation-related diseases are widespread. Nearly 250 million cases are reported every year, with more than 3 million deaths annually-about 10,000 a day. Diarrheal diseases impact children most severely, killing more than 2 million young children a year in the developing world. Many more are left underweight, stunted mentally and physically, vulnerable to other deadly diseases, and too debilitated to go to school.

This situation in today's world is humiliating, morally wrong, and oppressive. The global community has made advances in many fields but it has failed to ensure these most basic needs of deprived people. Worse still, if unprecedented global action is not taken, the lot of the poor is expected to worsen in the foreseeable future.

## Current Situations

In spite of hard work and laudable progress, the number of people without access to both water supply and to sanitation in developing countries remained practically the same throughout the 1990s: the increase in population served was just enough to keep pace with population growth. According to the Global Water Supply and Sanitation Assessment 2000 Report, the majority of the world's population without access to improved water supply or sanitation services lives in Africa and Asia. Two-thirds of people without access to improved water supply and more than three-quarters of those without access to improved sanitation live in Asia.

No figures are available on hygiene. However, experience has shown that clean water alone leads to only minor health improvements. The essential factor is sound personal hygiene, with adequate public sanitation and clean water as supporting components. While each of the three components alone has some health benefit, their combined effect is far greater. Hygienic behavior is virtually impossible without a source of safe water and a safe means to dispose of human and other wastes.

Access to water and sanitation services is closely related to each nation's economy. The economic gap between rich and poor countries has widened over the last 20 years. Many of the least developed countries have been caught in a downward economic spiral. Their governments can find it hard to sustain basic social programs, including water and sanitation. Furthermore, aid programs often lack the flexibility essential in such cases. This crisis is most apparent in Sub-Saharan Africa. In Asia, the Middle East, North Africa, Latin America, and the Caribbean, the situation is generally better, although growing cities represent a critical challenge.

The dissolution of the USSR has caused the quality of water services in large parts of Central Asia to slip backward. Throughout this region, institutional reform has become critically important to the goals of decentralization and encouragement of private initiative. In addition, collaborative mechanisms are badly needed to help promote common awareness and joint action across the diverse political, economic, and cultural philosophies and practices that these nations embrace.

### Future Needs

The Population Council predicts that world population will grow to 7.8 billion over the next 25 years, with most of the increase in urban areas. The urban population will roughly double, to approximately 4.5 billion people. After 2020, all population growth-and most poverty-in the developing world will occur in urban areas, as the rural population declines. Universal water supply and sanitation coverage by 2025-a now widely acknowledged goal-will mean that in urban areas an additional 1.9 billion people will need water supply and 2.1 billion will need sanitation services. In rural areas, 1 billion people will need water supply and 2.1 billion will need sanitation.

Field experience and studies suggest that a minimum quantity of safe water is required for a person to drink, prepare food, ensure personal cleanliness, and use a sanitary latrine. Drinking and cooking take 10 to 15 liters per day. Water needs for hygiene and sanitation are less precise, and vary from one culture to another. But a person who practices personal hygiene and uses a latrine needs an absolute minimum of 20 liters per day. Further health benefits accrue when communities move from public tap to house connections. Those with house connections usually use 40 or more liters per head. The total volume of water required to meet basic needs for all is thus relatively small, even for a city of 1 million, compared to agricultural and industrial uses, and even to household use by the wealthy. Thus the problem in domestic use is not water quantity.

Sanitation is one of the most important interventions in improving the human condition. Yet many agencies neglect hygiene and sanitation because they are not included in agency mandates. What constitutes good hygienic practice varies from culture to culture although the common aim is to break the fecal-oral transmission route of disease. Disposing of human wastes in a manner that does not contaminate the environment and that further limits the likelihood of disease transmission from person to person is a fundamental requirement. Minimum sanitation standards should be established at the national level.

## THE VISION 21 PROCESS

The process began with meetings in towns and villages in 21 countries, where local men, women, and children joined local NGOs, citizens' groups, and other stake-holders. The groups looked a generation ahead and asked, "What water, sanitation, and hygiene environment would we like to see in our community in the year 2025 and what is needed to attain this?" Following the local meetings, the national consultations reviewed the communities' answers, which started a dialogue (sometimes for the first time) among government, community representatives, and NGOs. Next, Vision 21 held five regional consultations. Contributors from the national meetings joined participants from countries that were not yet part of the national Vision 21 exercise. The final part of the process was a global consultation, where the final version of Vision 21 was endorsed by a gathering of stakeholders representing all the regions. All these people shared their aspirations and their strategies for practical action toward universal access to hygiene, sanitation, and water supply. Thus, Vision 21 opened the door to an approach that has the potential to reach everyone. What seemed idealistic has proved to be achievable.

## The Way Forward

The constraints for improvement are neither financial nor technical-they are political, social, and managerial. Business as usual has proven unable to produce adequate water services. Democratic thinking and action, one of the most essential changes, is a prerequisite for development.

To find solutions for the imminent crisis in hygiene, sanitation, and water supply the Water Supply and Sanitation Collaborative Council (WSSCC) undertook a democratic consultation process that developed Vision 21 (see Box). If the goal of hygiene, sanitation, and water supply for all people is to be achieved, people's roles must change. The most important actors will be individuals and groups in households and communities with new responsibilities for their own hygiene, sanitation, and water services, as part of a collective strategy.

Public authorities will need to provide enabling conditions, clearing large-scale obstacles, securing empowerment of people through self-reliance, supporting individuals and families in their efforts, and carrying out the work that households and communities cannot manage for themselves. Similarly, water-sector professionals must combine their technical skills with an ability to communicate with those they serve.

The fundamental premise is that people's initiative and management of their own quality of life must be at the center of planning and action. Visions and plans articulated at local levels are the building blocks for progress at the next levels of national, regional, and global action.

This approach demands collaborative action by empowered people in households and communities, and by authorities that support new roles for civil society. Fresh attitudes and commitments, reflected in new policies and activities, are needed at every level of society and governance. The foundation of the new approach is recognition that water and sanitation are basic human rights. Together, water and sanitation services can improve living conditions for all, and most particularly for children and women. They form a major component in poverty reduction. Such recognition can lead to systems that encourage genuine participation by men and women, resulting in the acceptance and practice of hygiene, coupled with safe water and sanitation at the household level.

## Investment Required

Earlier estimates of annual expenditures on water and sanitation ranged from US$10 to US$25 billion, most on higher level services in urban centers whose cost is not recovered from the users. The Global Water Partnership's more recent estimate is that an annual investment of US$30 billion might be needed for water supply and sanitation.

The WSSCC suggests that if the principles elaborated in the Vision 21 document are seriously applied, the total cost for providing a basic level of service over the next 25 years (in addition to the costs borne by households or communities) totals US$225 billion, or approximately US$9 billion per year. This estimate is within the range of current expenditures. It reflects the potential for cost recovery possible through political determination, to which participation is the key.

The controversy over large dams on the River Narmada has come to symbolise the struggle for a just and equitable society in India. The story is long and complicated and will take a long time to tell. In brief, the Government's plan is to build 30 large,

135 medium and 3000 small dams to harness the waters of the Narmada and its tributaries. The proponents of the dam claim that this plan would provide large amounts of water and electricity which are desperately required for the purposes of development.

Opponents of the dam question the basic assumptions of the Narmada Valley Development Plan and believe that its planning is unjust and inequitous and the cost-benefit analysis is grossly inflated in favour of building the dams. It is well established that the plans rest on untrue and unfounded assumptions of hydrology and seismicity of the area and the construction is causing large scale abuse of human rights and displacement of many poor and underprivileged communities. They also believe that water and energy can be provided to the people of the Narmada Valley, Gujarat and other regions through alternative technologies and planning processes which can be socially just and economically and environmentally sustainable.

Through this web site we shall endeavour to present the view of the poor and underprivileged affected by the dams and the people's movements they have created (primarily the Narmada Bachao Andolan) which are leading the crusade for justice and the Right to Life of the many inhabitants of the Narmada valley.

We recognise the complexity of the issues involved. However, once one cuts through all the rhetoric, lies and subterfuge of the vested interests, the gross inequities are clear. Large numbers of poor and underprivileged communities (mostly tribals and dalits) are being dispossessed of their livelihood and even their ways of living to make way for dams being built on the basis of incredibly dubious claims of common benefit and "national interest". For us, this is simply immoral and therefore unacceptable. No purported benefits can be used to justify the denial of the fundamental rights of individuals in a democratic society. And given the evidence of past megadam schemes in India and elsewhere and what has already happened in the Narmada Valley, we believe that the promised benefits will never be realised.

A quick look at the ground reality would disabuse anyone of the real nature of the dam-builder's enterprise. Large dams imply large budgets for related projects leading to large profits for a small group of people. A mass of research shows that even on purely technical grounds, large dams have been colossal failures. While they have delivered only a fraction of their purported benefits, they have had an extremely devastating effect on the riverine ecosystem and have rendered destitute large numbers of people (whose entire sustenance and modes of living are centered around the river).

For no large dam in India has it been shown that the resettled people have been provided with just compensation and rehabilitation. At a more abstract level, the questions that arise in the Narmada Struggle challenge the dominant model of development (of which Sardar Sarovar dam is a prime example) that holds out the chimerical promise of material wealth through modernisation but perpetuates an inequitous distribution of resources and wreaks social and environmental havoc.

We would like to emphasise that the water problems of drought-prone areas of Gujarat, like Kutch, Saurashtra and North Gujarat (the Government's raison d'etre for the dam) are admittedly real. However given the nature of the plans for Sardar Sarovar, it will never solve these problems. On the contrary, in the shadow of the costliest project ever undertaken in India, it is unlikely that alternative schemes that would genuinely address these problems would be implemented. Sardar Sarovar takes up over 80% of Gujarat's irrigation budget but has only 1.6% of cultivable land in Kutch, 9% of cultivable land in Saurashtra and 20% cultivable land in North Gujarat in its command area.

Moreover, these areas are at the tail-end of the command and would get water only after all the area along the canal path get their share of the water, and that too after 2020 AD. In summary, all available indicators suggest that these needy areas are never going to benefit from the Sardar Sarovar Project. In simple terms, the struggle over the river Narmada holds a mirror to our national face and challenges our commitment to professed ideals of justice, equality and democracy.

## Sites of Struggle

Of the 30 big dams proposed along the Narmada, Sardar Sarovar Project (SSP) and Narmada Sagar Project (NSP) are the megadams. The Maheshwar and Omkareshwar dams along with SSP and NSP, are to form a complex which would ultimately cater to the needs of SSP.

The struggle of the people of the Narmada valley against large dams began when the people to be displaced by SSP began organizing in 1985-86. Since then the struggle has spread to encompass other major dams in various stages of planning and construction chiefly Maheshwar, Narmada Sagar, Maan, Goi and Jobat. Tawa and Bargi Dams were completed in 1973 and 1989 respectively have seen the affected people organize post-displacement to demand their rights.

Official website of the Narmada Valley Development Authority :

- Sardar Sarovar Dam: Information about the Sardar Sarovar Dam
- Maheshwar Dam: Information about the Maheshwar Dam
- Maan Dam: Information about the Maan Project
- Indira Sagar Dam: A case study of a village affected by ISP
- Bargi Dam: The Human Cost of the Bargi Dam
- Goi Dam: Goi Project: A Critique
- Jobat Dam: Jobat Project: A Critique

## A Brief History

The Narmada river originates from the Maikal ranges at Amarkantak, 1057 m above the sea-level, now in Shahdol district of Madhya Pradesh. In its 1312 km long journey before joining the Arabian Sea, the Narmada flows through the three states of Madhya Pradesh (MP), Maharashtra and Gujarat. Nearly 90% of the flow is in MP, and most of the remaining is in Gujarat. It flows for a very brief stretch through Maharashtra.

The valley of the river Narmada (which means one who endows with bliss) has been the seat of an uninterrupted flow of human civilization dating from pre-historic times. The Narmada finds mention as one of the seven most sacred rivers in ancient Indian texts. A number of written accounts and ballads refer to this river. Its banks are dotted with temples, myths and folklore, the living symbols of a timeless Indian tradition. The river Narmada has supported a bewildering variety of people and diverse socio-cultural practices ranging from the relatively autonomous adivasi (tribal) settlements in the forests to non-tribal rural population.

The idea of damming the Narmada was discussed as far back as the late 19th century during the days of the British Raj. The first Irrigation Commission of India, in its 1901 report, mentions a barrage near Bharuch. However the black alluvial soil of the region was not considered suitable for flow irrigation from the point of view of investment.

The issue of damming the river was raised again after independence under the thrust of the Nehruvian Development policy which referred to dams as the "temples of modern India." It is said that the first Home Minister of India, Sardar Vallabhbhai Patel who hailed from the strong agrarian background of central Gujarat dreamt of harnessing the river for the benefit of his own people. This "dream" syndrome became very strong and was subsequently used by every politician in Gujarat to leverage political support for the Narmada project.

The Narmada valley project was mired in controversy and dispute right from its inception. In 1965, the Khosla committee planned a 530 feet high dam in Navagam (the site of the Sardar Sarovar dam today) while allocating 13.9 MAF (million acre feet) of water to MP and 10.6 MAF to Gujarat. This proposal was immediately locked in a dispute between the so-called riparian states i.e. Gujarat, Maharashtra and MP over the sharing of the costs and benefits of the project. The chief minister of MP, Mr. Govind Narayan Singh, objected to the unprecedented submergence as a result of the dam and contested the claims of Gujarat on the Narmada waters. Gujarat on the other hand claimed a higher share of water on the basis of the projected needs of the "drought prone area" in the far-off Kutch region. In this effort, Gujarat also made Rajasthan a party to give itself more bargaining power, although Rajasthan-a non-riparian state-had nothing to do with the project.

In 1969, the Government of India under Mrs. Indira Gandhi constituted the Narmada Water Disputes Tribunal (NWDT) to resolve this inter-state water dispute. The Tribunal itself was subjected to a series of wranglings between Gujarat and MP. While MP proposed a dam height 210 feet, Gujarat demanded that the height of the dam be 530 feet. While Gujarat put its water requirement at 22 MAF, MP would concede only 4 MAF. Finally in 1979, after 10 years of deliberations, the Tribunal gave its award which consisted of clear compromises between the claims of Gujarat and MP. Accordingly they allocated 9 MAF of water to Gujarat. and arrived at the 453 feet for the height of the dam. Subsequently, 2 extra feet were added to the dam height for completely unknown reasons to bring the height to round figure of 455 feet. After a token show of resistance, the main political formations in MP accepted the award.

The full contours of the Narmada Valley Development Plan (NVDP) appeared only towards the late 1980s. It is an ambitious plan which envisages the building of 30 big dams, 135 medium dams and 3000 small dams on the Narmada & its tributaries. If all of these dams ever get built then the river as we know it will disappear and all that will be left are a series of lakes.

## RECOMMENDED WATER HARVESTING AND WATERSHED MANAGEMENT WORKS

## AGRO-CLIMATIC ZONES

Based on the requirements of agricultural development, the country has been demarcated into 15 agro-climatic regions. However, for promoting rainwater harvesting with particular reference to augmenting drinking water availability in rural areas, these regions have been slightly modified and an additional region viz. "Himalayan foot hills" has been added. Broad features of these 16 regions and the recommended water harvesting measures for each region are discussed in the following paras.

## HUMID NORTHWESTERN HIMALAYAS

This region comprises hilly areas of Jammu & Kashmir, Himachal Pradesh and Uttaranchal. This cold region has skeletal soils, podsolic soils, mountain meadow soils and hilly brown soils. The terrain is highly undulating with steep slopes. The soils are generally silty loam and are prone to erosion. Landslides are common in denuded hill slopes especially where there are excessive human settlements with good network of roads and hill tracks. Water harvesting measures recommended for the region are:

(i) Roof water harvesting

(ii) Diversion of perennial springs and streams water in storage structures

(iii) Village ponds

(iv) Collection from hill slopes

## HIMALAYAN FOOT HILLS

The region is characterized by slope-wash material comprising loose soil deposits underlain by boulders and pebbles. These deposits generally have moderate to high percolation rates where the soil cover is thin. In topographic lows the thick soil cover provide scope for dug ponds with fairly good water retention capacity.

Often the ground water gradient is steep which is conducive to quick drainage of ground water into nearby streams. The region covers foothill areas of Jammu & Kashmir, Himachal Pradesh, Punjab and Uttaranchal in the west and parts of West Bengal, Assam and Arunachal Pradesh in the east. The recommended structures are:

(i) Collection from hill slopes

(ii) Village ponds

(iii) Contour trenching

## HUMID HIGH RAINFALL NORTH EASTERN ZONE

The region is characterized by complex geological formations with rocks either exposed on surface or under moderately thick soil cover. The soils are generally fragile and prone to severe erosion. The region covers large areas of Sikkim, Darjeeling hills, Arunachal Pradesh, Meghalaya, Nagaland, Manipur, Tripura, Mizoram, Assam, and Jalpaiguri and Cooch Behar districts of West Bengal.

These are high rainfall areas with high surface runoff. In some areas because of adverse topography and hydrogeological conditions, ground water development is not techno-economically viable while in some others the habitations do not have convenient access to the potential ground water sources, which are usually found in topographic lows like stream beds and intermontane valleys. The recommended measures are:

(i) Roof top harvesting

(ii) Diversion of perennial springs and streams in storage structures (tanks)

## HUMID ASSAM BENGAL PLAINS

The region covers parts of the lower Gangetic plains comprising alluvium with diverse mix of sand, silt and clay. The main topographic features of the region are the fluvial plains, and lower and upper alluvial terraces. The fluvial plains are characterized by abandoned river channels, ox-bow lakes and the land surface carved by numerous perennial and seasonal streams. Though the region receives good rainfall, there are often drought like situations due to long gaps between successive spells of rainfall especially in areas drained by small seasonal streams. The natural drainage channels and streams flowing through the alluvial terraces severely erode their banks. Because of excessive agricultural activity coupled with unscientific land management the topsoil is prone to erosion.

The ground water usually has excessive iron and mica. Excessive arsenic is found in about 1,000 habitations in West Bengal. However, ground water development in the region especially in Assam is constrained by, interalia, lack of reliable power supply. The recommended water harvesting measures are:

(i) Tanks

(ii) Check dams/ Anicuts

(iii) Gully plugging

(iv) Contour bunding

## SUB-HUMID AND HUMID SUTLEJ-GANGA ALLUVIAL ZONE

The region covers parts of Punjab, Haryana, Uttar Pradesh and Bihar and is served by middle reaches of the Sutlej basin and the lower and middle reaches of the Ganga basin. The eastern part of the region covering plains of Bihar and eastern Uttar Pradesh receives good rainfall but due to its uneven distribution in space and time, some areas face sub-humid conditions and even drought like conditions in the years of below-normal rainfall. The southern part of the Sutlej basin has sub-humid climate. During the last 5 decades the region has seen large-scale development of ground water for irrigation. This has resulted in lowering of ground water table in many areas. The problem of drinking water supply is, however, mainly because of non-sustainability of the water sources for various socio-economic reasons. The recommended water harvesting measures for the region are:

(i) Ponds

(ii) Check dams

(iii) Gully plugging

(iv) Contour bunding

## NORTH-WESTERN SEMI-ARID AND ARID ZONE

This zone consists of western Rajasthan, which is characterized by hot sandy desert, erratic rainfall, high evaporation, absence of any perennial rivers and scanty vegetation. Because of low rainfall and high evaporation the natural ground water recharge is negligible. The ground water table in most places is at considerable depth. Potable ground water at reasonable depths is found at a few locations. Agriculture in the area, except the command of the Indira Gandhi Nahar Pariyojna (IGNP) is rainfed. There is extensive ground water exploitation for drinking water supply in rural areas. The rainwater harvesting measures recommended for this zone are:

(i) Nadi/ Talab

(ii) Tanka

(iii) Khadin

(iv) Percolation tanks

(v) Anicuts

(vi) Gully plugging

(vii) Contour bunding

## CENTRAL SEMI-ARID VINDHYAN ZONE

This zone comprises southeastern districts of Rajasthan, southern districts of Uttar Pradesh and central parts of Madhya Pradesh. The area has diverse topography with ravines in some parts of Narmada Valley and hills in others. Nearly one third of the land is not suitable for cultivation. Irrigation and cropping intensities are low. While the rainfall in areas lying in Madhya Pradesh is fairly good being of the order of 900 mm, it is as low as 350 mm in the areas falling in Rajasthan and Uttar Pradesh. Because of the predominantly hilly terrain the monsoon runoff is high which causes extensive soil loss from hill slopes and erosion of riverbanks. Ground water movement from higher levels to lower levels is significant which is evident from the depletion of water levels in wells and hand pumps especially those along stream banks. The water harvesting and watershed development measures recommended are:

(i) Ponds

(ii) Check dams

(iii) Contour bunding

(iv) Gully plugging

(v) Sub-surface dykes

## HIGH RAINFALL HIGH RUNOFF CHHOTANAGPUR PLATEAU

This area is characterized by soils of medium to shallow depths and undulating topography. Because of steep slopes, high rainfall intensities and long rainy spells the surface runoff is high which causes extensive soil loss due to rill and gully formations and stream bank erosion. The problem is further compounded by unscientific agricultural practices. The region covers the entire Jharkhand state and adjoining hilly areas of Bihar, West Bengal and Orissa. Because of adverse topography and pattern of human settlements in the hilly terrain potential ground water sources are not within convenient reach of all the rural population. Improvement of watersheds and local rainwater collection and storage are considered necessary to improve water availability. The recommended water harvesting practices, therefore, are:

(i) Tanks/ Ponds
(ii) Check dams/ Anicuts
(iii) Gully plugging
(iv) Contour bunding

## MALWA PLATEAU & NARMADA BASIN

The region forms a major part of peninsular India with an annual rainfall of about 900 mm. The predominant soil type is deep black soil. Because of low permeability of soil natural ground water recharge is mainly through fissures and joints in exposed rocky strata and through streambeds. The water harvesting methods recommended for the region are:

(i) Ponds
(ii) Check dams
(iii) Sub-surface dams

## SOUTH-CENTRAL DECCAN PLATEAU ZONE

The region covering parts of Andhra Pradesh, Tamil Nadu, Karnataka and Maharashtra is typically semi-arid. The region is characterized by highly diverse geological setting with predominance of hard basaltic rocks and variable rainfall.

Ground water occurs under varying conditions in shallow and deep aquifers. Surface strata and soil types are by and large conducive to natural ground water recharge. The recommended water harvesting structures are:

(i) Ponds
(ii) Check dams
(iii) Percolation tanks
(iv) Bandhara
(v) Gully plugging
(vi) Sub-surface dams
(vii) Contour bunding

## CHHATTISGARH PLATEAU ZONE

The region comprises Chhattisgarh state and southwestern Orissa hills. The geological and geomorphological characteristics of the region are more or less similar to those in South-Central Deccan Plateau Zone. Even though rainfall in the region is relatively higher, the recommended structures are the same as those for the South-Central Deccan Plateau Zone.

## SOUTH-EASTERN BROWN/ RED SOIL ZONE

The region covers Pachamalai and Kadavur hills and pediplain areas of Tamil Nadu and Veligond hills and part of the plains (excluding the 4-5 km wide coastal belt) of Andhra Pradesh. The rainfall in the region varies from about 818 mm in Perambalur district of Tamil Nadu to 1,148 mm in Nellore district of Andhra Pradesh. Runoff coefficient varies from 6.64 to 10.67 percent in plains and from 20 to 45 percent in plateau and foothill areas. The recommended water harvesting structures for the region are the traditional ponds/ tanks. Besides percolation tanks and sub-surface dams are suggested in the vicinity of drinking water sources like dug wells, hand pumps and tube wells.

## SOUTHERN VARIABLE RAINFALL, MIXED SOIL ZONE

The region covers southern parts of Maharashtra and west-central parts of Tamil Nadu. It has a highly undulating and dissected landform with an elaborate natural drainage system. Distribution of rainfall is highly uneven. The land surface is diverse in composition, the main features being sandy or younger alluvial plains and rocky gravel pediments. The soils are friable and prone to erosion, which results in excessive gully formation. The recommend water harvesting and watershed development measures are:

(i) Ponds/ Tanks/ Kunta
(ii) Nadi
(iii) Check dams
(iv) Percolation tanks
(v) Sub-surface dams
(vi) Gully plugging

## SOUTHERN BI-MODAL RAINFALL ZONE

The region covers the southern most parts of Kerela, Karnataka and Tamil Nadu. The prominent physiographic features are the southern plateau and hills, east coast plains and hills and west coast plains and hills. The recommended water harvesting and watershed development measures are:

(i) Ponds/ Tanks
(ii) Percolation tanks
(iii) Check dams
(iv) Gully plugging
(v) Contour bunding

## EASTERN COROMANDAL

The region covers the entire coastal belt of Orissa, Andhra Pradesh and West Bengal. The recommended measures for water harvesting, ground water recharge and watershed development are:

(i) Ponds/ Tanks/ Kunta
(ii) Nadi
(iii) Check dams
(iv) Percolation tanks

(v) Sub-surface dams
(vi) Gully plugging

## WESTERN MALABAR

The region covers the western Malabar area of Kerela and coastal areas of southern Karnataka. The recommended measures for water harvesting, ground water recharge and watershed development are:

(i) Ponds/ Tanks/ Kunta
(ii) Check dams
(iii) K.T. Weirs
(iv) Bandhara
(v) Percolation tanks
(vi) Sub-surface dams
(vii) Contour bunding

**6**

# HARVESTING RAINWATER AND ITS MANAGEMENT

## INTRODUCTION

The famous water-diamond paradox may finally turn out not to be so. The use value of water was never undermined, but its about time that even its exchange value is given due importance. Fresh water today is a scarce resource, and it is being felt the world over. The reality of water crisis cannot be ignored. India has been notorious of being poor in its management of water resources. The demand for water is already outstripping the supply. Majority of the population in the cities today are groundwater dependent. In spite of the municipal water supply, it is not surprising to find people using private tube wells to supplement their daily water needs. As a result, the groundwater table is falling at an alarming rate. Extraction of groundwater is being done unplanned and uncontrolled. This has resulted in:

1. Hydrological imbalance
2. Deterioration in water quality
3. Rise in energy requirements for pumping

Uncontrolled disposal of industrial effluents and sewage of cities into rivers and other water bodies has also resulted in contamination of groundwater. Hence, immediate remedial actions need to be undertaken to avoid a national water crisis.

Rain Water Harvesting, is an age-old system of collection of rainwater for future use. But systematic collection and recharging of ground water, is a recent development and is gaining importance as one of the most feasible and easy to implement remedy to restore the hydrological imbalance and prevent a crisis.

Our focus is on the National Capital Territory (NCT) of Delhi, which is currently facing acute water shortage and drastic drop in the groundwater table over the last few decades. Technically speaking, water harvesting means capturing the rain where it falls. Experts suggest various ways of harvesting water:

- Capturing run-off from rooftops
- Capturing run-off from local catchments
- Capturing seasonal flood water from local streams
- Conserving water through watershed management

Local water harvesting systems developed by local communities and households can reduce the pressure on the state to provide all the financial resources needed for water supply. In addition, involving people will give them a sense of ownership and reduce the burden on government funds.

## NEED FOR WATER HARVESTING

The scarcity of water is a well-known fact. In spite of higher average annual rainfall in India (1,170 mm, 46 inches) as compared to the global average (800 mm, 32 inches) it does not have sufficient water. Most of the rain falling on the surface tends to flow away rapidly, leaving very little for the recharge of groundwater. As a result, most parts of India experience lack of water even for domestic uses.

Surface water sources fail to meet the rising demands of water supply in urban areas, groundwater reserves are being tapped and over-exploited resulting into decline in groundwater levels and deterioration of groundwater quality. This precarious situation needs to be rectified by immediately recharging the depleted aquifers.

Hence, the need for implementation of measures to ensure that rain falling over a region is tapped as fully as possible through water harvesting, either by recharging it into the groundwater aquifers or storing it for direct use.

## SCIENCE OF WATER HARVESTING

1 In scientific terms, water harvesting refers to collection and storage of rainwater and also other activities aimed at harvesting surface and groundwater, prevention of losses through evaporation and seepage and all other hydrological studies and engineering inventions, aimed at conservation and efficient utilization of the limited water endowment of physiographic unit such as a watershed. Rain is a primary source of water for all of us. There are two main techniques of rainwater harvesting:

(a) Storage of rainwater on surface for future use.

(b) Recharge to groundwater.

Directly collected rainwater can be stored for direct use or can be recharged into the groundwater. All the secondary sources of water like rivers, lakes and groundwater are entirely dependent on rain as a primary source.

### Hydrological Cycle

The term "water harvesting" is understood to encompass a wide range of concerns, including rainwater collection with both rooftop and surface runoff catchment, rainwater storage in small tanks and large-scale artificial reservoirs, groundwater recharge, and also protection of water sources against pollution. The objective of water harvesting in India differs between urban and rural areas. In urban areas, emphasis is put on increasing groundwater recharge and managing storm water. On the other hand, in rural areas securing water is more crucial. There the aim is to provide water for drinking and farming, especially for life-saving irrigation, and to increase groundwater recharge.

## ROOFTOP / RUNOFF RAINWATER HARVESTING FOR ARTIFICIAL RECHARGE TO GROUND WATER

Water harvesting is the deliberate collection and storage of rainwater that runs off on natural or manmade catchment areas. Catchment includes rooftops, compounds, rocky surface or hill slopes or artificially prepared impervious/ semi-pervious land surface. The amount of water harvested depends on the frequency and intensity of rainfall, catchment characteristics, water demands and how much runoff occurs and how quickly or how easy it is for the water to infiltrate through the subsoil and percolate down to recharge the aquifers. Moreover, in urban areas, adequate space for surface storage is not available, water levels are deep enough to accommodate additional rainwater to recharge the aquifers, rooftop and runoff rainwater harvesting is ideal solution to solve the water supply problems. Harvested rainwater can be stored in sub-surface ground water reservoir by adopting artificial recharge techniques to meet the household needs through storage in tanks. The Main Objective of such rainwater harvesting is to make water available for future use. Capturing and storing rainwater for use is particularly important in dryland, hilly, urban and coastal areas. In alluvial areas, energy saving for 1m rise in ground water level is around 0.40 kilo watt per hour.

## Advantages of Rainwater Harvesting

1. To meet the ever increasing demand for water. Water harvesting to recharge the groundwater enhances the availability of groundwater at specific place and time and thus assures a continuous and reliable access to groundwater.
2. To reduce the runoff which chokes storm drains and to avoid flooding of roads.
3. To reduce groundwater pollution and to improve the quality of groundwater through dilution when recharged to groundwater thereby providing high quality water, soft and low in minerals.
4. Provides self-sufficiency to your water supply and to supplement domestic water requirement during summer and drought conditions.
5. It reduces the rate of power consumption for pumping of groundwater. For every 1 m rise in water level, there is a saving of 0.4 KWH of electricity.

6. Reduces soil erosion in urban areas
7. The rooftop rainwater harvesting is less expensive, easy to construct, operate and maintain.
8. In saline or coastal areas, rainwater provides good quality water and when recharged to ground water, it reduces salinity and helps in maintaining balance between the fresh-saline water interface.
9. In Islands, due to limited extent of fresh water aquifers, rainwater harvesting is the most preferred source of water for domestic use.
10. In desert, where rainfall is low, rainwater harvesting has been providing relief to people.

**Design Considerations**

Three most important components, which need to be evaluated for designing the rainwater harvesting structure, are:

1. Hydrogeology of the area including nature and extent of aquifer, soil cover, topography, depth to water levels and chemical quality of ground water
2. Area contributing for runoff i.e. how much area and land use pattern, whether industrial, residential or green belts and general built up pattern of the area
3. Hydro-meteorological characters like rainfall duration, general pattern and intensity of rainfall.

**Design Criteria of Recharge Structures**

Recharge structures should be designed based on availability of space, availability of runoff, depth to water table & lithology of the area.

**How much Water can be Harvested?**

The total amount of water that is received in the form of rainfall over an area is called the rainwater endowment of that area. Out of this, the amount that can be effectively harvested is called the water harvesting potential. Water Harvesting potential = Rainfall (mm) X Collection efficiency.

## QUALITY OF STORED WATER

Rainwater collected from rooftops is free of mineral pollutants like fluoride and calcium salts that are generally found in groundwater. But, it is likely that to be contaminated with these types of pollutants:

1. Air Pollutants
2. Surface contamination (e.g., silt, dust)

Such contaminations can be prevented to a large extent by flushing off the first rainfall. A grill at the terrace outlet for rainwater can arrest leaves, plastic bags and paper pieces carried by water. Other contamination can be removed by sedimentation and filtration. Disinfectants can remove biological contamination.

### Cost Analysis

1. Cost of a Rainwater harvesting system designed as an integrated component of a new construction project is generally low.
2. Designing a system onto an existing building is costlier because many of the shared costs (roof and gutters) can be designed to optimise system.
3. In general, maximising storage capacity and minimising water use through conservation and reuse are important rules to keep in mind.
4. With careful planning and design, the cost of a rainwater system can be reduced considerably.

### Cost of Installation

1. An individual house of average area of 300-500 $m^2$, the average cost will be around Rs. 20,000-25,000. A recharge well will be constructed near the existing borewell. The roofwater through PVC pipe will be diverted to recharge well.
2. An apartment building, the cost will be less since the many people will share the cost. More over in apartments there are separate storm water drains, which join the MCD drains in the main road. Here

along with recharge well, recharge trench and percolation pits can be constructed. The cost will be around 60 to 70 thousand.

3. A colony, the cost will be much less. For instance, in Panchsheel Park colony, around 36 recharge wells were installed at the cost of 8 lakh, which is around Rs 500-600 per house. In many colonies in Delhi, storm water drains are present but it is difficult to isolate them from sewage drains because there has been violation of the drainage master plan. Also, these drains are not properly maintained. Hence, care needs to be taken while using storm water for water harvesting. Rooftop harvesting is preferred because the silt load is less. In storm water drain the silt load is high and generally the municipality does not maintain the storm drains properly.
4. An institution with campus, the cost was around 4 lac. Here two recharge wells and three trenches cum percolation pits were constructed.

Average annual maintenance cost would be around Rs 200-300 for two labourers once in a year to remove the pebbles and replace the sand from trenches.

**Rain Water Harvesting Structures in Urban Environment**

A typical Roof top Rainwater Harvesting System comprises of:

(a) Roof catchment

(b) Gutters

(c) Downpipes

(d) Rain water/Storm water drains

(e) Filter chamber

(f) Ground water recharge structures like pit, trench, tubewell or combination of above structures.

**Methods of Ground Water Recharge**

**Storage Tanks :** For harvesting the roof top rainwater, the storage tanks may be used. These tanks may be constructed on the surface as well as under ground by utilising local material. The size of tank depends upon availability of runoff and water demand. After proper chlorination, the stored water may be used for drinking purpose.

**Recharge Pits :** Recharge pits are constructed for recharging the shallow aquifers. These are constructed 1 to 2 m. wide and 2 to 3 m. deep which are back filled with boulders, gravels & coarse sand.

**Trenches :** These are constructed when the permeable strata is available at shallow depths. Trench may be 0.5 to 1 m. wide, 1 to 1.5 m. deep and 10 to 20 m. long depending upon availability of water. These are back filled with filter materials. In case of clay layer encountered at shallow depth, the number of auger holes may be constructed and back filled with fine gravels.

**Abandoned Dug Wells :** Existing abandoned dug wells may be utilised as recharge structure after cleaning and desilting the same. For removing the silt contents, the runoff water should either pass through a desilting chamber or filter chamber.

**Abandoned Hand Pumps :** The existing abandoned hand pumps may be used for recharging the shallow / deep aquifers, if the availability of water is limited. Water should pass through filter media before diverting it into hand pumps.

**Abandoned Tube Well :** Abandoned tubewell may be used for recharging the shallow / deep aquifers. These tube wells should be redeveloped before use as recharge structure. Water should pass through filter media before diverting it into recharge tube well

**Recharge Wells :** Recharge wells of 100 to 300 mm. diameter are generally constructed for recharging the deeper aquifers and roof top rain water is diverted to recharge well for recharge to ground water. The runoff water may be passed through filter media to avoid choking of recharge wells.

**Vertical Recharge Shafts :** For recharging the shallow aquifers which are located below clayey surface at a depth of about 10 to 15 m, recharge shafts of 0.5 to 3 m. diameter and 10 to 15 m. deep are constructed depending upon availability of runoff. These are back filled with boulders, gravels and coarse sand.

**Shaft with Recharge Well :** If the aquifer is available at greater depth say 20 or 30 m, in that case a shallow shaft of 2 to 5 m diameter and 5 to 6 m deep may be constructed depending upon availability of runoff. Inside the shaft, a recharge well of 100 to 300 mm diameter is constructed for recharging the available water to deeper aquifer. At the bottom of the shaft, a filter media is provided to avoid choking of the recharge well.

**Lateral Trench with Bore Wells :** For recharging the upper as well as deeper aquifers, lateral trench of 1.5 to 3 m. wide and 10 to 30 m. long depending upon availability of water with one or more bore wells may be constructed. The lateral trench is back filled with boulders, gravels and coarse sand.

### Typical Design of Trench cum Injection Wells

Above design is specific to location. Size of storage cum filter tank varies from place to place and depending upon the available runoff water from the catchment. Depth of the tubewell also varies from place to place and is normally taken down to the first granular saturated sandy formation. Recharge trench with tube well under construction. After the construction trench can be covered with detachable slabs. Vehicles can move over it and children can play without fear or lawn can be grown over after putting soil over the slabs leaving provision for periodical cleaning.

### *Cost of Recharge Structures*

The cost of each recharge structure varies from place to place. The approximate cost of the following structures is as under:

| S.No. | Recharge Structure | Approximate cost (Rs.) |
|---|---|---|
| 1. | Recharge pit | 2,500-5,000 |
| 2. | Recharge Trench | 5,000-10,000 |
| 3. | Recharge through hand pump | 1,500-2,500 |
| 4. | Recharge through dug well | 5,000-8,000 |
| 5. | Recharge well | 50,000-80,000 |
| 6. | Recharge shaft | 60,000-85,000 |
| 7. | Lateral Shaft with Bore well | Shaft per m. 2,000-3,000<br>Bore well 25,000-35,000 |

(Source: www.cgwaindia.com)

### *Success Parameters*

**Level of Water Table:** Increase in the level of groundwater is an obvious and visible parameter for success of rainwater harvesting systems.

**Quality of Water:** Rainwater is available as the purest form of natural water. The very process of dilution that occurs as rainwater mixes with the groundwater leads to an improvement in the quality of groundwater. Decrease in the following factors are taken into consideration to assess the groundwater quality before and after rainwater harvesting:

a. Salinity

b. Fluoride concentration

c. Nitrate concentration

d. Bacteriological and heavy metal concentration

## Agencies Actively Involved in Rainwater Harvesting

1. *Central Ground Water Board (CGWB) :* Established in 1954, the Central Ground Water Board (CGWB), a National apex organisation, functions under the Ministry of Water Resources. The Central Ground Water Board has been entrusted with the responsibilities to carry out scientific research, surveys, exploration, monitoring of development, management and regulation of country's vast ground water resources for irrigation, drinking, domestic and industrial needs.

   The Central Ground Water Authority (CGWA) was set up in 1997 under sub-section (3) of Section 3 of the Environment (Protection) Act, 1986 (Act of 1986) and has been given the mandate for the "Regulation and Control of Ground Water Development and Management" in the country.

2. *Centre for Science and Environment (CSE) :* The Centre for Science and Environment is a public interest research and advocacy organisation, which promotes environmentally sound and equitable development

strategies. CSE has been involved in raising awareness about the need of community based water management for a number of years. A water crisis that has come about because rain, as a source of water has been ignored. As a technological solution CSE is therefore promoting the concept of community and household based water harvesting as this decentralised technology can be adopted by all concerned and also promote a participatory paradigm of water management.

### *The Case of Delhi*

The National Capital Territory (NCT) of Delhi is facing a water crisis and is even likely to face a water famine. Rapid urbanization coupled with population explosion is attributed as the major cause. The situation becomes grimmer during dry seasons and large numbers of residents have to depend on groundwater to augment the municipal water supply. In South and Southwest districts of Delhi, the situation is explosive and water levels are declining at alarming rates. The Central Ground Water Authority has notified South and Southwest districts of Delhi in August 2000 for regulation of ground water development. Proper water management strategy is the need of the hour. A number of measures are also being promoted to arrest the falling groundwater levels. One of the foremost and essential measure is rainwater harvesting followed by artificial recharge of groundwater. Delhi has a population of roughly 14 million. Against the present requirement of about 3,324 million litres per day (MLD), the installed capacity is only 2,634 MLD.

There has been a widespread drop in the groundwater table in Delhi, especially in the south and southwestern localities of Delhi. Lack of regulation related to private and individual extraction of groundwater aggravates this situation.

Delhi has an annual average rainfall of 611.8 mm. Due to poor recharge and heavy extraction of groundwater, groundwater levels in Delhi have declined by as much as 8 metres in the past decade.

### *Hydrogeology of Delhi and Surrounding Areas*

The groundwater availability in NCT, Delhi is controlled by the hydrogeological situation characterized by occurrence of alluvial formation and quartzitic hard rocks. The following distinct physiographic units further influence the groundwater occurrence.

### *Physiographic Units and Ground Water Potential*

The Four physiographic units that influence and control the groundwater occurrence and movement are:

- o Alluvial plain on eastern and western sides of the ridge (low to moderate yield prospects 25-30 $m^3$/hr.)
- o Yamuna flood plain deposits (large yield prospects 50-100 $m^3$/hr.)
- o Isolated and nearly closed Chattarpur alluvial basin (low yield prospects 10-15 $m^3$/hr.)
- o NNE-SSW trending Quartzitic Ridge (limited yield prospects 5-10 $m^3$/hr.)

### *Depth to Water Levels*

The periodic monitoring of groundwater levels indicates deeper water levels in the range of 20 to 45 m below ground level (bgl) in southern parts of Delhi extending from Rajokri in the west to Kalkaji-Okhla industrial area including Chattarpur basin in the south. In the central part of southwest district, water levels are in the range of 12 to 16 m bgl. Shallow water levels within 5 m bgl are mainly in the flood plains of Yamuna falling in east and northeast districts. Most areas of north, central, New Delhi and northwest districts are having water levels in-between 5 to 10m bgl.

### *Decline in Water Levels*

A comparison of water levels from 1960 to 2001 shows that water levels in major part of Delhi are steadily declining because of over-exploitation. During 1960, the groundwater level was by and large within 4 to 5 meters and even in some parts water logged conditions existed. During 1960-2001, water levels have declined by 2-6 m. in most part of the alluvial areas. Decline of 8-20 m. has been recorded in south-west district and in south district the decline has been 8-30 m. Areas registering significant decline fall mainly in south and south-west districts and have been identified as priority areas for taking up artificial recharge to groundwater by roof top rain water harvesting.

## Ground Water Quality

Chemical quality of groundwater in NCT Delhi varies with depth and space. In alluvial formations, the quality of groundwater deteriorates with depth, which is variable in different areas. Brackish groundwater mainly exists at shallow depths in northwest, west and southwest districts with minor patches in north and central districts. Groundwater is fresh at all depths in the areas around the ridge in the central, New Delhi, south and southwest districts. In the areas west of the ridge, in general, the thickness of fresh water aquifers decreases towards northwest. In the flood plains of Yamuna, fresh water aquifers exist down to 30-45 m. In other parts of NCT, Delhi areas falling under central, New Delhi, east and north-east districts ground water is fresh and potable at shallow depths except in a few pockets around Nizamuddin and Connaught Place where ground water is marginally brackish to saline.

A Model for South and Southwest Delhi:

Total aerial extent of the district = 670 $km^2$

Total population = 40.07 Lac (Census 2001)

Yield Potential of fracture zones = 100-200 lpd

Groundwater level varies from = 5m-50m below ground level

Rate of decline of groundwater level = 1-4m per annum

(Source: Rainwater Harvesting: A necessity in south and southwest districts of NCT, Delhi, Central Ground Water Board, Ministry of Water Resources, GOI)

South and southwest districts of Delhi are comparatively at a disadvantage situation in terms of providing piped water supply, as the water treatment plants are located in northern part of Delhi. Though the government is supplying 148 lpcd (litres per capita per day), the demand and supply gap in these two districts is high because of being posh and economically developed nature. To meet this demand supply gap there has been an explosion of tubewells in this area leading to rapid depletion of groundwater table. Any man-made scheme or facility that adds water to an aquifer system may be considered to be an artificial recharge to groundwater. Artificial recharge to groundwater in south and southwest Delhi needs to be given top priority so as to make the groundwater resources sustainable and improve the quality, which is deteriorating because of over-exploitation.

The thickness of unsaturated zones (potential unsaturated aquifer system for recharge) in these areas varies from 12-50 m. The success rate of Water Harvesting Systems in south Delhi is high compared to other parts of Delhi due to deeper water levels. The intake capacity of the recharge well is good. Where as in Yamuna flood plain and in north Delhi where the water level is very shallow, the intake capacity is low. Water harvesting structures work effectively when the water is more than 15 m below ground level. Hence, south Delhi is ideal for water harvesting.

## GROUNDWATER RECHARGE FROM RAINFALL

Recharge from high intensity rainfall is not a rapid process, but occurs through stagnant pools that are left in low lying areas after significant amount of surface runoff from surrounding areas and farm lands. Thus, rainfall recharge being depression focussed, certain parts of groundwater recharge zones may never receive direct infiltration to the water table. Hence, there is a need to conserve this large amount of water which can be utilised for artificial recharge of groundwater. The annual precipitation over NCT of Delhi in volumetric terms comes out to be 910 MCM (Million Cubic Metres) .

The amount of runoff generated out of this is about 193 MCM. Thus, it is essential to conserve each and every drop of water falling on the territory so as to solve the problem of water supply through augmentation of groundwater resources in suitable areas of the territory. Nuclear Research Laboratory, IARI has estimated that direct groundwater recharge from rainfall infiltration has wide range of spatial and temporal variation, with most parts receiving less than 8 percent recharge from rainfall. But on an average only 10 percent 7 of the annual rainfall is considered as potential recharge without any artificial effort.

## Role of the Government Through the Eyes of the Media

To tackle the problem of drought that rocked the country, the Ministry of Water Resources has drawn up a programme for rainwater harvesting and recharge. A Rs 45-crore plan has been earmarked for rainwater harvesting and recharge in the Ninth Plan. The ministry has sanctioned Rs 25 crore for the Central Ground Water Board programme, which involves states and user agencies in rural and inaccessible areas. The Central Ground Water Authority is also issuing directives to the states and municipal bodies to undertake rooftop rainwater harvesting and its recharge to groundwater mandatory for every dwelling unit by amending city by laws.

At the state level, sensing the need to conserve water, the Delhi Development Authority has proposed amendments to building by-laws making it mandatory for city buildings to have in-built provisions for water conservation, rainwater harvesting, and energy conservation. The proposals, if accepted, would necessitate build-ups over 250 $m^2$ to have provision for rainwater harvesting, dual water supply system, limiting flushing equipment capacity to 5 litres, installation of waste water recycling plants and conservation of energy through passive climate control. Coimbatore has joined the select group of cities in the country which have made rainwater harvesting mandatory to reduce groundwater exploitation. Plans for all new structures within the corporation limit would be approved only if they satisfy the newly drafted guidelines of the corporation.

The corporation council has approved the resolution, which necessitates residential buildings, commercial and industrial structures to have proper rainwater harvesting systems. Over the years, the groundwater level has been depleting in the city and surroundings following large-scale exploitation. It is estimated that the level could be down to 200 to 350 feet in most of the areas. Moreover, increasing encroachments at 17 of the 28 tanks have aggravated the situation (The Financial Express, 26 June 2000). Experts point out that the scope of water harvesting is tremendous. An improvement in water conservation can also provide the foundation for a multitude of other problems. However, they opine that there needs to be a change in the governance of water systems-a decentralized system of water management is required.

## Arguments Against Water Harvesting

Despite the growing awareness about the benefits of water harvesting, there is another school of thought that argues that roof water harvesting systems (RWHS) are not alternative to public systems in urban and rural areas of regions receiving low rainfall. It says that very little empirical work has been done to assess the impact of roof water harvesting on urban and rural water supply situation.

Two important factors seem to be missed out. First, there is significant variation in rainfall in many arid and semi-arid regions and it can pose serious limitations on the amount of water that could be captured. Second: the roof area per capita that is available for capturing rainwater is quite limited and this again could pose a constraint on the amount of water that can be captured. Therefore, the estimates currently available over-emphasise the scope of this technique. Further, there has been no systematic inquiry into the technical feasibility of storing water captured from rooftop in the urban areas. The hydrological opportunities for roof water harvesting would vary significantly from year to year, as well as from location to location, and variation likely to be more in low rainfall areas.

The physical feasibility of RWHS in urban and rural areas is of great importance. To analyse this, M Dinesh Kumar studied the city of Ahmedabad, which falls within the semi-arid tropic of India. He showed that there could be major variations in the volume of water that could be stored across different housing stocks. In case of large individual bungalows (600 sq. m roof area), it can vary from 72 $m^3$ to 21 $m^3$. Assuming the per capita requirement for the upper class family as 500 litres per day, the water stored would be sufficient to meet the domestic water requirement for 5 months in a good year to one and a half months in a bad year. For a small bungalow (200 sq. m roof area), the amount of water that could be stored varies from 24 $m^3$ in a good year to 7 $m^3$ in a bad year.

Assuming the per capita water requirement to be 300 litres per day, the stored water would be sufficient to meet the requirements for 80 days in a good year to 23 days in a bad year. In the case of a 3-storeyed middle-income housing stock, the volume varies from a maximum of 7.5 $m^3$ to a minimum of 2.7 $m^3$ . For the lower income groups (320 sq. m roof area), it can vary from 4 $m^3$ to 1.2 $m^3$.

Assuming the per capita water requirement of the middle income group as 200 litres per day, stored water would be sufficient to meet the requirements for 5 weeks in a good year to 2 weeks in a bad year. Similarly for the lower income group, assuming a per capita water requirement of 150 litres per day, the stored water would be sufficient for just four weeks in a good year to just one week in a bad year. In the case of multi-storeyed apartments for the high-income groups, the volume of water per capita varies from a maximum of 5.3 $m^3$ to a minimum of 1.5 $m^3$ . Similarly for the middle-income groups it can vary from 2.4 $m^3$ to 0.70 $m^3$.

Taking the per capita water requirement for the high income group as 200 litres per day, the stored water would be sufficient to meet the requirements for less than 4 weeks in a good year and one week in a bad year. Taking the water requirement of middle-income groups as 150 litres per day, the stored water would be sufficient to meet the requirements for 16 days in a good year to 5 days in a bad year. RWHS require underground storage tanks. For an apartment with roof area of 320 sq. m, the maximum volume of water that can be stored is 416 $m^3$ to 112 $m^3$ for rainfalls of magnitude 1200 mm and 350 mm respectively. The capacity of existing storage tanks in a typical 10-storeyed apartment will be 30-40 $m^3$. Most urban housing stocks do not provide the kind of land area required for building such laıge tanks, which is necessary for storing the water for lean seasons.

The actual size of a new storage tank would depend on the time duration between two large rain spells, given the magnitude of rainfall. If there is good number of non-rainy days between two large wet spells, the capacity requirement would come down, provided water from the new storage tank is used up during this period. For this, two things are required. First: when rainwater is available, the public system will have to cut down its supplies, which means that both the systems have to be synchronised. Second: rainwater stored in the new tank will have to be lifted and put in the old storage tanks as and when it gets empty space.

This would pose complex management problem in case of large housing stocks with several users under one roof. The analysis shows that roof water harvesting is beneficial for those who are living in bungalows and flat systems, provided the available per capita roof area is quite significant, that is more than 6 sq. m. Hence, roof water harvesting systems are best suited to higher and middle-income groups. As such, it is not a substitute for urban public water utilities. RWHS is only one among many strategies for countering the growing urban water crisis.

## CONCLUDING REMARKS

It is no denying that sustaining and recharging the groundwater along with judicious use of the limited fresh water resources is the need of the hour. If sufficient measures are not taken up immediately, we will face a crisis which will be detrimental to the very survival of mankind. Efficient management of water resources and education about judicious utilisation of water resources along with measures of harnessing, recharging and maintaining the quality of water and water bodies has to be taken up on war footing.

One of the most logical steps towards this goal would be acknowledging the importance of rainwater harvesting. This should not only encompass rooftop rainwater harvesting but also stormwater harvesting systems.

Stormwater harvesting is yet to be acknowledged as a better alternative over rooftop water harvesting. One of the major hurdles in stormwater harvesting is the poor state of stormwater drain systems in India. A planned approach is hence needed in order to fully utilise the potential of rainwater to adequately meet our water requirements. Hence, an equal and positive thrust is needed in developing and encouraging both the types of water harvesting systems. We have to catch water in every possible way and every possible place it falls.

## Centre for Science and Environment, New Delhi

Centre for Science and Environment (CSE), a New Delhi based non-governmental organisation, through its "Peoples' management of water" campaign promotes the paradigm of community-based rainwater harvesting with the objective of 'Making Water Everybody's Business'.

Rainwater harvesting is a potential solution to address the water crisis in both rural and urban areas. The model projects: CSE is constantly deluged with queries, opinions and ideas from people who are concerned about the prevailing water crisis and are keen to play an active role in managing water. As a part of its initiative to spread awareness about community-based rainwater harvesting techniques, (CSE) has identified five model projects in Delhi, from among those that have been designed by it. These act as effective tools to establish the fact that rainwater harvesting can be taken up and implemented successfully in urban centres. This paper is a discussion on the rainwater harvesting systems adopted in these five model projects which are situated at distinct geographical and geological areas.

These sites include Jamia Hamdard University, Tughlakhabad; Panchsheel Park colony, Panchsheel park; The Shri Ram School, Vasant Vihar; Janki Devi Memorial College, Rajendra Nagar and Mira Model School, Janakpuri. They feature different forms of rainwater harvesting- rooftop harvesting and surface water harvesting. CSE have been monitoring these projects since its implementation to assess the impact of rainwater harvesting on the quality and quantity. Improvement of both quantity and quality at all these project areas has been remarkable.

**Quantity:** Measurement of water levels in the tubewells in project area is indicative of a positive trend. The details of the Pre monsoon, Monsoon, and Post monsoon water levels are as follows: (Note: All readings in metres)

| Name of the site | Pre-monsoon | Monsoon | Post-monsoon |
|---|---|---|---|
| Jamia Hamdard University | 45 | 38 | 40 |
| Janki Devi Memorial College | 35.8 | 22.1 | 27 |
| The Shri Ram School | 40 | 35.1 | 36.2 |
| Mira Model School | 7.6 | 5.2 | 7.1 |
| Panchsheel Park Colony | 28.6 | 26.7 | 27.1 |

**Quality:** It has been found that after rain water harvesting the quality of groundwater in general has improved. The following is the highlights of the water tests conducted by the Pollution Monitoring Lab (PML) of CSE. The average impact on different physicochemical parameters are as follows:

- o In all the samples pH (Hydrogen ion concentration) has improved and has moved towards neutral.
- o In 72 per cent and 82 per cent of the samples there is decline in Total Dissolved Solvents (TDS) and Total Solids (TS) values respectively, and the maximum improvement in value of TDS is up to 80 per cent in the sample from Panchsheel Club.
- o In 91 per cent of the samples alkalinity increased within prescribed limit and acidity declined after the monsoons.
- o Calcium (Ca), Magnesium (Mg) and hardness, these parameters are showing mixed results. In around 50 per cent of the samples, there is an increase in hardness after monsoon. In 50 percent there is decrease in hardness value after monsoon. Samples from the Mira Model School have shown a drop in the concentration of Calcium (Ca). While 64 per cent post monsoon samples show a declining trend in Ca content, the remaining 36 per cent follow the reverse trend. Again, sample from Mira Model School is shows 63 per cent decrease in Mg concentration. In general, around 55 per cent of the

samples are showing a decrease in the Mg content after the monsoons.

- o In 100 per cent samples there is decline in the values of oil and grease, turbidity and chromium content.
- o Nitrate concentration has shown a declining trend in all the post monsoon samples.
- o Nitrite was detected in two samples and mercury was detected in one sample pre monsoons, but post monsoon the traces of these two compounds were not detected in any of the samples.

**Conclusion:** It can be concluded from above findings that rainwater, if conserved and utilised using the rainwater harvesting technology, can be an effective tool of replenishing ground water resources

## RAINWATER HARVESTING AS AN ADAPTATION TO CLIMATE CHANGE

Extreme climate events such as aridity, drought, flood, cyclone and stormy rainfall are expected to leave an impact on human society. They are also expected to generate widespread response to adapt and mitigate the sufferings associated with these extremes. Societal and cultural responses to prolonged drought include population dislocation, cultural separation, habitation abandonment, and societal collapse.

A typical response to local aridity is the human migration to safer and productive areas. However, climate and culture can interact in numerous ways. We hypothesize that people may resort to modify dwelling environments by adapting new strategies to optimize the utility of available water by harvesting rain rather than migrating to newer areas. We review recent palaeoclimatological evidence for climate change during the Holocene, and match those data with archaeological and historical records to test our 'climate change-rainwater harvest' hypothesis. We find correlation between heightened historical human efforts for construction of rainwater harvesting structures across regions in response to abrupt climate fluctuations, like aridity and drought. Historical societal adaptations to climate fluctuations may provide insights on potential responses of modern societies to future climate change that has a bearing on water resources, food production and management of natural systems.

Complex and extreme climate events such as aridity, drought, heat wave, flood, cyclone, stormy rainfall or hurricane are expected to leave a much greater impact on human society than gradual changes in climate. As culture and climate are interlinked, there is a general human response to adapt and mitigate the sufferings associated with such climate extremes. Societal and cultural responses to prolonged drought include population dislocation, dwelling abandonment, widespread migration and state collapse. A documented and predictable response to local aridity is the human migration to safer and productive localities. However, climate and culture can interact in many ways. Here, we propose that rather than migration, people may also resort to modify the dwelling environments by adapting strategies to optimize the utility of available water by harvesting rain.

Where there is water on earth, virtually no matter what the physical conditions, there is life. Water has been important for the development of cultural complexity in human society during the Holocene and earlier. Human ancestors have always used aquatic resources to their benefit, as we see the earliest association of hominid ancestors with lakes and pools dating back to 6 and 7 m.y. ago (Upper Miocene) from northern Chad, central Africa. The earliest known hominids, Sahelanthropus tchadensis, may have exploited a significant aquatic fauna such as fish, crocodiles and amphibious mammals, along with primates, rodents, elephants, equids and bovids associated with gallery forest and savannah.

Natural springs, river valleys and coasts have remained favoured locations for both hominids and modern humans. Particularly, aquatic and maritime adaptations such as coastal occupation, fishing and seafaring played a significant role in demographic as well as geographic expansion of modern humans after about 150,000 years ago.

A comprehensive knowledge of climate fluctuations and corresponding adaptation by human society is crucial for our progress towards sustainability. We review published archaeological and historical records of rainwater harvesting systems and water management worldwide to understand the climate-rainwater harvesting link. Since we expect that adaptation through rainwater collection may be particularly effective in tropical monsoon regions, where the seasonal cycle in rainfall is large, we specifically examined both sacred and secular ancient texts as well as published scientific work to infer the relationships of 'climate change-rainwater harvesting' in India.

Taking water as a central issue, a chronological history of India beginning circa 4500 BC to the present was constructed from the available literature.

A review of high-resolution studies documenting the Holocene climate change from multi-proxy data helped us to examine the behaviour of past climate, including the monsoons. Additionally, in order to obtain the collateral evidence from primary data for climate change and fluctuating rainfall over India, we reconstructed the monsoon winds for the past 4500 years using fossil Glo.

## HOLOCENE CLIMATE VARIABILITY

For a long time, climate of the Holocene epoch (~ 11 kyr BP to present), compared to last glacial period (widely accepted dates for the Last Glacial are ~ 74 kyr and 14 kyr ago as given by the Intergovernmental Panel on Climate Change), was considered to be stable. But that belief has been broken as detailed and well-dated worldwide palaeoclimate records have provided evidence of climate variability and extreme climate events such as aridity, drought, flood, cyclone, stormy rainfall and millennial-scale variation in climate during the Holocene.

The most recent of these events was the Little Ice Age (LIA), which occurred during 1300-1850, reducing the subtropical sea-surface temperatures by 3 to 4 C. Indeed, pace of the Holocene events and of abrupt climate shifts during the last glaciation has been suggested to be statistically the same; together, they make up a series of climate shifts with a cyclicity close to 1470 500 years.

These changes may have influenced some of the most momentous revolutions-for instance, evolution of cultural diversity, domestication of medicinal plants, crops and animals, and adaptive innovations through socio-economic development- in human history during the Holocene.

Shifts in early Holocene atmospheric $CO_2$ concentration and abrupt early to mid-Holocene climatic transition have been registered both at the equator and the poles. Holocene climate fluctuations as inferred from proxy records worldwide, including North Atlantic, western Canada, southwest Ireland, North America and elsewhere are now well established. Records of sedimentation in Laguna Pallcacocha, southern Ecuador suggest El Nino/Southern Oscillation (ENSO) variability on millennial timescales throughout the Holocene.

It is notable that El Nino events influenced prehistoric cultural development in Peru. The onset of El Nino events at 5.8 kyr ago is coincident with the beginning of a monumental temple construction on the Peruvian coast, and the increase in El Nino frequency after 3.2-2.8 kyr ago correlates with the abandonment of monumental temples in the region.

In addition, several extreme arid events and droughts have been documented in Asia, Africa, North America, and South America38. These may represent individual episodes in a recurrent pattern of dry events, but some events may be consistent with greenhouse gas forcing.

For instance, failure of the winter and spring rains and increased temperatures led to drought during 1998-2002 over the Northern Hemisphere mid-latitudes across the United States, the Mediterranean, southern Europe, and Southwest and Central Asia. These droughts were linked through a common oceanic influence and were consistent with greenhouse gas forcing.

Climate fluctuations that we review here are not necessarily anthropogenic. Some proxies representing local climate at different places across the world reveal that the 20th century is probably neither the warmest nor a uniquely extreme climatic period of the last millennium. A variable sun through changes in solar irradiance and processes such as biological regime shifts may have caused the observed climate variability and climate fluctuations over much of the Holocene. Indeed, geophysical, archaeological and historical evidences support a solaroutput model for climate change44 during a large part of the Holocene. As inferred from biological and geological proxies, terrestrial palaeotemperature may have been higher due to natural variability.

Just before the Holocene, SSTs increased by 3.5-4.0 C during the last two glacial-interglacial transitions, synchronous with the global increase in atmospheric $CO_2$ and Antarctic warming, but the temperature increase occurred 2000-3000 years before the Northern Hemisphere ice sheets melted. Deglaciation lagged the melting of ice sheets in the Northern Hemisphere by millennia and may still be under way, and may remain so in the future.

Thus, before the twentieth century anthropogenic climate change and its impacts that we are witnessing, the last truly global climate change occurred between 20,000 and 10,000 years ago. At the last Glacial-Interglacial Transition rise in tropical temperature was felt first, for example in the Andes and the Indo-Pacific warm pool, propagation of warming signal from the tropics to drive ice-sheet melting in the Northern Hemisphere 2000 to 3000 years later that resulted in global rise in sea level of 120 m. There was a rise of atmospheric $CO_2$ by nearly 90 parts per million (p.p.m.), from a low of about 180 p.p.m. in glacial times and parts of the earth warmed up by 10-12 C.

## CLIMATE CHANGE AND HUMAN MIGRATION

The archaeological and historical records show many instances of societal collapse, attributed to a combination of social, political and economic factors. However, recent studies have implicated climate change and drought as the primary agent in human migration, cultural separation, population dislocation and the collapse of prehistoric and early historic societies.

Human migration due to climate change and environmental stress is a well resolved survival strategy across continents, including Africa, Eurasia, South America and Australia. Ice cores from Kilimanjaro provide an ~ 11.7 kyr record of Holocene climate variability for eastern equatorial Africa. The periods of abrupt climate change shown in ice cores include ~ 8.3, ~ 5.2 kyr ago, and a third period, ~ 4 kyr ago coinciding with the 'First Dark Age' known for the most severe drought in tropical Africa. In a more recent history, effects of variable precipitation and drought in equatorial east Africa during the past 1100 years bear links with climate change and cultural effects.

Oral traditions as well as scientific evidence both indicate drought-induced famine, political unrest and large-scale migration of native population, and establish strong connection between cultural development, climate change and water stress.

Recently, a robust study by Nunez et al.4 found widespread evidence for human occupation influenced by water availability in the Atacama desert in northern Chile from 13,000 calibrated 14C years before the present (cal yr BP) to 9500 cal yr BP, and again after 4500 cal yr BP.

Initial human occupation coincided with a change from very dry phase to a humid phase. Archaic open campsites at elevations above 3600 m show that humans lived around late Glacial/early Holocene palaeolakes on the Altiplano. Human use of these sites was terminated between 9500 and 4500 cal yr BP due to drying of the lakes. The fact that climate change was instrumental for human occupation and abandonment of the area also provides support to proposition that early people in the Atacama region focused on favourable, humid habitats such as lakes, springs and streams.

## CLIMATE CHANGE AND RAINWATER HARVESTING

We now turn to our proposed hypothesis that in a changing climate people may resort to rainwater harvesting and continue to occupy homelands rather than migration. History tells us that cultures do not give up until they have exhausted options for survival over the area they occupied for longer period.

Before we explore widespread evidence of rainwater harvesting as an adaptation to climate change in India, we briefly explore global evidence for possible correlation between heightened historical human efforts for construction of rainwater harvesting structures across cultural landscapes throughout the human history in response to aridity and drought conditions.

## South America

Several studies note climate variability over the continent. A 10,000-year simulation study over Mexico suggests that a 'megadrought' and thirteen other devastating droughts lasting over a decade resulted in 20 to 40% reduction in rainfall and occurred with a return period of less than 1000 years.

The Mayan civilization is a case in point, which developed around 3000 years ago in Mesoamerica, and faced recurrent droughts due to solar forcing before it collapsed due to climate deterioration towards the end of the Classic Period. A recent study has shown that the collapse of the Mayan civilization in the Terminal Classic Period occurred during a spatio-temporally extensive dry period in the region, interspersed by more severe droughts centred at about AD 810, 860, and 910. What was the Mayan response to these oscillations before collapse? Indeed, a water storage adaptation in the Mayan region.

Ancient reservoir technology developed by the Mayan people in the seasonally dry tropics of southern Maya lowlands reveals that rainwater storage was a major source of water supply during the dry season. Reservoirs were constructed, for example, in Tikal to cope with seasonal scarcity of water. There were at least three distinct types of reservoirs as documented by Scarborough and Gallopin: centrally located reservoirs, residential reservoirs and margin reservoirs. The nomenclature is essentially based on location of the reservoir and the differential capacity to store water. Similar water collection and storage have been documented in other areas of South America as well.

Ancient man-made earthworks of Bolivian Amazon are another example of adaptation. The crucial factor that facilitated early domestication of palms and harvest of fish was construction of large-scale earthworks such as documented by Erickson in the Bolivian Amazon. A complex man-made network of hydraulic systems and fish weirs covering 525 km$^2$ in the ancient landscape of Baures region of Bolivia is a classic example of rainwater collection that provided sufficient animal protein and palm fruits to feed large and dense populations in an arid savanna.

## North America

There are numerous studies that have documented abrupt climate change, extreme drought conditions and storminess over North America during the Holocene.

The 'Dust Bowl' drought severely impacted USA during 1934, 1936, and 1939-40. Recent studies of longer term US Great Plains drought variability over the past 2000 years with the use of palaeoclimatic data imply that no droughts as severe as those of the 1930s have occurred since the 1700s. A particularly notable example, supported by tree-ring climatic data, is the Lost Colony of Roanoke Island, which disappeared during the most extreme drought in 800 years (AD 1587-89). The appalling human deaths and the near abandonment of Jamestown Colony occurred during the driest 7-year episode in 770 years (1606-12).

In agreement with our hypothesis, existence of more than 2.6 million small, man-made water bodies accounting for ~ 20% of the standing water area in USA may be the result of adaptation response to climate fluctuations. In addition, on the Southern High Plains, when surface water sources dried up due to most intense drought, substantial adaptive strategies, including well-digging were employed by human society during the Holocene. Indeed, the discovery of a prehistoric well excavated in response to drought during the Pleistocene-Holocene transition by the Clovis people around 11,500 BC is the oldest prehistoric well in America. The Clovis well is also among the first evidence of water harvesting-groundwater in this case-as an adaptation to climate change. The excavation of wells near regions which had surface water shortly before has been posited as the evidence for drought during the Pleistocene-Holocene transition.

### Arabian Peninsula

Increasing depth of wells through time found at archaeological sites in Hili near Al Ain, United Arab Emirates, is in concordance with increasing aridity and consequent decline in groundwater levels for the past 4500 years. In southern Arabia's highland Southern Jol, McCorriston and Oches have documented and dated early water impounding structures, with important implications for prehistoric Arabian resource management and food production. In the Wadi Sana and its Wadi Shumlya tributary, checkdams (water-impounding structures) have been discovered buried in silts deposited 13,000-5000 years ago. While use of checkdams for agricultural activities in this region cannot be ruled out, the Wadi Sana archaeological remains of water storage adaptation are older than known ancient Arabian agriculture. Other purposes for which they might have been built could be flood control (another example of adaptation to extreme climate event), enhancement of pastures and promoting vegetation growth.

## CLIMATE FLUCTUATIONS AND RAINWATER HARVEST IN INDIA

Holocene climate fluctuations, including large spatial variation in Holocene monsoon and temperature over India are now well-resolved from various climate change proxies. Folk sayings such as 'capture rain where it rains' may have originated in response to increased aridity in the Indian region over the last few millennia. Such climate fluctuations may have given rise to traditional village tanks, ponds and earthen embankments numbering more than 1.5 million, that still harvest rainwater in 660,000 villages in India and encourage growth of vegetation in commons and agroecosystems.

A somewhat coherent, although unresolved, picture that emerges for India is as follows: as the aridity increased in the region as is evident from palaeoclimatic studies, people intensified rainwater harvesting as is seen from archaeological and historical evidences.

Indeed, a specific emphasis through the long sweep of history on management of rainwater harvesting systems in ancient texts, such as Rigveda (1500 BC), Atharva Veda (800 BC), Kautilya's Arthasastra (300 BC), Varahamihira's Brihatsamhita (AD 550), and Kalhana's Rajatarangini (AD 1148-1150) may document adaptation to fluctuating climate. We expect documentations in ancient texts of other continents as well, though we do not probe that in any detail.

In the Indian subcontinent, climate change in western India has been studied in relatively greater detail than in other parts. Detailed chronology of the Thar desert in western India based on lacustrine deposits suggests that the climate for the past 5000 14C years has remained dry. Yet, humans were present in the region during 55 years BP (2894-2643 BC) even before the Indus Valley Civilization (4100 to 3500 14C yr BP or 2600 to 2000 BC).

The antiquity of human occupation of Thar desert goes back to late Pleistocene as indicated by the discovery of hand axe from Late Acheulian site and microlithic site with pottery of early-to mid-Holocene (i.e. between 7 and 6 kyr ago). Even after the disappearance of river Saraswati due to drainage disorganization and subsequent increase in aridity, people continued to occupy the region by adapting to climate change through rainwater harvesting. Indeed, the post-Saraswati society that developed in the Thar desert is essentially a rain-harvesting society. For instance, archaeological evidence indicates presence of ponds, tanks and step-wells in several areas once occupied by the people of Indus-Saraswati civilization. Today, Thar is the most densely populated desert in the world and every settlement there has often more than one water collection pond and numerous earthworks to harvest rain developed over the last 5500 years of continuous and dynamic adaptation to climate change.

There is other evidence to support our climate change-rainwater harvesting hypothesis. Himalayan ice core data suggest several periods of drought in the South Asian region. Many of these were with modest rainfall failures (1230s, 1280s, 1330s, 1530s, 1590s and 1640s), but two (1790s and 1876-77) were the most severe with exceptional aridity in the last 1500 years.

Consequential cultural response to such a fluctuating climate is reflected in archaeological and historical records of heightened activity of widespread earthwork construction for rainwater harvesting across social strata. Majority of palaces and forts (perhaps all) constructed during the 13-18th century developed elaborate water-harvesting systems. A spurt in activity is also evident in large-scale efforts for repair of ancient earthworks, particularly during late 17th and 18th century.

During the Neolithic period (5000-3000 BP), people in the Deccan Plateau were just starting pastoralism and settled agriculture; it was also the time when aridity had started to set in during 5-2 kyr BP. No wonder then, people in the Deccan Peninsula developed some of the most extensive and intricate rainwater harvesting systems known to humankind.

## CONTEMPORARY RELEVANCE OF RAINWATER HARVESTING

As a sound adaptation, why does rainwater harvesting matter more today than any other time in the Holocene? There are several reasons, as Jackson et al. note:

(1) over half of the accessible freshwater runoff globally is already appropriated for human use;

(2) more than 1 × 109 people currently lack access to clean drinking water and almost 3 × 109 people lack basic sanitation services;

(3) because the human population will grow faster than increases in the amount of accessible freshwater, per capita availability of freshwater will decrease in the coming century;

(4) climate change will cause a general intensification of the earth's hydrological cycle in the next 100 years, with generally increased precipitation, evapotranspiration,

occurrence of storms and significant changes in biogeochemical processes influencing water quality.

Humanity now uses 26% of the total terrestrial evapotranspiration and 54% of the runoff that is geographically and temporally accessible. New dam construction could increase accessible runoff by about 10% over the next 30 years, whereas the population is projected to increase by more than 45% during that period. Under such circumstances, harvesting rain shall be crucial.

Furthermore, as mentioned earlier, the climate fluctuations which we review here are not essentially anthropogenic. However, in future the case may likely be driven perhaps more by humans than nature. Burning of the fossil-fuel and deforestation have emerged as principal anthropogenic sources of rising atmospheric $CO_2$ and consequential global warming observed in late 20th century. Recent anomalies in temperature, precipitation, snow cover, sea level and extreme weather conditions provide collateral evidence of anthropogenic global climate change.

Particularly, now globally coherent fingerprints of global warming and climate-change impacts across natural systems are becoming clearly visible. With more than 99.9% confidence level, it can now be said that the rate of annual warming for global land areas over the period 1901-2000 was 0.07 C per decade. As summers get hotter and hotter, and anthropogenic climate changes exert further strain on economic, social and natural systems, water scarcity is likely to grow in India and elsewhere. Addressing water problem holds the promise in future for a world compounded by climate change, growing population109 and decreasing water-impounding area of traditional tanks due to urbanization.

In addition, extreme climate events are registering an increasing trend. A significant proportion of the global land area has been increasingly affected by a significant change in climatic extremes during the second half of the 20th century. In India, wintertime rainfall may decline by 5 to 25% and may lead to droughts during the dry summer months in coming decades. Thus, we will have to take into account the large-scale, natural climate variations as well as human-induced climate change in the management of natural, social and economic systems. If extreme climate events increase in future due to climate change, human society will use different means of adaptation. Additionally, regardless of climate fluctuations, population growth will put extra stress on natural resources. Alternative to ecologically damaging, socially intrusive and capital-intensive water management projects that fail to deliver their desired benefits, it would be useful investing in decentralized facilities, efficient technologies and policies, and human capital to improve overall productivity rather than to find new sources of water supply.

Such efforts would need to be encouraged with innovative policy regimes that concurrently promote rainwater harvesting.

Traditionally, such systems have been integrated with agroforestry and ethnoforestry practices, and remain useful in contemporary conservation and ecological restoration of degraded ecosystems. A systematic support to local innovations on rainwater harvesting could provide substantial amounts of water.

For example, a hectare of land in an arid region with just 100 mm of rainfall annually, could theoretically yield 1 million litres of water per year from harvesting rainwater. Simple local techniques such as ponds and earthen embankments that we have reviewed here can help in harvesting and storage of rain.

Rural and urban water use, restoration of streams for recreation, freshwater fisheries, and protection of natural ecosystems are all competing for water resources earlier dedicated to food production. Under such circumstances, decentralized rainwater harvesting adaptations prove efficient.

For instance, in the Negev Desert, decentralized harvesting of water in microcatchments from rain falling over a 1 ha watershed yielded 95,000 l of water per hectare per year, whereas collection efforts from a single large unit of a 345 ha watershed yielded only 24,000 l per hectare per year. Thus, 75% of the collectible water was lost as a result of the longer distance of runoff.

Traditional systems would become more efficient if scientific attempts are combined to enhance the productivity of local knowledge115, as has been attempted in China. But some local technologies may already be at par with scientific attempts. For instance, the indigenous teras water-harvesting system in Sudan offers agricultural production security and also raises the nutrientlimited yield from ~ 150-250 to ~ 650 kg ha-1 through its nutrient-harvesting effects.

Widespread arsenic poisoning is another case in point where rainwater harvesting has great potential as a possible solution. In West Bengal and Bangladesh, alluvial Ganges aquifers used for public water supply are polluted with naturally-occurring arsenic, which adversely affects the health of millions of people by causing arsenicosis and increasing the risk of cancer. Millions of people are at risk in Bangladesh alone. Arsenic mobilization is associated with the advent of massive irrigation pumping that draws relatively young water directly into the aquifer.

Deep wells are being advocated as a remedy, that may provide a source of clean water; but the solution is only a provisional one. Rainwater harvesting is a better option to provide arsenic-free, safe water in a cost-effective and accessible manner, particularly for drinking and food preparation.

We must, however, address several challenges effectively to make rainwater harvesting efficient, particularly treatment of harvested rainwater in areas where pollution is rampant. For instance, it is now possible to use nanofiltration for the removal of hardness, natural organic material, micropollutants such as pesticides, viruses and bacteria, salinity, nitrates and arsenic.

With an insightful policy, rainwater harvesting can be promoted as a core adaptation strategy for achieving the global security and sustainability of water resources in an era of anthropogenic climate change.

## CONCLUSIONS AND THE WAY FORWARD

Clearly, over thousands of years, people living in various geographical and climatic regions of the world have evolved diverse, indigenous rainwater harvesting and management regimes as an adaptation to climate change. Some of these practices continue to remain in use, particularly in South Asia.

Rainwater harvesting in South Asia differs from that in many parts of the world-it has a history of continuous practice for at least the last 8000 years. As we noted, although hydraulic earthworks are known to have occurred in ancient landscapes in many regions, they are no longer operational systems among the masses in the same proportion as in South Asia.

The antiquity of rainwater harvesting as an adaptation to climate change in India is deep. In a fluctuating Holocene climate, rainwater harvesting by early farmers may have been pivotal for emergence and diversification of food production. Future studies should concentrate on cultural responses to climate change with economic implications, such as the role of rainwater harvesting in plant and animal domestication that may have shaped the evolution of cultural landscapes, agroecosystems and early agriculture.

Construction of early rainwater harvesting systems required simple scooping of the earth and putting up embankments or erecting elongated soil heaps along farm boundaries. But, the benefits of such innovations for early farmers may have been substantial.

Earliest examples of rainwater systems in India include the havelis of Jabalpur, bandh and bandhulia of Satna, virda of Gujarat, khadins of Rajasthan, ahar-pynes of Bihar, eri of Tamil Nadu, dhora of Aravalis and similar other earthworks throughout the country.

As these earthworks still continue to survive and serve society, scientific studies such as 14C dating of sediment cores of ponds, tanks and lakes would be useful to understand the dynamics of rainwater harvesting and climate relationship in diverse geographic regions across India.

Rainwater harvesting in response to climate extremes enhances the resilience of human society. In a world confronting local and global changes, building resilience of human society to absorb shock, learn and develop would depend on sound knowledge of the historical adaptive processes that are still functional. An integrated perspective of traditional knowledge on adaptation strategies, such as the rainwater harvesting system, is particularly useful to comprehend vulnerability and adaptation to environmental stresses at the local scale. Local studies on risk management and decision-making can complement global climate modelling exercises in order to fully capture the complexities of real life.

Although rainwater harvesting continues to be practised globally, and there is renewed interest in its revival, the system nonetheless has fallen to disrepair. It would be worthwhile to investigate whether declining interest in this time-tested adaptation, in India for example, is due to economic reasons or a climatic response to increasing strength of southwest monsoon during the past 400 years.

Whatever the case, climate policy and water policy would require to be streamlined to promote rainwater harvesting in the water-stressed regions of the world. We believe that neither the water policy nor the climate policy discussions seem to notice the worth of rainwater harvesting as an adaptation to climate change, especially in urban areas where water resources are fast depleting due to rapid increase in population and unrestricted use of water.

Studies of historical societal adaptations to climate fluctuations provide insights into possible responses of modern societies to future climate change and sustainable management of water resources.

7

# MANAGEMENT OF WATERSHED RESOURCES

## INTRODUCTION

Watershed is a geohydrological unit draining at a common point from a system of streams. 'A watershed is the area of land that drains into a body of water such as a river, lake, stream or bay. It is separated from other systems by high points in the area such as hill or slopes.

It includes not only the waterways itself but also the entire land area that drains to it'. From management perspective, a watershed is, in addition to the hydrological characteristics: not just an area, but a land mass and a point of reference along the main flow channel, with its own particular drainage area.

The Government of India in early seventies initiated integrated development of all land and water resources on watershed basis through Drought Prone Area Programme (DPAP), Desert Development Programme (DDP) and Integrated Watershed Development Programme along with externally aided projects, private initiatives of local communities and NGOs. However, all these schemes showed increase productivity of irrigated lands and rain fed lands in most of the states showed little or no sustained improvement.

In 1990-91 a 'Common Approach for Watershed Development' was jointly formulated and adopted by the Ministry of Agriculture and the Ministry of Rural Development (MoRD), through the National Watershed Development Project for Rain fed Area (NWDPRA).The objectives of each Watershed Development Project envisaged under it are(MoRD 1994) :

a. To promote the economic development of the village community which is directly or indirectly dependent on the watershed through :

   (i) Optimum utilisation of the watershed's natural resources like land, water, vegetation, etc. that will mitigate the adverse effects of drought and prevent further ecological degradation.

   (ii) Employment generation and development of the human and other economic resources of the village in order to promote savings and other income-generation activities.

b. To encourage restoration of ecological balance in the village through :

   (i) Sustained community action for the operation and maintenance of assets created and further development of the potential of the natural resources in the watershed.

   (ii) Simple, easy and affordable technological solutions and institutional arrangements that make use of and build upon, local technical knowledge and available materials.

c. Special emphasis to improve the economic and social condition of the resource-poor and the disadvantaged sections of the watershed community such as the asset less and women through:

   (i) More equitable distribution of the benefits of land and water resources development and the consequent biomass production.

   (ii) Greater access to income generating opportunities and focus on their human resource development.

In 1995, there were five groups of ongong government WSM project which vary considerably in their institutional and administrative framework, as well as in the size and natural resource endowment of the project area :

a. National programs under the Ministry of Agriculture (MoA) : the National Watershed Management Project for Rainfed Areas (NWMPRA);

b. National programs under the Ministry of Rural Development (MoRD) : the Drought Prone Area Program (DPAP), the Desert Development Program (DDP), the Integrated Wasteland Development Project (IWDP), the Jawahar Rozgar Yojana (JRY) and the Employment Assurance Scheme (EAS);

c. National programs funded by multilateral donors : World Bank, European Community etc.

d. State programs implemented by the State governments, often with foreign funding and NGO collaboration, e.g., the Karnataka WSM Program assisted by the Danish International Development Agency (DANIDA) or the Watershed Management Program in Maharashtra assisted by the German Development Bank (KfW) and

e. Operational research projects (ORP) or model watersheds under the Indian Council for Agriculture Research (ICAR).

Each Watershed Development Project is expected to achieve the following results by the end of the project period :

a. All the work /activities that are planned for the treatment and development of the drainage lines, arable and non-arable lands in the watershed areas.

b. All the members of the Watershed Development Committee and staff such as watershed secretary and volunteers have been given orientation and training to improve their knowledge and upgrade technical/ management and community organisational skills to a level that is appropriate for the successful discharge of their responsibilities on withdrawal of the Watershed

c. The village community would have been organized into several homogenous self-help groups for savings and other income generation activities which would have achieved sufficient commitment from their members and built up financial resources to be self-sustaining.

Impact evaluation studies both on the ground and through remote sensing techniques have shown that watershed-based interventions have led to increase in groundwater recharge, increase in number of wells and water bodies, enhancement of cropping intensity, changes in cropping pattern, higher yields of crops and reduction in soil losses.

## INTEGRATED WATERSHED DEVELOPMENT PROJECTS

Watershed programmes are being viewed as a 'rural livelihood' for people inhabiting the fragile eco-system experiencing soil erosion and moisture stress. It aims at integrating soil conservation measures, ensuring the availability of drinking water, fuel wood & fodder and raising income and employment for farmers and landless labourers through improvement in agriculture production and productivity.

In this context, it would be appropriate to cite and derive lessons from the success stories of Sukhomajri village in Haryana, Pani Panchayat in Maharashtra, Ralegaon Siddhi in Maharashtra, Rajsamadhiyala village in Gujarat, Thanagazi area in Alwar district of Rajasthan, Direct well-recharge in Saurashtra etc. Sukhomajri project evolved the concept of 'Social fencing', the fundamental way of forest conservation of any degraded forest area (Mishra 1998 & Sarin 1996).

Due to the efforts of 'Hill Resource Management Society', dedicated efforts of a team of Govt. officials, consistent institutional, technical & financial support by Govt. and international agencies, grass production increased from 0.1 ton to 2.05 ton per hectare, wheat 0.275 ton to 0.58 ton per hectare, production of milk from 334 litres to 579 litres per day and annual household income increased from Rs.10,000 to Rs.15,000 from 1975 to 1986. However critics to social sustainability highlighted the unequal distribution of water (Secklar 1983 & 1990),unequal distribution of income, increase in disparity among rich and poor, cases of conflicts, corruption charges against few leaders, failures of Dairy Cooperative, bio-gas plants

& community sprinkler irrigation system, non-participation of women etc. (Teotia 1994,Gopal Krishna 1996,Grewal et al.1995) in the project. Vilasrao Salunke evolved the institution of 'Pani Panchayat' and established a trust called 'Gram Gaurav Pratisthan' in village Naigaon, Maharashtra in 1974.

He accepted on lease a 16 hectare plot on hill slope, constructed a percolation tank at the bottom of the hill and dug well downstream of this tank. The well water was then lifted to a height of 12 metres for irrigating the farm area on the hill slope. As the result, yield of the farm increased tenfold from 10 qtls to 100 qtls of grains.

With the efforts of Shri Annasaheb Hazare and villagers, 44 micro-percolation tanks or Nala bunds, five check dams and three subsurface barriers were constructed in village Ralegaon-Siddhi of Maharashtra. About 500 hectares of land are now receiving irrigation and 400,000 trees have been planted. The village has not only became self-sufficient but is exporting grains & vegetables and per capita income recorded increase of tenfold from a meager Rs. 225 to Rs.2,250.

In Rajsamadhiyala village, Gujarat under the leadership of Shri Hardevsingh Jadeja (sarpanch) constructed 45 water harvesting structures, increased plantation from 1600 to 50000, earned Rs. 2.5 crore from the sale of village farm produce, constructed buildings & roads and took several steps to improve the economic condition of the villagers. In Alwar district of Rajasthan, volunteers of Tarun Bharat Sangh (TBS) led by Rajendra Singh with the active participation of villagers revived the traditional practice of constructing 'Johads' by building a barrier across an ephemeral stream or by excavation of a pond at a natural depression.

At the end of 1977, about 3000 water harvesting (WHS) were constructed in about 650 villages, which were accompanied by other activities such as farm and contour bunding, construction of anicuts, check dams and afforestation etc. The synergistic effect of these activities are rise in water table, multiple cropping, increase in fodder & milk, availability of drinking water in wells, cessation of migration to cities, improved income & living standard of villagers and perennial flows in five streams namely, Arvari, Ruparel, Sarasa, Bhagani-Tildeh and Jahajwali. Shyamjibhi Antala, founder of Saurashtra Lokmanch and Panduranga Shastri Athavale, spiritual leader of the Swadhyay parivar popularise the practice of recharging wells from the farm runoff water in the Saurashtra peninsula in the western State of Gujarat. Studies claimed that the costs of recharging 10,000 wells during 1993-1994 were Rs.5 million and increased value of agriculture output was Rs. 80 million.

Apart from these, the various innovative water harvesting techniques being used at the experimental stages are :

**Fog Dip:** In the Atacama desert, a Canadian research scientist constructed 75 double-layered net, each 12m by 4m, which were hung about 4m above the ground. Millions of droplets from the fog condense on the net fibres, coalesce into a large drop and then fall into a trough. This system provides around 1000 liters of fresh water per day (Anonymous 1998b)

**Artificial Glaciers:** In a cold arid plateau of Ladakh, the snowmelted water is stored in a small reservoirs and distributed to farmers during sowing seasons.

**Berries:** A beery is a rectangular step well or circular open well having a parapet constructed inside or on the bank of a surface water tank. These are meant for providing water when the tank bed gets dry. The lower well walls are left open to receive the recharge water.

**Surungams or Tunnels:** This practice is found in the Kasargod district of Kerala wherein percolated water within the lithomarge is drained through a tunnel to a small reservoir for domestic use or for irrigation.

**Lined Ponds:** In the Bhal area of Gujarat, The Mahiti-Utthan NGO under the leadership of Nafisaben Barot used a novel idea for preventing pond water turning brackish and drying up in summer seasons. He used a low-density polyethylene sheet (LDPE) for preventing contact of water with the low brackish or saline soil deposited at bottom of the pond. Rain water falling directly or from the surrounding area is stored in the pond and used for domestic purposes by the people.

Apart from these, some water harvesting techniques touched through research and development are augmentation of spring, optimal design of a percolation tank, aquifer storage and recovery, development of ASR techniques in hard rocks, use of non-toxic polymer liquid in the catchment areas to increase the amount of runoff received by the water harvesting structures, runoff generation efficiency of rooftops, use of monomolecular films of alcoxyethanols for reducing evaporation from surface water bodies.

**Sustainability Issues in Watershed Management**

The UNDP Report (1994) defines 'Sustainable Development is development that not only regenerates economic growth but distributes its benefits equitably, that regenerates the environment rather than destroying it, that empowers people rather than marginalising them. It gives priority to the poor, enlarging their choices and opportunities and providing their participation in decisions affecting them. It is development that is pro-poor, pro-nature, pro-jobs, pro-women and pro-children'. It focuses on establishing linkages between ecology, economic and social life.

The ecological rehabilitation of the degraded land characterised by deforestation, soil erosion, depletion of ground water, ecological imbalance etc. has been the main focus of the watershed projects. The issue of ecological sustainability is related with major stages of human development: gathering, nomadic pastoralism, settled cultivation and industry.

The ecological destruction in the industrial societies is rapid and the victim in this process are village-based systems of community forests and pasture management (Gadgil & Guha 1992).It includes regeneration of forest cover, reduction in soil erosion, increase in surface and ground water potential and involving efficient natural resource management (Lyer & Roy 2005). The economic sustainability has been identified with increase in food grain production, fodder production, milk & livestock production and increase in employment opportunities.

Experience has shown that unless the people receive any tangible economic benefits, the people's participation and social sustainability of the project remained causality. The focus on 'social sustainability' is on the formation of the new socio-cultural institutions, strengthening of the traditional socio-cultural institutions, promoting equity and social empowerment through community/people's participation.

This concept has emerged from the literature review of the watershed management programme in different regions, eg 'social fencing' emerged from Sukhomajri (Mishra & Sarin 1987),charismatic leadership in Ralegaon Siddhi (Pangare 1992),bureaucratic model of development in Jhabua (Rajoura 1999),blending of technical and social ideologies for judicious use of water in Salunkhe's experiments of Pani Panchayat (Salunkhe 1998), people's participation in the construction of johads (ponds) & its replication resulting in revival of several rivers (Singh 1999).The success of watershed management in these villages is due to social factors like, equity in terms of caste, class gender in the distribution of generated benefits, timely guidance and support from the government and development agencies, role of dedicated leaders,creation and smooth functioning of the local institutions etc.

## CAPACITY BUILDING INITIATIVES IN WATERSHED MANAGEMENT

'Capacity building 'has been variously termed as capacity development or capacity strengthening targeted at four levels: personal, organisational, institutional and community level as donors increasingly support community-driven development. This paradigm shift of development strategy from 'what the project can do to help the people' to 'what the project can do with people's participation' in 1980s and 1990s was the outcome of a number of flaws and resulting poor performance exhibited by the NWDPRA along with the early large scale watershed development programmes of GOI: evaluation according to biophysical factors without regarding people's livelihoods, operation in a top-down fashion, little commitment to the maintenance of water harvesting structures so created and a syndrome of dependency on govt.(Turton 2000), soil conservation works on rain fed plots are much better maintained were participatory approach is adopted and farmers themselves have made a financial contribution towards their cost, neglect of women and poor (Kerr et al.1998), etc.

The comprehensive framework for capacity development in environment (CDE) published by DAC (OECD-DAC 1995, OECD-DAC1997a,OECD-DAC 1997b,OECD-DAC,nd) defined it as 'the ability of individuals, groups, organisations and institutions in a given context to address environmental issues as part of a range of efforts to achieve sustainable development'. In watershed context, it focused on empowering communities with technical facilitation support from the technical staff & making them responsible for all steps of project cycle (identification, planning, management, implementation, monitoring and evaluation of activities) both on the private as well as community land. There are certain principles that are integral to the approach to capacity development: stake holder's involvement and ownership; programme /project flexibility in adjusting or adapting to local contexts and varying views/needs; integrated, multi-disciplinary perspective going beyond sectoral boundaries; networking among various institutions/ organisations and access to and sharing of information. Capacity building initiatives in watershed development programmes should promote stakeholders, involvement in planning and implementation; facilitate networking for consultation and experiences sharing, develop a practical participatory system built into the project /programme cycle and provides feedback for planning.

There are four main categories of stakeholders associated with the watershed programme namely,

(a) Administrators and managers including officers from various organisations namely at Directorate of Agriculture, District Nodal Agency, heads of PIA and heads of the registered societies of micro-watershed etc.

(b) Implementers include WDT belonging to respective PIAs, office bearers of registered societies at micro-watershed level, other participating members including land owners and landless families in the micro-watersheds.

(c) Trainers include full time existing faculty members of the identified training organisations in the public and NGO sector, part-time external resource persons who are identified as trainers (as per need) to assist the above organisations; para-professionals at village level etc.

(d) Farmers, landless labour, women etc.

Bhan and Pandey (2005) found limited evidences of participatory approach, mismatch between the training needs of clients and capacity of training institutions, inexperienced trainers, ineffective short duration courses, limited emphasis on action research, lack of motivational aspects in training courses etc. However a well designed course based on sound guidelines as evident from covering technological, management and social aspects would enhance the skill of stakeholders associated with watershed programme.

## DROUGHT PRONE AREA PROGRAMME IN JAMMU & KASHMIR STATE

The Drought Prone Areas Programme was reviewed by Task Force set up by Ministry of Rural Development, Govt. of India, headed by Dr. M.S. Swaminathan during 1980-81. In 1987, the Central Sanctioning Committee narrowed and priorities the range of activities relating to soil conservation, land shaping and development, water resources conservation and development, afforestation, plantation and pasture development to sharpen the focus on more productive agriculture and vegetable cover. The DPAP was started in district Udhampur & Doda during 1973-74, as a part of DPAP Agency Doda. In April 1982 , it was separated and started functioning independently under the chairmanship of Udhampur District Development Commissioner in eight blocks namely, Udhampur, Chenani, Panchari, Reasi, Pouni, Arnas, Mahore and Gool. The areas specific objectives assigned to it were :

a. To minimise the adverse effects of drought on production of crops, livestock and productivity of land, water and human resources through integrated development of natural resource base of the area and adoption of appropriate technologies.

b. To minimize occurrences of drought and control desertification of the desert areas through integrating and dovetailing other related state/central programmes with DPAP programme.

c. To conserve, develop & harness land, water and other natural resources including rainfall for restoration of ecological balance in the long run.

During 1990-91 to 1997-98, 25 Watersheds were treated fully with thrust on activities related to soil conservation, land shaping & development, afforestation, pasture, fodder and grass land development. The proportionate weightage assigned to various sector/activities under DPAP funding was land shaping & development,soil moisture conservation (30%), water resource development (20%),afforestation and pasture development (25%),minor sectors (15%) and project administration (10%). The funds were shared equally by the Centre and State government on 50:50 basis and the target was area predominantly inhabited by the SC/ST families and other economically backward classes. DPAP works preferably are taken during lean agriculture period so that additional employment opportunities could be provided to the landless agricultural labour. In 2001, new guidelines were implemented wherein local people's participation was made mandatory both in plan formulation and execution of works under the technical guidance of Watershed Development Team.

| | | | | | |
|---|---|---|---|---|---|
| 1 | Udhampur | 1. Sue-Chaker | 1993-94 | 1997-98 | 42.21 |
| | | 2. Himbra Gandala | 1990-91 | 1995-96 | 45.53 |
| | | 3. Garnai | 1993-94 | 1997-98 | 27.71 |
| 2 | Pouni | 1. AlayaDehari | 1992-93 | 1997-98 | 19.59 |
| | | 2. Mari Nalla | 1991-92 | 1997-98 | 35.51 |
| | | 3. Narloo | 1990-91 | 1995-96 | 20.81 |
| 3 | Reasi | 1. Kotli karwa | 1990-91 | 1995-96 | 15.57 |
| | | 2. Bhabber | 1993-94 | 1997-98 | 21.22 |
| | | 3. Kanjali | 1992-93 | 1997-98 | 35.64 |

| | | | | | |
|---|---|---|---|---|---|
| 4 | Panchari | 1. Badhota | 1990-91 | 1997-98 | 13.71 |
| | | 2. Lander | 1991-92 | 1997-98 | 43.57 |
| | | 3. Moungri | 1990-91 | 1997-98 | 23.53 |
| 5 | Arnas | 1. Thakra Kote | 1993-94 | 1997-98 | 24.99 |
| | | 2. Kansar | 1993-94 | 1997-98 | 19.47 |
| | | 3. Thuroo | 1990-91 | 1997-98 | 29.01 |
| 6 | Mahore | 1. Sarh Bathoie | 1993-94 | 1997-98 | 21.19 |
| | | 2. Hassote | 1990-91 | 1995-96 | 36.81 |
| | | 3. Bhagga | 1993-94 | 1997-98 | 9.6 |
| 7 | Chenani | 1. Kud Madda | 1990-91 | 1995-96 | 48.92 |
| | | 2. Pattan Garg | 1993-94 | 1997-98 | 10.64 |
| | | 3. Gouri Kund | 1993-94 | 1997-98 | 29.29 |
| 8 | Gool | 1. Ind Mahakund | 1990-91 | 1997-98 | 23.7 |
| | | 2. Budhan | 1990-91 | 1995-96 | 13.2 |
| | | 3. Ashmer Famrote | 1993-94 | 1997-98 | 29.12 |
| | | 4. Chassana | 1993-94 | 1997-98 | 7.96 |

*Source: Evaluation Report regarding impact of DAPA(2000), block Udhampur, 13

## REVIEW OF RESEARCH METHODOLOGY

In recent decades, more and more developed countries and developing countries have increasingly adopted watershed management to establish an enabling environment for integrated use, regulation and treatment of water and land resources of a watershed based ecosystem to accomplish resource conservation and biomass production objectives (Jensen et al. 1996) and thereby sustaining social and economic development (Kneese & Brower 1984, Newson 1992, Spulber & Sabbaghi 1998).

In India, since the inception of WDP funded by the Ministry of Rural Areas and Employment in 1995-96, an estimated US $ 3.5 billion have been invested by the Govt. for Rehabilitation and Development of Micro-Watersheds, the World Bank, Danish Development Agency (DANIDA), State Institute of Rural

Development (SIDA), Swiss Development Corporation (SDC), Department for International Development (DFID) and Indo-German Watershed Development Programmes (WDPs) through direct funding support as well. It is, therefore, the need of the hour to review the impact of watersheds on conserving and developing natural resources, capacity building, empowerment of the village community etc, observed by different scholars and policy makers in India and abroad.The crux of the various research studies and reports carried on the aforesaid topic is as follows:

Ram, Balak (2004) emphasised on a systematic characterisation and mapping of bio-physical resources viz. climate, landform, soil, vegetation surface and groundwater, transport network and village settlement, land use etc. using conventional and remote sensing techniques, correlates with socio-economic data, integrate them and formulate sustainable land use planning zones for optimizing production potentials in watershed. Based on UMA (Unique Mapping Area) system of Australia, CAZRI has evolved a concept of composite mapping system called Major Land Resource Units (MLRU)for development planning and applied on 5426 ha area around Kailana near Jodhpur for waste land development. Out of total 5000 ha area found worth for development, 74.32% has been proposed for regeneration and ecological management,1.08% for rehabilitation forestry, 2.36% silvipastoral revegetation, 14.76% agro forestry, 6.96% agri-horticulture and 0.52 % for vegetable cultivation.

Khan, M.A (2004) assessed and exploited specific technology package such as nadi, tanka, khadin, anicut, gully plugging, water harvesting dams, water spread, percolation tank, sub-surface barriers and sand-filled dam for sustainability in agriculture production in water deficit regions such as western Rajasthan. In Barmer district, the development of trees with supplemental irrigation from the nadi has improved the environment, besides providing fodder and fuel.Tanka water was utilized for raising forest nursery and establishment of fruit orchards. Improved design of khadin have been used to optimise the process of infiltration, runoff generation and routing, as well as soil and water storage capacity.Construction of anicuts in Ujalian watershed (Jodhpur district) has helped in regeneration of plants of different species and grasses in the upstream area.In Pali district,its presence has increased aquifer recharge from 5.2% to 38.5%. Studies conducted for 3 year at Kalawas in Jodhpur district revealed that with the construction of a sub surface barriers, the rate of depletion of ground water was reduced from average 1.0m to 0.3m per year.Studies carried out for four years at Jodhpur revealed that evaporation reduction in sand filled reservoir was about 92 %, although reduction in storage capacity was nearly half.

Joshi, N.L (2004) focused on agro-forestry such as agro-horticulture system, agro-silivicultural system and silvo-pastoral system to increase total productivity per unit areas and simultaneously for conserving and improving the natural resources of soil. In drought years when annual crop fails or their production is highly depressed, fruit tree species yield considerable food, feed, land fuel thereby greatly obviate the sufferings from general shortages. In agro-silvo systems, agricultural crop provide seasonal revenue, while trees are managed at 8 to 10 years rotation giving extra return of timber, fuel wood and fodder. Silvo-pastoral by emphasing on top feed tree species carrying grasses or legumes increases fodder supply in rural areas. Agro-pastoral maintains balance between fodder crops and pastures. He suggested that sustainability in production can better be achieved by optimally combining cropping system, alternative land use systems and live-stock systems and the means available to the farmer to raise them profitability. Such system interacts adequately with environment without dislocating the ecology and socio-economic balance on one hand and attempts to meet the national goals on the other.

Tejwani, K.C (2005) probed at the agents of deterioration in watersheds and concluded that the farmers /beneficiaries will participate (and even contribute) to watershed management as long as they get short term/on-site /direct /tangible benefits. They do not get enthused by the prospect or promise of soil conservation for the next generation or availability of timber ten years or more down the time, indirect benefits of betterment of environment and under ground water recharge (which occurs elsewhere as springs and benefits others).Since farmers / beneficiaries are the agents of change, discussing the local needs and benefits will trigger enthusiastic and committed participation by them. Having identified the needs, the goods and services have to be delivered in cost-effective and efficiently, preferably through a single window delivery so that farmers /beneficiary does not have to run to many functionaries. Only when the farmers/beneficiaries and the agents of change function in unison, then alone success of development activities is possible.

Singh, Singh & Sharma (2005) highlighted the achievement of Chenani Watershed Project of district Udhampur and provide suggestions on self observations basis for other ongoing watershed activities. On 1300 hectares of watershed project,500 ha of land was afforested for fuel wood and fodder, 400 ha of land was used for pasture development, 200 ha of land was planted with various agro-forestry horticultural tree and rest of 200 ha is planted with shrubs, grasses and legumes to conserve moisture and to control erosion. To harness the benefits of micro watershed, suggestions offered are decentralise and initiate micro-planning on the individual village basis, promoting enterprise like sericulture, mushroom growing, horticulture etc., ensuring accountability of work done, raising carrying capacity of the area, coordinating activities of various department and timely release of funds to check undue delays and ensuring efficiency of activity implementing channels.

Wittayapak,Chusak & Philip Dearden (1999) examined four case studies of community-based watershed management with emphasis on their operational decision making arrangements in Northern Thailand. All the case studies established community-based regimes as a results of declining resource abundance, but differ in their operational rules, administration, effectiveness and satisfaction among stakeholders. Ban Luang Watershed suffered from being too large,with too many stake holders and not very restrictive operational rules, leading to internal conflicts among the different stakeholders. Thung Hang, watershed being too small , though helped in terms of village input to decisions and recognising fellows users,but was under severe resource pressure and outside recognition from the govt.

Although Ban Lung is smaller than Thung Hang in terms of both the size of watershed and number of users, the long history of community awareness of the importance of maintaining water supplies from the watershed, the richness of the forests and increased dependence on off farm employment.But this robust institution can soon be weakened in the face of users discarding their obligations for reciprocity. The authors suggested that with establishment of legal forest communities comprising officials and provincial forest inspection committees chaired by the provincial governor would strengthen the weak institutions who apparently look for greater degree of reliance on outside authorities.

Webler Thomas et al. (2003) explored the decision of New England local governmental officials (LGOs) to participate (or not)in regional collaborative environmental policy making on watershed management planning. Factor analysis resulted in five perspectives but consider three important. The study found that LGOs make their decision to participate or not based on three general considerations : they feel they can help make a positive difference, they see working on the problem as consistent with their environmental ethic and it is in their community's interest that they participate in the process.

Dawel He and Chen Jingsheng (2001) focused on watershed management issues in China such as divided jurisdiction and overlapping responsibilities of water management agencies, water pricing,lack of attention to non-point sources, absence of legislation regarding both watershed organisations & public participation, illegal implementation of existing environmental laws and national policies concerning agriculture & farmers. They suggested that a multi-objective, multi-functional development programme should be constituted for integration of emigrant resettlement, poverty elimination, regional development and environmental protection.

Sharma,Giridhari Paudel (2002) surveyed on farmers changing land use and management practices in two mountain watershed namely, Phewatal Watershed (project area) and Yamdi Mardi (non project area)Watershed confronted with shrinking landholding size and scarcity of non-farming employment opportunities. Based on the survey of 300 households, the study found that farmers in both watersheds have gradually intensified land use and cultivated new crops to increase farm production and income. They have shifted from cereal crop to livestock husbandry, particularly along the road in the project watershed and to vegetable and other cash crops in the accessible foot hills of the non-project watershed. The degree of the adoption of various structural and biological measures to control soil erosion, landslides, gully expansion to increase farm production was higher in the project watershed than in the non project watershed.

Ghanbarpour,Hipel & Abbaspour (2005) provided a framework for Strategic Watershed Management Planning (SWMP)to satisfy long-term objectives of a majority of stakeholders belonging to Kan Watershed located north of Tehran, Iran. Within SWMP framework, a set of strategies was established and group decision analysis techniques were used to rank different strategies and alternatives that would best satisfy stakeholders' objectives. From the analysis made, water resource development emerged out to be important strategy both by governmental personnel and community leaders.

SWMP imparts a degree of rationality to watershed planning as it provides an opportunity to learn from the vast range of knowledge and expertise of the community, identify many stakeholders' preferences, furnishes a forum in which watershed managers can clarify and resolve conflicts before the implementation stage. They suggested establishment of Watershed Council later coordinated governmental plans with community preferences and experts judgments in the initial stage of planning process. Such organisations would have representatives from different parties in a watershed.

Li,Wang &Tang (2006) conducted field experiment about transfer mechanism of nutrients in soil on sloping lands influenced by natural and artificial factors on the soil collected from a sloping land at upstream of Taihu Lake basin, China.

Result showed that the rainfall intensity had a small influence on nutrient concentrations in runoff, but a significant influence on the runoff flow on sloping lands. The slope length influenced the nutrient loss by soil erosion on areas that receive rainfall. They suggested different management practices for different sloping lands including changing fertilization, improving fertilization technology, adjusting vegetation coverage and cultivation system of arable land on different sloping lands within a watershed.

Ravnborg,Helle Munk (2002) explored the relationship between poverty, soil quality and soil management strategy based on field research carried in Rio Saco, Cuscateca & Tascalapa Watersheds in Honduras,Central America.

The result showed casual relationship between poverty & soil degradation. Neither were the poor found to be more likely to clear forest for agri. purposes than the less poor in any of three watersheds. Second, poor farmers were constrained by lack of capital, labour and land but capital constraint significantly affected the choice of soil management strategy of poor farmers, in that it inhibited them from using chemical fertilizers. Use of velvet bean as a green manure crop was found to be within reach of poor farmers and built on the available resources.

Sharma et al. (2001) assessed the impact of remote sensing and GIS techniques to arrive at cost-effective plans for conservation and development measures for watersheds based on a part of Jasdan Taluka (district of Rajkot) in Gujarat. In the watershed studied, the actual implementation of soil and water conservation measures recommended along with the alternative land use systems resulted in a considerable decrease (up to 55% at sub-watershed level) in runoff , thereby improving the soil moisture regime. Multiple agriculture production system such as agro-horticulture, agro-silviculture etc.were found to be very effective in conserving rainwater. After conservation measures, the runoff yield was found to decrease by 42.88% of the pre-conservation value for the entire watershed.

Moore, Elizabeth & Koontz (2003) developed a typology of collaborative groups classified as: citizen-based, agency-based and mix type based on the examination of 64 watershed groups in Ohio, USA.

The study found the influence of collaborative groups on policy differs across the group types and different types of groups are likely to report different accomplishment. Citizen based groups more often relied on traditional ,adversarial means such as lobbying and petitioning, the impact of mixed and agency-based groups was more such subtle and less visible, through technical advice and changes in individuals decision making.This helped the govt. to allocate its scarce resources by knowing which type of groups were inclined to achieve particular outcome. More over choice of collaborative group had implications for what the group was likely to accomplish.

Shrestha (Vaidya) & Pushpa Lata (1998) investigated the women's management role in the Shivapuri watershed which earlier was characterised by excessive environmental degradation, poverty, underemployed and population pressure. With the formation of the Forest User's Group Network and Women's User Group Network, a number of training and workshops were conducted to resolve resource mgt problem. Increase is the use of improved cooking stove, coupled with private plantation to economise and make effective use of fuel energy along with income generating scheme were initiated which contributed in raising family status. It further led to improved water flow from 0.08 m3 to 0.17 $m^3$ per second from 1963 to 1990. It was suggested that fragile mountain area cannot provide enough land productivity but the tremendous resources under management can support an industrial complex. Therefore, industry must be started to supplement land productivity in Nepal.

Lokesh (2004) estimated the total economic value of Kallambella Watershed Development Program (WDP) employing 'with and without project' framework using field data for 2001-01.He found that due to WDP, the value of rain fed dry land increased by 17 percent (Rs.5,371 per acre) over non-watershed project area.The contribution from rain fed field crops,agri-horticulture, agro-forestry and silvi-pasture was 46%, while contribution from groundwater irrigation was 49 percent of the total economic value of Rs.20,375 per acre. Intangible benefits formed one percent and livestock three percent net return per acre of dry land field crops (ragi and groundnut) in watershed area was Rs.1,437 which was Rs 719 in non-watershed project (NWP) area. Due to recharge of ground water, gross irrigated area per irrigation well increased by 53 percent (by 24 acres).The perennial crops in agri-horticulture and silvi-pasture contributed almost equally (around 45 %)to ground water irrigation in this watershed. While groundwater irrigation is investment intensive, perennial crops in agri-silvi system are not. Hence higher budgetary allocation in watershed be made for this sector to augment farm incomes. This also complements environmental goals through carbon sequestration.

Sripadmini,R lauded the role of National Watershed Development Programme for Rainfed Agriculture (NWDPRA) which covered 4400 micro watershed covering an area of 4.2 m.ha with an outlay of Rs.9,800 lakhs in the nineth plan. An evaluation study conducted of Mendhwan Watershed Project under IGWDP in Maharashtra State showed a phenomenal change in land use pattern, a substantial increase in the number of families owning wells, a increase in water table to the extent of 10 feet and the net incremental income estimated at Rs 1,680 per hectare with family labour. He suggested that sustainability issues in rain fed areas demand both conservation of resources and enhancement of productivity on a continuous basis.

Report on 'Paraticipatory Watershed Development under Integrated Watershed Development Project (Hill-11)', evaluated community empowerment and income generation activities carried under the IWDP (Hills-11) project implemented in Kandi areas of Punjab in the districts of Gurdaspur, Hoshiarpur, Nawanshahar, Ropar and Patiala with the World Bank support covering 17 sub watershed, 3,.27 lakh population with a total outlay of Rs. 214 crores. Under this watershed VDC and Women's Self Help Groups accumulated a total saving of about Rs.60 lakhs. Women's Self Groups were trained in tailoring, football making, detergent making, book binding, dari making etc. and IGAs linkages were created with local market and also markets in Ludhiana/ Jalandhar. For poors, activities such as backyard poultry, bee keeping, small scale milk processing units etc. were taken. Three year programme was chalked out and provision for trainings, tools and raw material for income generating activities for enhancing training for community. Exposure visit of beneficiaries outsides the State and India was undertaken.

Report entitled 'Unscaling of Successful Experiences in Mainstream Watershed Programme in India-Mechanism Instruments and Policy Consideration' synthesised the detailed case studies of watershed projects funded by DANWADEP in three states namely,Orissa, Karnataka & M.P and experiences under innovative watershed project funded by various organisations like Govt. of India, bilateral projects and NGOs. The lessons from studies were analysed under five themes/sub-themes:(i) user right (ii) capacity building (iii) equity for resources among poor families (iv) participatory monitoring and evaluation system and (v) withdrawal strategy/ post project sustainability. In its review report, it highlighted that policy attention is required to improve coordination both at the central policy level & between ministries & departments at Central & State level, better Go-NGO collaboration to improve the operation of the various project implementing agencies, careful policies regarding degree of subsidies & contribution involved in the financing of investment by the different parties participating, strengthening of the real participation by the poor and ensuring that benefits from watershed development accrue to the poor and women.

Farrington & Lobo (1997) evaluated Indo-German Watershed Development Programme (IGWDP) covering 92000 ha of private and other land in 20 districts in Maharashtra, involving 50 NGO working in 74 watershed. They concluded that cases of participatory micro-watershed management especially those managed by NGO are becoming abundant. Yet, almost without exception, they are small in scale and can be expanded only by repeating the same slow, costly, in-depth techniques in successive villages. By contrast, many government-sponsored approaches have expanded rapidly, but often lack the local ownership and group coherence necessary for sustainable management of the common pool components of watersheds. If approach to micro watershed rehabilitation are to be participatory and rapidly replicable, then a close engagement of stakeholders is needed in creating local watershed planning methodology, framework for local-level collaboration among NGO, CBOs & Govt. departments and creation of mechanisms which channel funds to local organisations with as few intermediate stages.

WASSAN report (2000) analysed the role perceptions, capacity building needs and enabling systems in place (with respect to participatory processes) at various stakeholder groups in a sample of 10 watersheds selected randomly from DPAP 3rd and 4th batch of the programme in A.P. The study found that training & community organisation budgets were centralised and programs were centrally organised in Hyderabad or at Mandal level. The capacity building efforts in no way matches the requirements of demands of the program both in quantity and in focus. Most of training programs conducted were 'lecture/ speeches oriented' without using any appropriate training methods. The report suggested creation of multi-stakeholder group & entrusting more responsibilities on Project Director DPAP to extend necessary coordination with PIAs, WDTs, MDTs & watershed community for the purpose of survey and organising stakeholder workshops.

Bhattarai et al. (2006) observed allocation of fixed proportions of land to develop agriculture, forest, other uses in a watershed and modeled as an optimisation problem faced by single user. Two time period cross-sectional data for 60 watersheds were used in the analysis. A multinomial logit model was used to explain the effect of population density, mean age, market concentration, travel time to work, road accessibility, personal income, education level and longitude & attitude of watersheds developed. Land use share was positively related to higher market concentration and road accessibility, but with a higher average time to work, suggesting a rural-urban job interface.

Turton and Farrington (1998) appreciated the Watershed Guidelines of the Ministry of Rural Area and Employment towards institutionally and ecologically sustainable enhancement of rural livelihood. They found that watershed development is not yet being planned strategically in the context of other rural development initiatives. At the project implementation (PIA), funding is insufficient for NGOs to attract and maintain quality staff. At the community level, there is inadequate effort to engage weaker groups in the process of WSD procedures for selecting (and de-selecting) villages. WSD work best where it is integrated with other means of enhancing livelihood & needs to be tailored to local agro-ecological, socio-economic and infrastructural conditions. For imparting the effectiveness and efficiency of state and nation, Govt. programme should include (i) support for a programme of capacity building at all levels (ii) support for cross-learning across project (iii) strengthening monitoring and (iv) strengthening strategic planning at the state and district levels.

Ahuja, Reena (2005) highlighted the pivotal role of women in management of natural resources, involvement in effective implementation and equitable distribution of the benefits of watershed management which at present is constraint by a number of socio-economic factors : involvement in less remunerative activities, loss of access to common pool resources, denial of land ownership rights, inconsideration to gender differentiated impacts of forest protection and lack of technical expertise.

The intervention strategies suggested by her for improving decision-making as resource users and poverty alleviations are : preparation of watershed plan with an understanding of gender needs and implementations; developing watershed plans on the basis of existing use & dependence pattern; reformulation of watershed guidelines to specify mechanisms for institutional arrangements for involvement of poor & women; development of micro-credit / self help groups; shifting focus from watersheds to livelihood development and organising gender sensitisation programmes.

Arya and Samra (2001) evaluated the role of participation during planning, designing, implementation, redesigning and maintenance of 27 watersheds inhabited by 2070 families in

Haryana Shivalika. They found that the examples of Bunga, Dhamala, Sukhomajri, Gobindpur, Mandappa and Lohgarh though showed a shift from self destruction to rejuvenation but was a short flip unless people are drawn into social programmes and given control of resources.

The formation of 'Hill Resource Management Societies' were encouraging and turned around economy of most villages. Immediate and direct economic benefits in the form of fodder and water provided to be attractive incentives for generating momentum in community participation dynamics.

These reviews have suggested site/area specific benefits, underlining the need for supporting them at macro level to sustain agriculture and economic development.

## RESEARCH GAP

GOI through a range of schemes, projects and programmes falling under three Central Govt. ministries (agriculture, forest and rural development) initiated watershed development to ensure the availability of drinking water, fuel wood & fodder and raise income & employment for farmers & landless labourers through improvement in agriculture production and productivity (Rao,C Harmantha 2000).Benefits from water harvest structures ranged from increased acquifer recharge from 5.2% to 38.5% (Khan 2004), intensified land use with emphasis on cash crops & livestock husbandry (Sharma 2002),income generating schemes contributing in raising family status & improved water flow (Shrestha 1998),increase in the value of rain fed dry land by 17%(Lokesh 2004), increase in the net incremental income at Rs.1680 per hectare with family labour (Sripadmini), asset building by SHG (IWDP report) etc. have spatially touched the various aspect of watersheds besides being area specific.

An integrated Approach under one nodal agency (DPAP) in sub-tropical zones has remained untouched. The area specific problems of Sue-Chaker Watershed, collected through survey were:

a. Low soil moisture conservation,excessive runoff,severe soil erosion leading to gully formation.

b. Low level of crop yield,fuel and fodder production. Improved agriculture practices were missing.

c. Unchecked grazing had rendered the lands denuded with poor soil moisture retentivity.

d. Forest cover was poor and damaged due to increased biotic pressure and

e. People were under employed and their level of income was abnormally low.

are addressed systematically along with cost benefit arising from individual crop,employment generation, participation and sustainability of watersheds.

## RESEARCH METHODOLOGY

The concept of watershed management envisages planning agricultural activities with due respect to conservation of natural resources of soil and water,taking watershed as a hydrologic unit. The specific objectives of the book are :

a. To quantify the impact of watershed technologies on agriculture productivity in respect of major crops and production of userfructs like fodder, grass, fuel wood etc.

b. Evaluation of achievements in enhancing in-situ moisture conservation, reduction in run off, flash floods and in checking erosion of top soil.

c. To measure the socio-economic development of the community directly or indirectly dependent on the watershed.

d. To evaluate the impact of watershed technology on restoration of ecological balance in the project area.

e. To examine as to how can people's participation in watershed programme and management of resources could be ensured.

Based on these objectives, following twelve impact variables adopted by Deshpande and Narahayanmoorth (1999) while reviewing the implementation of NWDPRA across studies in India, supplemented by area specific variables outlined under DPAP projects for J&K State are examined.

**Table : Impact Variables for Evaluating Agriculture Productivity in Sue-Chaker WDP**

| S.no | Impact variables |
|---|---|
| 1. | Improvement in productivity per hectare |
| 2. | Improvement in employment |
| 3. | Shift towards higher remunerative crops |
| 4. | Cost-benefit analysis |
| 5. | Adoption level of new technology |
| 6. | Effectiveness of administrative machinery |
| 7. | Efficiency of the multi-disciplinary approach |
| 8. | Sustainability of the project |
| 9. | Adequacy of the project |
| 10. | Relevance of the project |
| 11. | Environmental impact |
| | a) Moisture conservation |
| | b) Biomass generation |
| | c) Ground water repletion |
| | d) Arresting soil degradation |
| 12. | People's participation |
| | a) Planning process |
| | b) Implementation |
| | c) Sustenance |

## Research Design

In the first phase, physical and financial assessment of various agronomical and engineering measures carried in the project area were conducted. For this, office of the Project Officer, DPAP Udhampur/Chairman of Watershed Committee/ Team Leaders of the respective watersheds of Block Udhampur were contacted for collecting information about the present and neighbouring watersheds. The break-up of physical/financial activities carried in Sue-Chaker watershed development project was as under

***Table : Physical /Financial Activities Carried in Sue-Chaker WDP***

| | | | | |
|---|---|---|---|---|
| 1 | **Agriculture Department** | **44.11** | **44.11** | **44.11** |
| | Construction of diversion drains, gulley plugging/Check dams/Nallah bank erosion control (in hects) | 232.1 | 14.8 | |
| | Const. of water harvesting tanks (in no.) | 5 | -- | |
| | Pasture development (hects) | 40 | 3.82 | |
| 2 | **Department of SC (Forest)** | | | **50.14** |
| | Contour trench plantation (no.) | 1,76,260 | 12.45 | |
| | DRSM works(in $M^3$) | 400 | | |
| | Afforestation (in no.) | 14,000 | | |
| | Minor engg. works (in no.) | 630 | 5.54 | |
| | Social forestry(in no) | 18,000 | 3.13 | |
| 3 | **Sericulture Department** | | | **4.81** |
| | Mulberry tree planted (in no) | 1,17,000 | 2.03 | |
| | Area covered under mulberry plantation (in hect) | 30.7 | | |
| 4 | **Horticulture Department** | | | **1.04** |
| | Fruit plantation (in no) | 6,998 | 0.44 | |
| | Area covered under plantation (in hect) | 35.29 | | |
| | **Total** | | **42.21** | **100** |

* Source:Office Record DPAP,Udhampur

Map of the project area was drawn (2.1 &2.2) and photograps of watershed technologies-Bench terracing, nallah bank erosion, gulley plugging, diversion drain and water harvest structures were clicked (Plates 2.1-2.15).

In the second phase, a schedule needed for collection of primary data from farming community was developed from review of literature and through discussion with knowledgeable people, encompassing twelve impact variables. Apart from descriptive and open ended questions, some questions were also kept on 5-point Likert scale(5<........>1. The same after pre-testing, got filled from 10% male population, selected systematically from three villages namely, Sue, Chaker and Sambal.The distribution of 201 male respondents village-location wise are as under.

***Table : Distribution of Male Respondents***

| Location /village | Sue | Chaker | Sambal | Total |
|---|---|---|---|---|
| Upper | 29 | 57 | 10 | 95 |
| Middle | 31 | 42 | 18 | 92 |
| Lower | 2 | 8 | 4 | 14 |
| Total | 62 | 107 | 32 | 201 |

In the third phase, to enlarge the scope of net benefits in agriculture allied activities, 10% female respondents in the project area was contacted, the distribution is as under.

***Table : Distribution of Female Respondents***

| Location /village | Sue | Chaker | Sambal | Total |
|---|---|---|---|---|
| Upper | 23 | 52 | 33 | 108 |
| Middle | 9 | 32 | 22 | 63 |
| Lower | 2 | 25 | 2 | 29 |
| Total | 34 | 109 | 57 | 200 |

## Data Purification

To quantify the impact of effective administrative machinery, relevance of the WDP and people's participation in planning, implementation and sustenance of the WDP, responses collected on Likert scale were further purified using factor analysis (12.00 version). The results of confirmatory factor analysis using principal component extraction and Verimax-Kaiser Normalization rotation method yielded 17 factors from 21 items with Eigen value = 1. The communalities for items were 1 indicative of higher degree of linear association among variables.The factor loading ranged from 0.559 to 0.968 and cumulative variance extracted ranged from 51.54 to 65.63.

***Table :Multiple Operational Factors Purified Through Factor Analysis***

| | | | | |
|---|---|---|---|---|
| **1 Effectiveness of administrative machinery** | **200** | **200** | **200** | **200** |
| • Sufficient confidence building measures were carried by WDT | 2.99 | 0.854 | | |
| • In your opinion sufficient publicity was given to WDP by Rural Development Agency | 2.77 | 0.613 | | |
| • WDT is sufficiently trained for the project | 2.97 | 0.859 | 51.54 | 51.54 |
| **2 Relevance of the project** | | | | |
| • WDP has led to the optimum utilisation of natural resources | 3.14 | 0.821 | | |
| • WDP has reduced the adverse affect of drought | 2.88 | 0.853 | | |
| • WDT has restored the ecological balance in the village | 2.84 | 0.752 | 55.03 | 55.03 |
| **3 People participation in planning and implementation of WDP First factor** | | | | |
| • Separate SHG were organized for women SC, ST, agri. labour etc. | 2.68 | 0.968 | | |
| • SHG meets regularly to take decisions relating to the project | 2.66 | 0.949 | 27.21 | |
| ***Second Factor*** | | | | |
| • You are represented in at least one user group | 2.67 | 0.968 | | |
| • You have made voluntary donations to the project | 2.66 | 0.754 | 20.24 | |
| ***Third Factor*** | | | | |
| • All the project related works were completed with the active participation and contribution of user group | 2.85 | 0.693 | | |
| • Your village is represented adequately in the WDP | 2.86 | 0.599 | | |
| • Local participation in decision making and programme implementation was carried on voluntary basis | 3.28 | 0.628 | 20.24 | 67.69 |

(No. of iteration= 4)

The value of Kaiser-Meyer-Olkin measure of sampling adequacy and Bartlett's Test of Sphericity indicated construct validity of the construct (Hair et al.1995). The reliability of the scale items was tested using Cronbach's Alpha method, the value ranged from 0.309 to 0.706.

The book is of great value to the policy makers, govt. agencies and voluntary organisations associated with planning, implementing and improving watershed projects in sub-tropical zone. It would improve the relationship between govt. agencies at different levels-central, state and local with respect to agriculture activities. Identification of area specific socio-economic problems would provide input for directing future researches.

## GENERAL DESCRIPTION OF UDHAMPUR DISTRICT

District Udhampur has been named after Raja Udham Singh, the eldest son of Maharaja Gulab Singh who was the founder of Dogra Rule in Jammu and Kashmir State. Situated in the southern part of the State, it has a geographical area of 4550 sq. km which lies between 32°45' to 33°30' north latitude and 75°35' to 75°55' longitudes, accounting for about 2.05% of total provisional area and forming the fifth largest district of Jammu & Kashmir State.

It is bounded in the west by Rajouri district; in the north by Anantnag district, in the north-east by Doda district, in south-east by Kathua district and in south-west by Jammu district.

The district has mountainous topography with altitude varying from 600 metre to 3000 metre above sea level.The climate of Udhampur varies from sub-tropical in Majalta, Reasi, Pouni, parts of Udhampur and Ghordi blocks to temperate zone in Mahore, Gool, Dudu, parts of Chenani, Arnas, Ramnagar and upper reaches of Ghordi block. Mean temperature varies form 1.°c-42°c.

The mean annual rainfall ranges between 2.30 mm to 485.14 mm and most of the perception is received during months of March,July and August. Rich mineral deposits like coal, bauxite, magnetite, gypsum and limestone are found in upper reaches. The district has 618 inhabited and 624 uninhabited villages.The villages are grouped into 216 number of panchayats,12 community development blocks, 5 tehsils(Udhampur, Ramnagar, Reasi, Chenani and Mahore)and 3 subdivisions.

Out of these three sub divisions one each at Mahore and Dudu Basant Garh have been declared as the bad pockets.The administrative headquarter is located at Udhampur at a distance of 66 kms from Jammu on Jammu-Srinagar National Highway No. 1 A.

The population of the district is 7435 lakhs as per census 2001. 84% of the population is rural based and the remaining 16% is urban. Majority population is Hindus (72%) and Muslim(26.23%).Scheduled caste constitute about 19.1% population while Schedule tribes is 14.80%.The literacy rate is 54.16%. Density of population is 162 person per sq. kms and sex ratio 871 female per 1000 male.

The major economic activities undertaken in the district are agriculture, horticulture, sericulture, dairy, poultry, fisheries,handicraft, handloom, Khadi and other village industries etc. The district is mostly hilly and has inaccessible terrain.

It is estimated that 90% of the population is rural and dependent on agriculture sector.

The landholdings of the farmers are small & marginal ranging from 0.5 to 2.0 hectares, the cropping intensity around 164% and only 0.064 lakh hectares area is irrigated accounting just 6% of the total cultivable area.

Agriculture is rain fed with frequent occurrence of moisture stress / draught like situations. In few cases excessive rains cause flood havocs.

To boost economic activities, there are two Industrial Estates one each at Battal Ballian & other at Reasi. Financial services are rendered by 7 nationalised /private sector banks with a network of 72 branches covering 54 service areas. The district has the world famous Hindu Shrine of Sri Mata Vaishno Devi located in sacred Trikuta hills.

The present Sue-Chaker Watershed Development Project lies in block Udhampur of district Udhampur.

## SUE-CHAKER WATERSHED DEVELOPMENT PROJECT

Sue-Chaker Watershed Development Project spreads over an area of 796.36 hectares in Sue, Chaker and Sambal villages of Chaker panchayat in DPAP block of district Udhampur. It is about 6-8 kms. from block head quarter Udhampur on the left side of Jammu-Udhampur road.

The elevation of the area varies between 800-1250m above MSL. The topography of area is undulating, cut up, rolling type and the general slope of the area ranges from 10-80% towards North-West.The area is traversed with numerous dry nallahs and depth of gullies so formed ranges from 4 metres to 20 metres. The water of the area drains into the Barhma nallah which ultimately merges into river Tawi. Due to the erosion on the bank of nallahs, numerous land slides during rainy season causes damage to the soil as well as to the vegetation. The watershed area is divided into three physiographic units: upper, middle and low.

A brief topographic,demographic and economic description of Sue-Chaker WDP as under :

### Topography of Sue-Chaker WDP

#### *a. Land Capability Classification*

According to Roman numerals, land as per its suitability for cultivation is classified into different classes.

**Class-I :** Soils in this group are deep, well drained and can be cropped intensively. There are practically no soils of this class in the present watershed area.

**Class-II:** These soils have inadequate soil depth, less than ideal soil structure and somewhat restricted drainage. Area under paddy crop and maize near the farm house belong to this class.

**Class-III:** Soils of this class has moderately steep slope, restricted root zone, low water holding capacity, low fertility or unstable soil structures.

**Class-IV:** Soils of this class can be put to cultivation, if proper soil conservation measures are adopted.

**Class V-VII :** Soils which are stoney or rocky and recommended only for pasture cultivation falls under this class. Land which can not be used for any kind of commercial plant production is graded under class VII.

### *b.Climate*

The project area falls in sub-tropical to temperate zone. About 80% of the rainfall occurs during monsoon season and the number of rainy days ranges from 51-188 days. During the rainy season, the frequency is about 10-15 days per month but in extreme cases it may prolong to 30 days. During March-April the hail storm adversely affect rabi crops of wheat, mustard and fruit trees. During winter snow fall is experienced in higher reaches. The mean annual temperature varies from 30 to 400. During winter the range of temperature varies minimum from 10-20c to maximum 100-150c whereas in summer the range of fluctuation is 400c to 200c.

### *c. Natural Vegetation*

The forest area is scrub, thick patches of Banj (fodder tree), Kamaloo (bushes) and Champ could be seen in isolated areas. The common tree species seen are Banj(Quercus semicarpifdia), Dhak(Butea monosperma),Chir (Pinus roxburghii & Pinus Longifolis), Dhaman (Grewia optiva),Tun (Red cedar), Daruni (Runica gernatum),Keu(Oilea Cuspidate),Santha(Dodonaea viscosa), Brankad (Adhotoda vasica)and Willow (Salix alba).Bushes of varying varieties such as Kambila (Mallotus philippensis,Kakoe(Barbares),Garna(Carissa opaca),Ber (Ziziyphus mauritiana lamk), Kikar/Babul (Acacia nilotica),Carissa Opaca, Colebrookia oppositifdia are seen in patches.

Among the varieties of grasses Dub(Cynodon dactylon) and Bathu(Chenopodium album) is common.

### *d.Present Land Use*

Of the total 796.35 ha of the pre watershed development land , its land use pattern was as follows:

***Table : Land Use Pattern under Sue-Chaker WDP****

| S.N. | Nature of area/village | Sue | Chaker | Sambal | Total |
|---|---|---|---|---|---|
| 1. | Total area as per village papers | 144.47 ha | 552.00 ha | 99.55 ha | 796.02ha |
| 2. | Forest area | - | 131.93 ha | - | 131.93ha |
| 3 | Irrigated area | - | 6.07 ha | - | 6.07ha |
| 4. | Rain fed area | 76.89 ha | | 63.54 ha | 282.07ha |
| 5. | Cultivable waste land | 26.71 ha | 146.50 ha | 23.06 ha | 196.27ha |
| 6. | Area not available for cultivation. | 40.87 ha | 125.86 ha | 12.95 ha | |

* Source:Office record,panchay at Chaker,Udhampur.

### *e. Croping Pattern*

Maize is the principal Kharif crop and is also the staple diet of rural masses. Pulses like mash & mong etc. were also grown. Due to lack of irrigation facilities, paddy was grown on limited areas.

Farmers generally hesitate to grow wheat because of its long duration and likely damage at the time of maturity during April-May. The cropping pattern practiced during pre-watershed was as under :

i. Maize-Fallow

ii. Mustard-Fallow

iii. Mustard-Maize

iv. Maize-Mustard

v. Fallow-Rice

vi. Mash-Wheat

vii. Potato-Wheat

viii. Maize-Barley.

The area was devoid of fruit trees except some indigenous varieties of citrus were found.The vegetables grown in the area were peas, brinjals, radish, knol-khol, lady finger, cowpease, beans, curcurbits for own consumption.

### *f. Manure and Fertilizers*

The usage of chemical fertilizer was negligible. The use of farm yard manure (FYM) was found only in those fields which were nearer to the farm houses and cattle sheds. The use of pesticides and insecticides was almost non existent.

## Socio-economic Profile of Sue-Chaker WDP

The total number of families in the project area were 2865 (census 2001) of which 54% belonged to schedule caste. The landholdings were small and marginal even less than 2.00 ha.The primary occupation of people was farming and during off seasons, they work as casual labourer. There were two primary and one middle school within the watershed area.In spite of 270 nos. of buffaloes 610 nos. of cows and good number of fowls, there was no Animal Husbandry/Veterinary Centre. There was no fertilizer dealer centre and the net work of govt. functionaries and banks were almost negligible. People were depended upon money lenders to meet their current and future financial needs. There was no primary health care unit and poverty was pervasive.

A brief description of the aforesaid variables is as follows:

### *a. Location of Fields*

The area covered by the sample respondents was divided into three reaches namely, upper, middle and lower. Accordingly, of the total fields of 201 respondents,47% lie in upper region, 46% middle and 7% constitute lower region of the watershed.

### *b. Caste*

The social institutions prevailing in the WDP were categorised into four classes : Brahmin, Kshatriya, Vaishya,Schedule caste and Schedule tribes. The percentage of respondents falling in each caste were Brahmin (13), Kshatriya (2),Schedule caste (69) and Schedule tribes (16).

### *c. Qualification*

On the basis of responses, five qualification categories have emerged : illiterate, below-matric, middle-matric, matric-graduation and above graduation. Majority of farmers are illiterate (69%), followed by matric graduation (19%), below matric (12%) and least constitute above graduation (6%) level of qualification.

### d. Religion

The respondents are found to be the followers of two religion namely, Hinduism and Islam. The percentage of Hindus in the total respondents is 84 compared to 16 Muslim.

### e. Number of Dependents

On the total 201 respondents, the numbers of dependent male and female were 612 and 516 respectively. 30.5% of dependent male are engaged in agriculture and animal husbandry; 28.86% agriculture, 21.40% agriculture labourer;1.99% not engaged in any vocation;1.50% animal husbandry & labourer and negligible proportion in job, shopkeeper and casual labourers. Of the 516 dependent female, 42.79% are engaged in agriculture and animal husbandry; 25.37% are not engaged in any vocation;18.41% in agriculture; 5.47% animal husbandry; 4.98% agriculture labourer and insignificant proportion in jobs and casual labourers.

### f. Allied Occupation

29.35% of the total 201 respondents are not pursuing any allied vocation; 28.86% are engaged in agriculture; 19.40% casual labourer; 11.44% agriculture labourer; 3.48% private job; 2.99% are shopkeepers; 2.49% agriculture and animal husbandry and 1.99% engaged in Govt. job.

### g. Annual Income

96.51% respondents have subsistence income from agriculture.1.49 % each have income from Rs.1000-Rs.5000 & Rs.5000-Rs.10,000. Only one respondent constituting 0.50% has income in the range of Rs.10, 000-Rs.15,000.Majority of the farmers are practising subsistence farming. 56.72% respondents did not have any income from agriculture. Income of 20.40% respondents ranged between Rs.5000-Rs.10,000; 11.44% respondents between Rs.1000-Rs.5000; 2.98% respondents Rs.15,000-Rs 45,000 to Rs. 55,000 Rs.-60,000. Thus majority of respondents have fields in upper region of the watershed falling in village Chaker. They were primarily schedule caste, illiterate and followers of Hindu religion. They carrying more dependent male compared to female population. They practice subsistence agriculture and their income from agriculture allied activities is negligible.

### *h. Land Tenure Pattern*

Of the total population, 32% farmers have landholdings below 0-0.50 ha, 58% 0.50-1.00 ha and 10% 1.00 to 2.00 ha.

The sources of credit availed by the respondents are grouped under three classes namely, non-institutional(money lenders & landlords), relatives & friends and institutional (banks).Within each class, different credit slabs were created on the basis of credit source availed and its utilisation behaviour exhibited by the respondents during survey. In the non-institutional credit source, maximum borrowings are seen in the slab of Rs. 1000-Rs.2000 and the amount borrowed was used for agriculture. Borrowings from relatives and friends are maximum in three slabs : Rs.1000-Rs.2000, Rs. 2000-Rs.3000 and Rs. 4000-Rs.5000.The funds availed were mainly in the form of short and medium term loans borrowed for agriculture development. Funds borrowed from institutional sources mainly from banks are maximum in the slab of Rs.11000-Rs.12000 used for purchase of animals during pre WDP compared to Rs.10,000-Rs.11,000 borrowed for poultry in the post WDP.

Maximum people in village Sue had borrowed funds from friends and relatives the slab of Rs. 2000-Rs.3000. The funds were used for agriculture development in pre & post WDP. Borrowings both in number and size declined in post compared to pre-WDP in village Chaker. Credit availed from friends & relatives ranked first followed by non-institutional and least by institutional sources. From the above analysis, following conclusions can be drawn:

Funds borrowed from non-institutional sources for agriculture and purchase of animals showed a declining trend both in number and size in post WDP activities compared to pre WDP. Borrowings from friends & relatives decreased both in number and size in post WDP.

Borrowings from banks were used for agriculture allied activities such as animal husbandry, poultry etc.

Borrowed funds were used for agriculture purposes in all the three villages. Borrowings from friends and relatives declined in number but size continue to increase in village Chaker. They also remained dominant in village Sambal in pre WDP but subsequently disappeared in post WDP.

## COMPARATIVE ANALYSIS OF WDPS OF DISTRICT UDHAMPUR

District Udhampur of J&K State has more than 17 percent area under wasteland.The district had been identified for Integrated Watershed Development under Drought Prone Area Programme in 1983-84 with the main objectives for increasing production & availability of food, fodder and fuel; restoration of ecological balance; improvement in the economic status of farmers & rural communities and generation of sustainable rural employment opportunities.Under revised guidelines two WDPs namely, Sundrani & Kawa-Baryal were selected for comparative analysis and evaluating the progress of Sue-Chaker and thereafter suggesting strategical measures for adopting more successful WDPs in the district.

Table shows comparative pre-post agriculture productivity of various crops including vegetables and fodder for Sue-Chaker,Sundrani and Kawa-Baryal Watershed Development Projects.Average productivity of paddy improved considerably and recorded as 1.48qtl/ha in Sue-Chaker,1.55qtl/ha in Kawa-Baryal and 2.02qtl/ha in Sundrani. In case of Jowar, the average productivity rose by 6.34qtl/ha (Sue-Chaker), -0.01qtl/ha (Sundrani) and 0.25qtl/ha (Kawa-Baryal).Average productivity of maize from pre-post development activities in the watershed rose from 10.10qtl/ha to 11.31qtl/ha, 6.24qtl/ha to 6.33qtl/ha and 9.41qtl/ha to 15.07qtl/ha in Sue-Chaker,Sundrani and Kawa-Baryal WDPs respectively.

Maximum increase in the productivity of wheat was recorded at 12.87qtl/ha in Kawa-Baryal followed by 1.42qtl/ha in Sundrani and least at 0.09qtl/ha in Sue-Chaker WDPs. Average productivity of barley rose by 1.6qtl/ha whereas rape and mustard recorded an increase of 1.44qtl/ha in Sue-Chaker WDP. Similarly, increase in average productivity was recorded in respect of vegetables and fodder in all the three WDPs. Average productivity of bajra declined in Sue-Chaker, whereas it remained almost static in Sundrani even after the Watershed Development Project activities.

Table depicts comparative percentage i.e increase /decrease in employment status measured in terms of mandays in three WDPs covering three sets of activities namely, agriculture, agriculture allied (apiculture, mushroom, horticulture, dairy, poultry, sericulture & direct marketing)and non agri. activities (weavers, cobbler, carpenter & casual labour).Percentage increase in the agriculture activities of male in the family was found to be maximum at 18.42 (Kawa-Baryal), 9.29 (Sue-Chaker) and least at 4.16(Sundrani).Among female maximum percentage increase was found at 919.85(Kawa-Baryal),10.77 (Sue-Chaker) and 4.16 (Sundrani).Similarly among hired male & female, Sue-Chaker WDP showed maximum increase at 225 & 200 percent followed by Kawa-Baryal WDP at 143.33 & 143.33 respectively.

In the agriculture allied operations,apiculture, mushroom, poultry and sericulture activities were missing in pre and post WDP.Horticulture activities were initiated during post watershed in Sue-Chaker WDP and found to engage 2000 mandays for male and 850 mandays for female.Mandays generated by family male became negative in post WDP of Sundrani but was 150 mandays for hired male.3.06% increase in family male mandays was recorded in Kawa-Baryal WDP. In dairy, percentage increase in family male mandays in decending order was 61.46 (Sue-Chaker),7.50 (Kawa-Baryal) and 4.77 (Sundrani). Among family female, Sue-Chaker and Sundrani showed negative trend whereas Kawa-Baryal recorded an increase of 111.11 percent in mandays. Mandays generated by family male showed a negative trend in Sue-Chaker and Sundrani WDPs during post watershed period but generated 150 mandays for hired male in Sue-Chaker WDP. Non-agriculture activities recorded increase or decrease only for family male.Weaving, carpentry and casual labour activities earlier done by family male were discontinued during post watershed period in Sue Chaker WDP. Mandays generated by cobbler recorded an increase of 87.5 percent in Sue-Chaker WDP. Percentage of mandays generated through casual labour for family male in Sundrani and Kawa-Baryal WDPs were 30.77 and 75 respectively.

Area under local variety of paddy declined in Sue-Chaker but recorded an increase of 37.23% in Sundrani and 3.33% in Kawa-Baryal WDPs.Usage of improved variety showed maximum increase at 200 % in Sue-Chaker, 37.23% Sundrani and 3.33% Kawa-Baryal WDPs. Percentage increase in area under local variety of Jowar was reported maximum at Sue-Chaker (126.22),Sundrani (15.79) whereas Kawa-Baryal showed negative trend. Area under improved variety of Jowar rose by 164.29 percent in Sue-Chaker WDP.

Area under local variety of maize showed negative trend , whereas under improved rose to maximum at 1175 percent in Sue-Chaker followed by 360 percent in Sundrani WDP. Area under local wheat declined in Sue-Chaker but recorded increase in the remaining two WDPs. Area under improved/hybrid variety of wheat recorded maximum increase in Kawa-Baryal (400%). Usage of local variety of barley declined in Sundrani and its improved /hybrid cultivation was reported to be discontinued in all the three watersheds.Local variety of rape and mustard declined in Sue-Chaker but reported increase in Sundrani WDP.Usage of improved/hybrid varieties of vegetables, fodder and bajra were found to be non-existent in all the three WDPs.Area under local variety of vegetable recorded maximum increase in Sue-Chaker followed by Kawa-Baryal and least in Sundrani WDPs.

Local variety of fodder and bajra continued to be cultivated more intensively in Sundrani as compared to Sue-Chaker WDP.

Tables 5.4. & 5.5 shows net income from Sundrani & Kawa-Baryal WDPs and crop-wise net income in all the three WDPs under study. The net income obtained from paddy, jowar, maize, wheat, rape and mustard, vegetables, fodder and bajra was Rs 62,637.5,Rs.-2324, Rs. 51590,Rs.140271,Rs. 3855, Rs.55788, Rs.199038 and Rs. -137 respectively in Sundrani WDP.

Similarly a comparison of pre & post watershed income from Kawa-Baryal WDP revealed that crop wise net benefits were paddy (Rs.98,880),jawar (Rs.-500),maize (Rs.85,743),wheat (Rs. 2,51,730),vegetable(Rs. 1,14,852) and fodder (Rs.2,93,025).In both these WDPs there has been marginal increase in gross area under different crops due to undertaking of different activities.A perusal of Table reveals that compared with other WDPs, farmers of Sue-Chaker WDPs derived maximum income from jowar (Rs.6,679),maize (Rs. 3,61,529),wheat (Rs.2,48,796), barley (Rs.210),rape and mustard (Rs.22,292), fodder (Rs. 2,06,729) and bajra (Rs. 681).

Whereas maximum income was to the tune of Rs 64,015 (paddy) and Rs. 56,857 (vegetable) was reported by the farmers of Kawa-Baryal WDP.Overall maximum increase in the net income was recorded from the farmers of Sue-Chaker (Rs.8,94,687) followed by Kawa-Baryal (Rs.4,98,850) and least by Sundrani (Rs. 3,27,655.5) by cultivating various crops under study.

Comparative adoption level of technology in the WDPs of district Udhampur reveals that usage of owned seeds declined in all the WDPs except in Kawa-Baryal and increased reliance are being placed on the HYV seeds sold by Dept. of Agriculture and local market. Similarly increased use of DAP and Urea has been observed during post WDPs.The number of farmers using FYM declined in Sue-Chaker but registered marginal increase in Sundrani and Kawa-Baryal WDPs. Among implements, farmers using desi plough decreased considerably (except in Sundrani) whereas in case of improved plough, tractors, chaff-cutter (except in Sundrani)and wheat thrasher, increased usage by farmers were recorded under post WDP conditions.

Farmers of Kawa-Baryal WDP revealed highest level of mean satisfaction regarding completion of project works with their active participation (3.32),maintenance of assets by the user group/panchayat (2.88),sufficient training to WDT(3.12), generation of financial resources for self sustaining by SHGs (3.28), SHG meets regularly to take project related decisions (3.42),SHG transacts business related to the resources generated among the members(3.60),SHG maintain their accounts up to date (3.40),adequate representation of the village in WDP (3.08) and sufficient appraisal of village land and its needs was carried by WDT (3.22).Farmers of village Sue-Chaker were highly satisfied with the parameter that WDT is sufficiently trained for the project (3.16) and sufficient confidence building measures were carried by the WDT (3.13).Overall mean level of satisfaction regarding effectiveness of administrative machinery for all the three WDPs is 2.96 whereas individually it ranged at 3.20 (Kawa-Baryal),2.86 (Sue-Chaker) & 2.83(Sundrani).

People participation has been judged by comparative effectiveness of community organisation, insufficiency of WDPs in fulfilling existing and future needs of farmers, effectiveness of agencies in generating awareness and motivation among farmers, training needs of WA/WT in WDPs and reasons for non-participation in WDPs by farmers. Farmers of village Sue-chaker gave highest rank to SHG &UG (3.81) and least to Mahila mandals / Charcha mandals /Youth clubs (1.56).The mean satisfaction level of farmers of village Sundrani ranged highest between 3.41 for participatory rural appraisal to lowest 2.44 for exposure visits and programmes on literacy, social welfare and income generating activities. Farmers of Kawa-Baryal gave high rank of 3.44 to participatory rural appraisal and lowest 2.50 to awareness camps.Overall mean for each WDP was found to be 3.00 (Kawa-Baryal),3.00 (Sundrani) and 2.99 (Sue-Chaker).

Several reasons were identified by the villagers for the insufficiency of WDPs in fulfilling existing and future needs of farmers.The mean response and its rank in descending order was non existence of any formal group (5.42), non involvement in planning and execution of watershed programme (4.52),inadequate knowledge to utilise the benefits of the project (4.14), fields are scattered in the watershed area (4.00),unawareness about the existence of the watershed (3.78),lack of personal contact by field functionaries (3.27) any other including illiteracy, poverty etc. (2.87).Comparative effectiveness of four agencies in generating awareness and motivation among farmers in WDPs reveals that the most effective agency proved to be informal groups (Sue-Chaker),WDT

(Sundrani) and any other including media by (Kawa-Baryal).Print or electronic media has proved to be least effective for the farmers of Sue-Chaker & Sundrani and WDT for Kawa-Baryal.

A perusal of Table regarding the training needs of WA/WT reveals that knowledge about technical aspect of in situ soil and moisture conservation technique (2.72) was prefered most followed by operation and maintenance of civil works (2.51),awareness about agri., horti., social forestry, nurseries, dairy, livestock mgt., fodder and pasture mgt.,pisciculture & other land uses (2.01), record keeping & conducting meeting (1.48) and least administrative and accounting procedure. Reasons for non-participation in WDPs by farmers identified various reasons which in order of importance response were the project was not as per our local need (4.78), non existence of informal group (4.67), participation need was not felt (4.48),unaware about WDP (4.13),absence of strong panchayat (3.99),insufficient awareness generation by PDA (3.22) and suggestions made were not accepted (2.91). From the above data, it is concluded that to maximise potentials from WDPs specifically Sue-Chaker, emphasis should be laid on popularising improved /hybrid varieties of crops;inducing agriculture allied activities such as mushroom, poultry, sericulture; motivating villagers to form formal groups such as SHGs, Mahila mandals/ Charcha mandals/Youth clubs etc; strengthening contact with field functionaries and reorienting training programmes for WA/WT.

## WOMEN EMPOWERMENT IN WDPS

Women constitutes an integral and an inseparable segment of stakeholders in any natural resources conservation, management & development project. The success of any programme of rural upliftment has direct relationship with effective and useful participation of rural women.The participation of women may however cannot be assured without due motivation and cannot be taken for granted. Rajora (2002) has identified four main reasons, each of which is exerting a cumulative, negative impact on the lifestyle of rural women.

Firstly, in many areas due to desertification and deforestation multipurpose tree species are becoming scarce causing women to collect fuel wood and other forest products from distant areas, which adds more hours to their already stretched working hours. Secondly, as men are employed as casual labourers in towns and cities, women are forced to carry out jobs previously done by men thereby leaving little time for the lengthy business of collecting and processing natural products.Thirdly, new technologies are changing land use, reducing the availability of minor forest products that women have traditionally used to supplement their family income. Fourthly, development projects often improve conditions for men, leaving women in their traditional roles. Lack of access to technical education & training; scarcity of land, time & money; poor organisation, restricted access to political power & a limited opportunity to influence decision-makers etc. are the hindrances in their effective participation in watershed development projects.

Dairy sector topped in employment generation and constitute 63.40% (Sue-Chaker), 55.51% (Sundrani) and 39.14% (Kawa-Baryal) of the total employment generation. This was followed by agriculture 35.29% (Sue-Chaker), 22.49% (Sundrani) and 37.10% (Kawa-Baryal).Mushroom and poultry were observed only in Sue-Chaker and percentage of post watershed mandays generated were 0.47 and 0.48 respectively. Horticulture created maximum mandays in Kawa-Baryal (23.76) followed by Sundrani (22.00) and least in Sue-Chaker (0.36).

Table depicts assets in the form of house, land, animals & consumer durable purchased by women in post WDPs of district Udhampur on account of enhanced income inflow arising from farm and off farm activities. Despite high no response, majority of women 18.5% (Sue-Chaker),32.0% (Sundrani) & 30.00% (Kawa-Baryal) renovated their houses followed by 17.00 % (Sue-Chaker),8% (Sundrani) and 30% (Kawa-Baryal) reported to be repaired. Land improvement through watershed technologies and improved agriculture inputs was practised more compared to purchase of land. Of the total, the percentage of respondents purchasing animals were 16.5(cow),15.0

(buffalo),4.5 (pig),2.0 (goat), poultry bird (2.0) and ass (0.5) in Sue-Chaker WDP. In Sundrani, the percentage of respondents purchasing cow, buffalo and pig were 52.0, 22.0 and 8.0 respectively. The percentage of respondents purchasing buffalo was 30 compared to 20 for cow in Kawa-Baryal WDP. Among consumer durables, T.V accounted for 24.5% respondents followed by small machines (18.5)%,furniture (6.0)%,refrigerator (2.0)% and least household utensils (0.5)% in Sue-Chaker WDP. Similar trend was observed for Sundrani WDP. In Kawa-Baryal WDP, the percentage of respondents purchasing consumer durable in descending order were furniture (30)%, small machines (20)% and T.V(10)%.

Awareness regarding various watershed technologies such as bench terracing, nallah bank erosion, gulley plugging, diversion drain,water harvesting structures (tanks) etc. as evident from Table reveals that women of Sue-Chaker possessed moderate level of awareness regarding bench terracing & nallah bank erosion and low awareness regarding diversion drain & water harvest structures. Similarly majority of women falling under Sundrani WDP possessed moderate level of awareness regarding various watershed technologies and their awareness about nallah bank erosion, gulley plugging, diversion drain was found to be high where as regarding watershed harvest structures was low.

Satisfaction of existing and future family needs in the form of food, fodder, fuel, horticulture, agro-forestry, soil-conservation, dairy, poultry, sericulture, social, employment, communication and marketing among women in three watershed areas is tabulated in Table.In case of food, the average family deficiency figure came out to be 1.44qtls (Sue-Chaker), 0.78qtls (Sundrani) and 2.10qtls (Kawa-Baryal).In fodder Sundrani (11.69qtls) ranked first followed by 11.11qtls (Kawa-Baryal) and least by 5.73qtls (Sue-Chaker).Fuel deficiency needs of Sundrani was 3.25qtls ,Sue-Chaker 2.17qtls and Kawa-Baryal 2.00qtls.

No existing and future needs in respect of agro-forestry and soil conservation were reported by the three WDPs. Dairy, poultry and sericulture needs though quoted but the extent of these was found to be meagre. Existing social, employment, communication & marketing needs were found to be deficient and respondents of all the three WDPs emphasised on its improvement.

The raw data obtained from 300 women from Sue-Chaker (200),Sundrani (50) and Kawa-Baryal (50) after proper editing and adjustments was purified and reduced through Exploratory Factor Analysis (EFA) using SPSS (version 13.0) that yielded as many as 32 statements falling within the working domain of WDP. Since the criteria for the study was finalised at FL>0.50, 18 factor solution was obtained in 7 iterations and 3 round explaining total variance of 64.789%.The value of Kaiser Measure of Sampling Adequacy (MSA) and Bartlett's Test of Sphercity were also satisfactory at 0.890 and X2 (153)=2.667.056 & p<.001. The table further shows the component loadings, communalities and % of variance explained by each factor by an orthogonal varimax rotation.

The composite reliability coefficient of the 18 scale items within all the four factors ranged from 0.53 to 0.75. As depicted in Table, the reliability coefficient for F1,F2,F3 were at 0.90,0.83,0.70 respectively indicating high consistency for being nearby to the criteria of 0.77 obtained by Gorden and Naryanan (1984). Nevertheless F4 also obtained necessary internal consistency which was at a minimum acceptable level of 0.50 as recommended by Nunnally (1978).The F1,F2,F3 & F4 yielded construct reliability (CR) higher and equal to 0.50 and KMO was also very much satisfactory at 0.733, indicating high construct validity of the construct (Hair et al 1995). Moreover all the inter-construct correlations were found to be (r>0) providing support for the convergent validity. Discriminant validity was obtained through cross-construct correlation (using Cronbach's alpha reliability analysis) compared to unity and all were significantly (p< .001) smaller than (1.0), showing the discriminant validity of the measures (Philips 1981).

The mean level of satisfaction among women in Sue-Chaker WDP fluctuated between minimum of 2.93 for compulsory training to women panchayat members would encourage participation among women to maximum of 3.19 for sufficient awareness and motivation carried for securing participation of villagers by Govt. agencies. Women from Sundrani WDP were highly satisfied with mean level at 3.12 for appraisal of village lands and its needs by agencies will induce participation in the project and lower mean at 2.68 felt the need for valuing and implementing suggestions given by women would induce their participation in the project. Similarly mean level at 3.30 shows that women of Kawa-Baryal WDP were highly satisfied with sufficient awareness and motivation carried for securing women participation by govt. agencies but were dissatisfied regarding the manner watershed training for women are being organised in the village. On the whole women in all the three WDPs felt that the existence of Mahila mandals /Charcha mandals/Youth clubs and watershed training would improve their participation in the project. Overall WDP wise mean level of satisfaction in descending order for the 18 statements is 3.02 (Sue-Chaker),2.95 (Kawa-Baryal) and 2.92 (Sundrani).

Thus, it may be concluded that ambit of watershed needs to be enlarged to satisfy secondary needs apart from basic needs of food, fodder and fuel to supplement the earnings of inhabitants in watershed area.

## CONCLUSION AND SUGGESTIONS

Soil and water conservation measures adopted under Watershed Development Programmes play a vital role in resource management and improving socio-economic condition of the rural folk.The present study pertains to Sue-Chaker Watershed Development Project which spreads over an area of 796.36 hectares in Sue, Chaker and Sambal villages.The area falls under panchayat Chaker of DPAP block Udhampur of district Udhampur in J&K State. The area falls in sub-tropical to temperate climatic zones. The topography of the area is undulating, rugged, cut off and rolling type. Maize is the staple food crop and for its cultivation usage of improved agri imputs is negligible.

The landholdings are small and marginal even less than 2.00 ha. The population is dependent on agriculture for livelihood. The specific problems of the area were diagnosed as low soil moisture retention,poor conservation,excessive runoff, severe soil erosion leading to gulley formation; low level of crop yield, fuel &fodder production and unchecked grazing rendering the land denuded with poor soil moisture retentivity. The income level of masses is abnormally low.

The total expenditure incurred on the project during 1992-98 was Rs.42.21 lakhs, with sector wise proportion as 44.11% (agri),50.14% (soil conservation), 4.81%(sericulture) and 1.04% (horticulture).Primary data was collected from 201 male respondents and 200 female respondents using questionnaire based on descriptive,ordinal and open ended questions.The data was purified using factor analysis (SPSS 12.00 version) and Cronbach's Alpha reliability values ranged from 0.309 to 0.706. Impact evaluation of the WDP was carried on twelve variables adopted by Deshpande and Narahaynmoorth while reviewing the implementation of NWDPRA across India and area specific variables outlined under DPAP projects for J&K State. The results of the study are analysed under following sub-heads:

### *Agriculture & Allied Activities in Watersheds*

Agriculture productivity in rain fed areas is a function of level of both monetary and non monetary inputs and is generally constraint by several factors such as scarce & uncertain water supply, low soil fertility, widespread land degradation and soil translocation through erosion. Consequent upon application of WDP technology in the fields, crop productivity per hectare in respect of major crops namely, paddy, jowar, maize, barley, rape & mustard and bajra showed noticeable improvement in post WDP compared to pre Sue-Chaker WDP. Local varieties continued to remain popular in pre-post WDP phases.

Productivity in respect of improved as well as local variety seeds continued to remain low as compared to standardised yield due to non-availability of monetary and non-monetary inputs required to achieve higher levels on sustainable basis. Location of field wise, crop productivity of local variety of paddy was higher in upper regions of watershed. Improved varieties registered higher increase in middle as compared to upper regions of watershed. Local variety of jowar registered higher productivity in upper followed by middle and least in lower.

Improved varieties of maize namely, Kanchan, Pioneer and Mansar were extensively introduced in post WDP phase and the productivity of these varieties tends to approach near standardised one. The productivity of barley was high in middle followed by upper and lower reaches in village Chaker in post WDP.

Productivity of vegetables in middle regions of watershed was more compared to upper and lower regions. Productivity of local varieties of rape and mustard, fodder and bajra increased marginally in post WDP phase compared to pre WDP. Comparative crop productivity in three watersheds namely, Sue-Chaker, Sundrani and Kawa-Baryal revealed increase in productivity during post WDP compared to pre-WDP. Crop-wise maximum increase in paddy productivity was recorded at 1.4qtl/ha (Sue-Chaker), Jowar at 6.34qtl/ha (Sue-Chaker), maize at 11.31qtl/ha (Sue-Chaker), wheat at12.87qtl/ha (Kawa-Baryal),barley 1.6qtl/ha and rape & mustard 1.44qtl/ha respectively (Sue-Chaker). Average productivity of bajra declined in Sue-Chaker, whereas it remained static in Sundrani in post WDP.

With the advent of watershed technologies, there was continuous surge for higher improved/hybrid seeds among farmers primarily on economic consideration. Farmers continued with cultivation of local varieties in respect of barley, rape & mustard, fodder and bajra, with corresponding increase in area during the post WDP compared to pre WDP. Number of farmers cultivating local variety of paddy declined in post WDP. Improved / hybrid variety registered increase usage in middle region of Sue and Chaker villages during post watershed development period. Farmers continued with more local and less with improved/hybrid variety of jowar during the period under study. In wheat crop, the number of farmers cultivating local variety fell from 188 to 153 and area declined from 64.2 ha to 56.9 ha. The number of farmers cultivating improved / hybrid variety rose from 15 to 39 and area increased from 14.25 ha to 18.6 ha.

Comparative tables revealed that area under local variety of paddy declined in Sue-Chaker but recorded an increase of

37.23% in Sundrani and 3.33% in Kawa-Baryal WDPs. Usage of improved variety showed maximum increase at 200 % in Sue-Chaker, 37.23% Sundrani and 3.33% Kawa-Baryal WDPs. Percentage increase in area under local variety of Jowar was reported maximum at Sue-Chaker (126.22), Sundrani (15.79) whereas Kawa-Baryal showed negative trend.

Area under improved variety of Jowar increased by 164.29 percent in Sue-Chaker WDP. Area under local variety of maize showed negative trend, whereas under improved variety rose to maximum at 1175 percent in Sue-Chaker followed by 360 percent in Sundrani WDP. Area under local wheat declined in Sue-Chaker but recorded increase in the remaining two WDPs. Usage of local variety of barley declined in Sundrani and the improved /hybrid cultivation was reported to be discontinued in all the three watersheds. Local variety of rape and mustard declined in Sue-Chaker but reported increase in Sundrani WDP. Usage of improved/hybrid varieties of vegetables, fodder and bajra were found to be non-existent in all the three WDPs. Area under local variety of vegetable recorded maximum increase in Sue-Chaker followed by Kawa-Baryal and least in Sundrani WDPs. Local variety of fodder and bajra continued to be cultivated more intensively in Sundrani compared to Sue-Chaker WDP.

Cost and benefit for Sue-Chaker WDP was calculated by subtracting average five years' cost of cultivation from average five years' price of a crop. The area under paddy increased by 0.35 ha and net benefit also increased from Rs. 6,918 in pre WDP to Rs.26,281 during post WDP. Area under Jowar increased in village Sue & Chaker resulting corresponding increase in income during post WDP compared to losses reported in pre WDP. Income from maize increased significantly in all the three villages in post WDP. In village Sue and Chaker, area under wheat declined marginally but income continued to increase in post WDP compared to pre WDP. In cultivation of barley, the pre watershed losses incurred by the farmers of village Chaker shifted towards profits in the post WDP.

In village Sue, though the area under rape and mustard remained intact but net income increased significantly during post WDP. In village Sambal new areas were brought under cultivation yielding additional net income to the farmers.Area and income from cultivation of vegetables increased whereas cultivation of bajra continued to yield marginal income only in post WDP. Cultivation of local variety of paddy entailed losses, which after watershed development activities when replaced by Ratna or China 1039, recorded significant increase in net income. Area and net income from Jowar improved during post WDP. Improved varieties of maize were introduced more in middle regions of watershed in village Sue and Chaker compared to corresponding upper and lower.

Area under local wheat declined but income continued to increase in all the three regions i.e upper, middle and lower of watershed.The net income improved marginally from the earlier losses incurred on cultivation of local variety of barley during post WDP. Income from rape seed ,mustard, vegetable and fodder by cultivating local varieties recorded increase in post WDP compared to corresponding pre WDP. The net benefit from the cultivation of 9 varieties of crops fluctuated between minimum of Rs. 210 for barley to the maximum of Rs. 23,61,529 for maize. Crop-wise net income in descending order was in case of maize (Rs.3,61,529), fodder (Rs.2,06,729), vegetables (Rs. 28,408), rape and mustard (Rs.22,292),paddy (Rs.19,363) ,jowar (Rs. 6,679), bajra (Rs.681) and barley (Rs. 210). In the cultivation of Jowar, barley and bajra the pre watershed losses subsided and marginal profits occurred in post Watershed Development Project.

The cost-benefit arrived from paddy, jowar, maize, wheat, rape & mustard ,vegetables, fodder and bajra was Rs 62637.5, Rs.-2324,Rs.51590, Rs.140271, Rs.3855, Rs.55788, Rs.199038 and Rs. -137 respectively in Sundrani WDP. Similarly crop wise net benefits were paddy (Rs.98,880), jawar (Rs.-500),maize (Rs.85,743),wheat (Rs.2,51,730), vegetable(Rs.1,14,852) and fodder (Rs.2,93,025) in Kawa-Baryal WDP. Compared with Sundrani & Kawa-Baryal WDPs, farmers of Sue-Chaker WDPs derived maximum income from jowar (Rs.6,679),maize (Rs.3,61,529), wheat (Rs. 2,48,796),barley (Rs.210), rape & mustard (Rs.22,292),fodder (Rs. 2,06,729) and bajra (Rs.

681).Whereas maximum income was to the tune of Rs 64,015 (paddy) and Rs. 56,857 (vegetable) was reported by the farmers of Kawa-Baryal WDP.Overall maximum increase in the net income was recorded from the farmers of Sue-Chaker (Rs. 8,94,687) followed by Kawa-Baryal (Rs.4,98,850) and least by Sundrani (Rs. 3,27,655.5) by cultivating the various crops under study.

Adoption level of technology in terms of agriculture input namely, seeds, fertilizers and technical know how for crop production revealed that compared to pre Watershed Development Project, farmers were using more certified seeds purchased from sale centres maintained by the Dept. of Agriculture than owned sources. Open market was relied only when seeds in needed quantity were not available with the sale centres. Usage of DAP, Urea, MOP and FYM recorded an increase in all the three villages under study in post Watershed Development Project. Maximum increase was observed in case of Urea followed by DAP and least FYM.Of the 9 implements used by the farmers in district Udhampur, 5 were found to be used by farmers in Sue-Chaker Watershed Development Project. Use of Desi plough declined and was compensated by increased usage of improved plough and tractors on hired basis. Similarly number of farmers using chaff cutter and wheat thrasher increased during post WDP. Number of farmers utilising technical know how through disseminating agency was found to be in descending order as fortnightly visit of JAAs, training, demonstration and least by personal field visits by the farmers.

Comparative adoption level of technology concluded that usage of owned seeds declined in all the WDPs except in Kawa-Baryal and increased reliance was being placed on the seeds sold by Dept. of Agriculture and local market. Similarly intense usage of DAP and urea was observed during post WDPs.The number of farmers using FYM declined in Sue-Chaker but registered marginal increase in Sundrani and Kawa-Baryal WDPs. Among implements, farmers using desi plough declined (except in Sundrani) whereas in case of improved plough, tractors, chaff-cutter (except in Sundrani) and wheat thrasher recorded an increase by farmers.

Watershed management is a holistic multi-institutional approach. In Sue-Chaker WDP coordination of activities of various Govt. departments namely, Dept. of Agriculture, Dept.of S.C (Forest),Dept. of Sericulture & Dept. of Horticulture were secured and the amount allocated in the project was Rs. 18.62 lakhs,Rs. 21.12 lakhs, Rs. 2.03 and Rs. 0.44 lakhs respectively. An indepth analysis of the project area and contact with the farmers highlighted following facts: Construction works of soil & conservation wing of dept. of agriculture were undertaken without people's participation, with deplorable present state requiring huge maintenance funds; afforestation was restricted to middle &lower reaches of watershed; mortality rate in case of mulberry trees was found to be very high due to water scarcity though some patches can be seen in middle Chaker village and existence of horticulture plants almost negligible in Sue,Chaker and Sambal villages.

An analysis of training needs of WA/WT revealed that knowledge about technical aspect of in situ scil and moisture conservation technique (2.72) was preferred most followed by operation and maintenance of civil works (2.51), awareness about agri., horti., social forestry, nurseries, dairy, livestock mgt., fodder and pasture mgt., pisciculture & other land uses (2.01), record keeping & conducting meeting (1.48) and least administrative and accounting procedures. Reasons for non-participation in WDP listed by farmers were:The project was not as per our local need (4.78), non existence of informal group (4.67), participation need was not felt (4.48), unaware about WDP (4.13),absence of strong panchayat (3.99),insufficient awareness generation by PDA (3.22) and suggestions made were not accepted (2.91).Following strategies are suggested to improve the state of agriculture in Sue-Chaker WDP :

Selection of right crop and variety is the first step in any successful crop production. To bring about improvement in productivity per hectare, three things should be available in time i.e funds, input & technology. When any of these is not available on time, production suffers otherwise crop production benefit farmers. Besides these, following measures are needed to improve agriculture production:

a. The Dept. of agriculture should make arrangements for timely procurement and distribution of required HYV seeds among farmers.

b. Developing better methods of seed selection and distribution can promote the technology. Farmers do not know which of the traits such as a taller plant, bigger size, colour, shine or shape of the grain, size of the pod, etc. are important. A study can be undertaken to select seeds according to these different parameters and the results can be disseminated among farmers through agri. extension agency.

c. Undertake a breeding and local germplasm development programme to select and spread local high-yielding varieties which are in tune with specific local agro-climatic conditions.

d. The conditions of existing seed stores should be improved so that any chance of deterioration in viability & quality of seeds is avoided.

e. A comparative study on the efficacy of different traditional and modern methods of seed storage may be made. The results should be disseminated among farmers.

f. Minimum support price for crops in watershed areas should be kept on higher sides. Fertilizer, plant protection material and implements should be subsidised and made available through single window system.

Awareness about improved farm operations should be created among farmers through agri. extension agency and mass contact by following ways:

a. Since paddy needs more water, it should be grown on limited areas.

b. Farmers must be educated to use only improved varieties of Jowar. If possible, the crop should be replaced with maize as it is more profitable, less water consuming and three crops in a year can be taken.

c. Farmers must be encouraged for timely sowing of maize crop and area recommended varieties as given by SKUAST.

d. Since no improved variety for barley is recommended for this area, farmers should possibly replace it with wheat or mustard.

e. As the yield and area under bajra is declining, farmers must be motivated to replace it with wheat which is the staple food of the region.

f. Agriculture universities should be associated to undertake plant breeding keeping in mind the synergy of different crops for mixed farming.The results of mixed farming and crop combinations must be popularised among farmers.

g. To minimise the adverse effect of weather, contingency plan for crop production is needed. Unfortunately, the alternate varieties of crops are not available with the farmers and the time they are managed, it becomes too late. To overcome this problem and to develop alternate land use systems, nurseries at site should be developed so that suitable plant species are readily available to farmers.

Besides focusing on conservation activities, efforts must be laid on strengthening of production systems by encouraging cultivation of vegetables, fruit & flowers training in organic farming techniques like composting, manufacture of vermicompost or biofertilizers etc.

Improved agriculture tools, implements and machinery of new design are of vital importance for increasing farm production, reducing the cost of farm operation & maintenance etc. Their timely and proper application and above all reducing or eliminating the human drudgery and conserving energy are essential to optimise the land productivity. Following suggestions can be made in this regard:

a. Demonstration on improved Implement Resource Management such as use of diesel and electric pumps, maize thrasher, chaff cutter, mechanised plough should be made in the respondents field to make them virtually understand the real benefits. Improved ploughs must be popularised as it increases the efficiency of drought animals.

b. Since the area is rain fed, Dept. of agriculture should popularise drip irrigation system and sprinklers. Govt. authorities should take up active steps by initiating these on demonstration basis.

c. Machines which produce sound and scarce away the birds need to be developed as it would protect grains from losses.

d. The design and material used in the Datri and other harvesting tools may possibly be improved to make it more efficient.

e. Partial mechanisation of operations, before, at and after sowing seems to be a perquisite in sub tropic regions where crop growing season is limited. Perhaps a custom-hiring services is required to cater to the need.

All water conservation technologies under watershed should aim at minimising loss of water through runoff, transpiration, evaporation and percolation. Some basic principles needs to be followed to tackle the problem of run off water & erosion are:

a. Intercepting a long slope into several short ones so as to maintain less than a critical velocity of the run off water. Such practices will increase the time of concentration thereby allowing more runoff water to be absorbed and retain in soil profile.

b. Use of watershed approach in the catchments area by afforestation & contour bunding to regulate peak inflow and reduce silt load, eviction of encroachment from the runoff water contribution areas & watershed areas and afforestation in the upper areas should be popularised. The current practice of allowing biomass growth in the tank bed area should be done away with as it results in avoidable evapo transpiration losses.

c. Upper regions of watershed must be covered with permanent vegetation with trees to check soil erosion. Maximum water harvest structures be constructed in top and middle regions to increase the area under life saving irrigation. In lower regions, maximum cultivation could be carried as the water is readily available for irrigation.

d. Studies can be made regarding the type and intensity of irrigation required for protection of crops from frost. The farmers do not make a distinction between normal irrigation and irrigation for 'frost protection' purposes.

e. Farmers must be taught about the productive ways of diverting the excess water, such as diverting it to open bolies, under ground recharge and sharing water with neighbours.

f. At middle & lower regions of the watersheds, training must be given to the farmers for the construction of farm pond. They can be financial assisted where heavy investment is required. They may be taken on tours to places where farmers have successfully constructed and using the farm ponds.

g. Agriculture land in watersheds on the hill slopes and ridges are vulnerable to moisture loss during the winter and early spring season. To prevent this, farmers must be educated to cover the land with crop residues, leaves & twigs.

h. Emphasis should be placed on vegetative barriers and filter strips as a potential means of checking/ minimising soil erosion.

i. In shallow soils having clay layer in the soil profiles, deep ploughing once in three years is called for.

j. The govt. land in the watershed area should be provided with permanent vegetative cover.The forest department at the district level should be motivated to take up these development works.

k. As a confidence building measures, selected farmers may be taken to successful watershed areas especially in H.P, A.P & Karnataka.

To supplement farmers income, the agriculture department and sericulture department can jointly organise education and training programme to start sericulture.The department of sericulture should distribute mulberry trees at nominal cost and provide free guidance & protection in the early stage of development. The department of horticulture should organise awareness generation camps for motivating and popularising among farmers about growing of suitable horticulture plants including citrus fruits.

The diversification of agriculture in watershed areas is must for increasing the income of the family. Mushroom cultivation, bee keeping, cultivation of medicinal plants could be the main components of this proposed diversification.

Scientific study for introduction of medicinal plants may be made to increase ground coverage by increasing biomass and source of income to the farmers.

Remote sensing techniques needs to be intensively used in the field ,land use/land cover mapping, geology and geomorphology, land degradation studies-salt affected, erosion, soil conservation planning, water resources-surface & ground water, forest & natural vegetation mapping, agriculture outcrop, human settlement, monitoring /change detection etc.

In an integrated watershed management system, horizontal and vertical coordination of line departments and natural resources, viz., soil, water, vegetation, livestock etc. are extremely important. It has been experienced that poor linkages & cooperation among line departments,lack of trained & experienced staff often results in increased cost of production , delayed adoption and lesser production levels. Therefore, a committee comprising members of different govt. departments, NGOs and villagers should be formed to assist in the overall development of the area.

Sub optimal production, meagre resources and poverty are the major problems, on the part of farmers in accepting the technology and other recommendations pertaining to watershed management programme/project. Since monetary inputs are expensive and beyond the reach of majority farmers, more emphasis should be laid on non monetary inputs also as these alone can increase agriculture output by 10-20%.

Credit plays a vital role in agrarian economy especially in rain fed agriculture.To meet the credit needs of farmers, watershed projects need to be linked with credit institutions particularly NABARD, Regional Rural Banks (RRBs), Cooperative banks ,commercial banks etc. that ensures free flow of shcrt and medium term loans for dairy animals, credit support to SHGs etc. Besides the lengthy and cumbersome loaning procedures deter the farmers in availing credit facility resulting in failure to undertake capital intensive & high return programmes.Therefore,lending procedures needs to be simplified with sensitising bank staff for extending training in agriculture sector.

Rain-dependent production programmes are high risk-prone and due to poverty people hesitate to invest heavely in monetary inputs especially in fragmented holdings. To minimise this, consolidation of land holdings and other reforms should be taken on priority basis. Marketing facilities provide a necessary incentive in resorting to crop diversification and growing high value oilseed, fruits and off season vegetables besides medicinal plants. Encouragement to Cooperative marketing and linking remote villages with towns would go a long way in bringing prosperity of the area.

There is no doubt that research system has generated vast knowledge and the appropriate technologies. But there is a strong feeling that the technologies generated are not being adopted due to various factors. Various programmes including operation research projects, lab to land and on-farm research be launched on extensive scale to bring the research system face to face with the farming community.

The Forest Department through association with PIA of WDP need to organise exhibition and campaign to generate awareness, training and guidance in Joint Forestry Management among stakeholders.

Green manure an essential component for maintaining organic matter, improvement of soil structure and soil fertility level was not adopted in the project area. The extension functionaries should take effective steps to educate farmers for the cultivation of green manure crops so as to enrich the soil with the important organic manure. Besides farmers must be motivated to use FYM as it would reduce dependence on fertilizers.

Capacity building at central & local levels through extension activities including training, workshop and seminars should be organised periodically.

The village level organisation should be reviewed periodically and its linkages between village communities and govt. departments should be strengthened.

Effective communication techniques must be evolved so that gap between the known technology and people's knowledge could be bridged. This can done by:

a. Farmers have to be made aware that conservation works should be undertaken over a wider area so that the harmful effects from excessive soil heat due to low rains is minimised.

b. Selected fields may be marked for seed production instead of grains. A social system may be created for enabling exchange of seeds of the best fields between different villages and farmers.

c. Research should be evolved around developing and demonstrating crop-friendly species of trees among farmers.

d. Farmers must be educated about the significance of using standardised seeds only through a process of pre-testing a variety of seeds whether bought or home grown. State Agri. Dept. may also undertake demonstration for testing of seeds before recommending for the project area.

e. Department of agriculture must make available reliable local seeds in packed form.

f. A social consensus along the lines of Joint Forest Management should be built for the proper maintenance and use of forest lands. Panchayat are valuable for promoting democracy. But democracy itself work only if there is non-political agency to define the public good and spread its awareness among the people.

g. One major problem is the availability of the biomass for food and fuel. Previously farmers used to bring biomass from grazing lands, panchayat or forest lands. Now the grazing lands have mostly been cultivated and this source has dried up. Now some boimass is available from wild plants and shrubs that grow in the fields though in limited quantity. Possible action in this regard would be to encourage the use of alternative domestic fuel such as solar energy or LPG gas.

Soil conservation measures, afforestation and grassland improvement may be taken in catchment areas. Beside these, following steps should be taken:

a. Watershed development strategies should emphasise on the human development and poverty reduction.

b. Due to low grazing potential, alternative people-friendly uses of left over common lands should be promoted.The suitability of fruit trees of Amla, Lasoda and other horticulture plants may be examined.

c. Quick maturing varieties may be promoted.Such varieties should be located that can mature before the moisture in the bed dries up.

The alternate land-use systems are of great value to achieve sustainable production on marginal lands under sub tropical conditions.Several forms of agro-forestry such as agro-horticultural system, agro-silviculture system and silvo-pastoral system are practised as a major alternative land use systems for rain fed regions.

## Agro-horti System

Fruit trees if suitably integrated in rain fed farming system could add significantly to overall agriculture production including food, fuel and fodder, conservation of soil & water, stability in production and income as the trees being deep-rooted can better tolerate monsoonal aberrations than short duration seasonal crop. Following steps should be taken to popularise horticulture among farmers:

a. Varying fruit-based cropping patterns, such as monoculture of a fruit species and intercropping of fruits with fruits, tubers and fodder should be popularised.

b. Several species of Lime (citrus aurantiifolia Swingle), phalsa, Jujube (ziziphus mauritiana Lamk) etc. are suited for the area. Their propagation from seeds and seedlings, layering, pruning, manuring should be demonstrated by the Dept. of horticulture to motivate the farmers.

c. Since majority of farmers are poor, fruit trees should be subsidised to cultivate interest among farmers.

d. A fruit nursery must be maintained in the area so that farmers can easily purchase the plants besides getting necessary guidance for rearing plants.

## Agro-silvi System

Agro-silvi system involves intercropping with trees and shelter-belts. Agriculture crops are normally grown between rows of trees planted at spacing of 5 m to 30 metres. The agriculture crops provide seasonal revenue, while trees are managed at 8 to 10 years rotation giving extra returns of timber, fuelwood and fodder.

a. Awareness may be generated among farmers for several kinds of crops such as maize, legumes etc. which can be under planted. Such cropping is also a form of conservation farming which enhances fertility and prevents erosion. One very strong argument in favour of such cropping is its ability to produce useable material even in years of severe drought.

b. Shelter-belts and wind beaks on farm lands are a form of agro-forestry which can be adopted in some parts of the rainfed region essentially to protect farmlands and to to enhance environmental values. Farmland shelter belts improve the farmland's microclimate. The shelter-belts can reduce the wind speed by 20% to 50% on an average and slow the evaporation rate by 10% during the day time and 4% by night. The moisture content of the soil,at 0-50 cm depth,could be upto 20% higher than of the control plot. Shelter-belts also favourably influence temperature. The nutrient status of the soil is improved by the addition of dry leaves from trees.

c. Researches on the optimal spacing between trees and between lines of these trees must be initiated. Trees and medicinal plants which give high value /return are more economical in comparison to crop cultivation has to be identified and popularise among farmers.

**Silvi-pastoral System**

Silvo-pastrol system essentially consists of top feed tree species carrying grasses or legumes (preferably perennial) as understorey crops. This system is suited to marginal lands and is most preferable where the fodder shortages are experienced frequently.

a. A few trees/shrubs,grasses and legumes which may be suitable for silvo-pastoral system in sub-tropical areas are:

   Trees : Acacia tortillas, Prosopis cineraria, Albizzia amara, A. lebbeck, Dichrostachyys nutans, Colophospermum mopane

   Grass:Cenchrus ciliaris,C.setigerus,Lasiurus sindicus, Panicum turgidum

   Legumes :Macroptelium atropureum (Siratro), Stylosanthes hamata, S. scabra, Atylosia scarabaeoides, Desmanthus virgutus,etc.

b. Community lands comprising panchayat land,sham lat (govt.) wasteland should be brought under fodder cultivation. Rotational grazing practices should preferably be practised to ensure availability of grasses to cattles.

c. The natural grasslands,cultivable waste and fallow lands provide some grazing during the favourable growth periods in the monsoon seasons. Such lands must be enclosured to provide protection from stray cattle & animals.This will also ensure green grass throughout the year.

d. The most effective way of protecting grasslands will be to convince the local population of the benefits of the plantations of grasses & trees and to ensure their active participation in this programme so that they do not allow their livestock to damage the plantation raised. Such a fencing is termed as 'Social Fencing' and has proved to be effective in so many areas.

Rainfed farming systems traditionally represent subsistence farming, with little room for high cost inputs i.e chemical fertilizers and pesticides.Crop under this system are subjected to soil pests, surface feeders (grasshoppers, crickets,etc.) & hairy caterpillars, armyworms, etc. Following suggestions are made for carrying an Integrated Pest Management in watershed:

a. Practise summer ploughing to expose early stages of pests and soil borne diseases.

b. Ensure seed treatment to check the attack of pests and diseases because it is cheap and requires very less quantity of pesticide.

c. Timely sowing and optimum spacing for healthy crop should be adopted.

d. Balanced dose of fertilizer be adopted for optimum crop yield and generating the resistance in the crop.

e. Use of biological and mechanical controls such as hand weeding, clipping of larvaes, manual destruction of eggs & larvae and use of pheromone traps should be given priority.

f. Termites are the most common soil pests adversely affecting crops in rainfed agriculture. This is also the only group of pests against which insecticidal location will continue to be the sole feasible management approach. Routine soil treatment with dusts or other soil insecticides usually take care of caterpillars.

g. A comparative study of the long term effects of weedicides on traditional crops may be undertaken. For achieving sustainability in farming, extension functionaries should identify the location specific indigenous plant protection measures adopted by farmers and include the same after evaluating effectiveness along with bio-pesticides for integrated approach.

Wood is the main source of energy and its existing & future shortages has been identified by all the stakeholders.To meet the increasing demand of fuel wood and to bring more areas under forests, following measures are suggested:

a. Undertake block planting-as fuel wood plantation.
b. Intensify bund plantation on the boundaries of agriculture fields.
c. Encourage silvi-pastoral system on marginal lands.
d. Motivate Agri-silviculture system wherever practicable.
e. Improve shelter belt plantation (roadside, farm boundaries).
f. Practise block rotational planting in which the rotation between tree/crop are done.
g. Develop fuel farm within this strategy-select species suitable for kandi areas.
h. A rural fuel policy with stress on renewable sources of energy has to be developed.
i. Use of solar cookers and solar PV pumps for drip irrigation in water scarcity areas should be popularised.

Man and animals are complementary to each other. To keep themselves alive, mankind has to depend on animals to meet its various requirements like milk and milk products, meat, eggs, hides, wool etc.

The animals have also been used for ploughing fields, drawing water from wells, transportation, manure for enhancing crop productivity, dung for cooking food, etc. Following measures are suggested to improve livestock production in the watershed area :

a. Livestock production in number and quality would be sufficiently high if the existing rangelands are well managed on scientific basis. Livestock production is optimum from August to December when herbage on the rangelands possesses good nutritive values. Provision on the supplemental feeding for productive livestock, during lean periods of the year(December to June), is recommended.

b. For solving the problems of feed and nutrition deficiency and ensure feed availability during lean period a 'Non-Conventional Silage Process' could be popularised. Unlike traditional silage, non-conventional silage making does not require green fodder of high nutritive value, but can be made from crops and grasses harvested at matured stage, poor quality agro-by-products like straw,stovers etc. and even tree leaves with incriminating taste, texture or organic waste of domesticated animals can be used.

c. The animals in order to produce must have access to enough feed and water round the year. Thus water in ponds must be preserved for stock and human consumption.

d. In the arid regions, mineral deficiency in livestock are very common and these should be controlled by providing mineral mixtures and Urea molasses mineral mixture bricks.

e. Improvement of native breeds can be done in two ways. Firstly by selecting breeding in which the best bulls of the same breed are used for improving the native breed. Secondly,by cross breeding with exotic breeds. In the former method the improvement is slow and takes very long period, whereas, in the later method, the improvement is very quick and is reflected in the next generation.

f. Dept.of Animal Husbandry through proper extension strategies like video films & demonstrations should popularise standard procedures for the optimal use of farm animals.These animals not only ease farm operations but also are helpful for maintaining the soil structure.

g. The veterinary authorities should organise periodic free camps in the villages as the respondents have strong faith in the traditional economy.

h. The shifts from draught animals to tractors has reduced the need to provide grazing land for these stock. But the farmers does keep other livestock-buffalo, goat and sheep-for milk, meat and cash income. Therefore production & utilisation of fodder available from crops is needed. Grazing land is required during rains for livestock. Moreover livestock generate income and employment as long homestead is located in the fields.

j. Though the respondents have maintained one or more animals but the milk producing capacity is very less.It is suggested to educate them in the use of concentrated feeds like oil cakes and cotton seeds as they are believed to increase the milk yield.

**Employment Potentials in Watersheds**

Agriculture in watershed areas is dominated by unorganised sector activities offering almost zero (negative) rate of growth and elasticity of employment Further, subsistence farming of low value crops on marginal lands, has resulted in the problem of under employment, low wages and poverty. An analysis of man days generated in agriculture, agriculture allied and non agriculture activities showed marginal increase in post Sue-Chaker WDP compared to pre WDP period. Agriculture remained lucrative both for male and female.

Several agriculture allied activities such as apiculture, mushroom, poultry and sericulture remained non-existent in Sue-Chaker WDP. Horticulture activities though initiated in post WDP registered increase in man days both for family and hired labour. In dairy activities, man days generated for family male increased but declined for female which was compensated by increase in man days for female hired labour. Man days generated by direct marketing activities for family labour declined but increased for hired male. Among the non agriculture activities, man days generated for family especially male in mason and cobbler activities increased compared to decline for carpenters and weavers during post WDP.

Comparative percentage increase in mandays among family male in agriculture activities was found to be maximum at 18.42 (Kawa-Baryal), 9.29 (Sue-Chaker) and least at 4.16 (Sundrani). Among family female maximum percentage increase was found at 919.85(Kawa-Baryal),10.77 (Sue-Chaker) and 4.16 (Sundrani).Similarly, among hired male & female increase in mandays were 225 & 200 (Sue-Chaker) followed at 143.33 & 143.33 (Kawa-Baryal) respectively. In the agriculture allied operations, no activity was observed in apiculture, mushroom, poultry and sericulture in the three watersheds under study. Horticulture recorded marginal increase in mandays in Sue-Chaker and dairy among family male and female belonging to Kawa-Baryal WDP. Weaving, carpentry and casual labour activities earlier done by family male were discontinued during post watershed development period in Sue Chaker WDP and mandays generated by cobbler recorded an increase of 87.5 percent. Percentage of mandays generated through casual labour for family male in Sundrani and Kawa-Baryal WDPs were 30.77 and 75 respectively. The existing watersheds must include following set of activities to enhance employment opportunities for rural folk.

1. Most of male family members were engaged as casual or hired labourer during lean agriculture period. In such cases, they may be trained properly in the execution of effective management and supervision jobs.
2. Since agriculture is rain fed, farmers must be trained for generating additional income opportunities by adopting vermicompost, cultivation of medicinal plants etc.
3. Credit at nominal rate of interest should be provided by banks and financial institutions to the SHGs, UGs,

panchyats and individuals who create additional employment opportunities in watershed areas.

4. Manufacture of simple farm implements/machines which remove drudgery among farm labourers must be encouraged by providing suitable financial incentives and trainings.
5. Manufacture of solar candles, rope & basket making should be encouraged by SHGs and rural cooperatives.
6. The project area being scarce of water, the availability of green vegetables throughout the year at reasonable rates is not possible. Rural masses can be trained in preserving dehydrated vegetables using solar dryers during production period. Such vegetables can be made available at reasonable prices during lean period.
7. Due to erratic rains and repeated moisture stress situations people of this region depend to a large extent on the naturally growing plants for fuel, food and fodder. A promising endeavour in the direction is to identify plants capable of yielding products of economic value which would not only provide much needed vegetative cover but would also help in generating employment and providing extra income.

## People's Participation in Watersheds

Participation in watershed management is recognised as a preferred tool to address the issues associated with balancing environmental concerns and consumptive use of water.It consists in the fulfillment of the ingredients of equity, empowerment, decision making and the active involvement (participation) of the disadvantaged sections of society and stake holders in the major social institutions and development programmes.

This communication may be passive, functional, interactive etc. which may relate to specific action for a limited purpose (Peabody 1965), enhancement of income, personal growth, self reliance or self development (Poul 1987), purposeful construction of public work (Heap 1976,Mumtaz & Soyal 1966), self motion (Giovanni& Sartori 1970), adherence to a set of rules

(Schotter1981) etc. In India Watershed Associations (WA),Watershed Committee (WC), Users' Group(UG),SHG (Self Help Group) and Gram panchayat ensures people's participation in the selection of the schemes, role in executing it , partaking in the fruits of development and has the potentials to transform the society ecologically, economically & socially.

Data from Sue-Chaker Watershed Development Project indicated that of the 201 respondents, 23 participated and 178 did not participate.. The non response rate though high was attributed to the various reasons and the basic cause was found to be 'participation need was not felt'. The other reasons in the descending order were 'unaware about the Watershed Development Project','the project was not as per local needs', 'non existence of informal group', 'absence of strong panchayat', 'insufficient awareness generation by Project Development Agency' and 'suggestions made were not accepted'.

Among the ranking of agencies generating awareness and motivation among respondents of Sue-Chaker WDP,the mean response for Watershed Development Team occupied first rank among the respondents of village Sue and second in Chaker (3.51) and Sambal (3.13) respectively. Informal groups/ leaders were preferred more in Chaker and least in village Sambal. Overall ranking in descending order was informal groups/leaders (3.73), Watershed Development Team (3.54), specialised team of govt. department (3.18) and others (2.64).

To evaluate the efficacy of existing community organisations, respondents were asked to assign ranks to SHG & Users Groups, participatory rural appraisal jointly carried by farmers and Govt. officials, awareness camps organised by Rural Development Agency, exposure visits carried by various Govt. departments and Mahila mandals/Charcha mandals/Youth clubs existed in their respective villages.

The tabulated results revealed that mean response for Self Help Groups & Users Groups (4.28) were found to be more in village Sambal followed by 3.81 in Sue and least at 3.69 in Chaker. Participation in rural appraisal was found to be more effective in village Chaker, followed by Sambal and least among respondents of Sue.

Awareness camps were favoured more by the respondents of Sambal and least by village Sue. The mean value for exposure visits was found to be 2.70 (Sue), 2.45 (Chaker) and least at 2.25 (Sambal). Mahila mandals/Charcha mandals/Youth clubs ranked least village wise and in overall ranking.Non existence of any formal group and lack of personal contact by field functionaries were found to be the major reasons for insufficiency of Sue-Chaker Watershed Development Project to meet the existing and future needs of respondents.

These were followed by scattered fields in watershed areas, lack of awareness about the existing watershed development programme and inadequate knowledge to utilise the benefits of the project. Low ranks were assigned to non involvement in decision making and others. The respondents expressed that training in technical aspect of in situ soil and moisture conservation technique were required to be imparted to members of the WDT. This was followed by operation and maintenance of civil works and agriculture allied activities in an integrated manner. Record keeping, conducting meetings, administrative and accounting procedures were least preferred. From the above analysis, it can be concluded that:

1. High level of illiteracy among farmers resulted in their inability to understand the significance and their role in participation for carrying development activities envisaged under the watershed development project
2. Non-existence of strong panchayat and social institutions were also found to be responsible for blocking communication linkages within villages and with Govt. functionaries.
3. Limited activities carried by the Rural Development Agency in generating interest and creating urge for participation among respondents.
4. Absence of formal organisations resulted in lack of coordination in agri. allied activities. Due to multiplicity of view points, unanimity was seldom reached among respondents as the results even the viable and useful view points were seldom implemented.

5. Informal groups/leaders were able to evoke better interest in watershed because of their sphere of influence, speedy communication and faith among members/ followers.
6. Specialised teams of Govt. departments and other agencies were less preferred for awareness generation and motivation because of their infrequent visits, lack of coordination in works and time constraints.
7. Self Help Groups and Users Groups were found to be more popular as they provide direct benefit to respondents besides satisfying their participation needs.
8. Mahila mandals /Charcha mandals/Youth clubs proved to be less effective in awareness generation and motivation because of limited participation of women owing to scattered fields, illiteracy and poverty.
9. The preference for awareness camps and exposure visits were found to be low as their reach were confined to lower regions of the watershed.
10. Technical aspect of in situ soil and moisture conservation techniques and maintenance of civil works were most preferred aspects of training desired by members of WTD/Association.
11. Majority respondents favoured existence of formal group and close contact with field functionaries for utilising the benefits of watershed technologies.

Integrated watershed management is a holistic concept and to strengthened people's participation for the planning, implementation & future management of the created structure and distribution of benefits in equitable & sustainable manner, following suggestions are being offered:

1. A participatory micro-plan at grass root level must be prepared for the overall development of cluster villages covering all socio-economic and natural resources management dimension. The participation of women and weaker sections of society must be ensured in planning, implementation and evaluation of watershed

project. People potentially affected by the project need to be more actively involved at project design stage.Strengthening institutional arrangement should receive highest priority.

2. To actualise the concept of watershed management, encouragement must be given to self-less leadership. The organisation of the people in the homogeneous caste composition villages in comparison to the heterogeneous caste composition village must be encouraged.

3. The interests of small and marginal farmers, landless labourers, women and other weaker sections of the society which were earlier neglected must be included in designing diversified income generation activities. Special training programme be planned for rural youth and women.

4. The tribal/rural communities living inside the reserved forests must be given some legal position and stake in the forests management. Van-Panchayats and Van Samiti should be formed and few positions must be reserved for women members. Social rules for harvesting of forest products must be framed.In this,villagers fix a particular day and period on which everyone in the village would harvest the fruits thereby minimising chance of destructive harvesting as the work is done under communal gaze.

5. The bureaucratic control on planning and management of forest resources under the present guidelines and situations should be relaxed and decision-making power should be extended to the local people also.

6. Indigenous knowledge and local material should be better utilised in the design and implementation of the project activities. This is particular true in case of vegetative barriers and forestry models, which emphasised fodder & fuel production.

7. For development of the capacity and achieving sustainable development, the staff must be trained both in technical skills and institutional development with

change of attitude from local Govt. control to joint management. The extension expert must also follow the participatory approach to empower the local people by transferring the technical and managerial capabilities.

8. The integrated concept of the project could be utilised by taking better technical guidance from the institutions like PAU Ludhiana, CSWCRTI Chandigarh, Forest Research Institute Dehradun etc.
9. Evolved catalysts and leadership in the effective functioning and sustainable management of VDC (Village Development Committee), WUS (Water Users' Society), FPC (Forest Protection Committee), NGO (Non-Government Organisation) and other social institutions should be strengthened. Since VDC are the integral part of the village protection force,they must be given the status of sub-committee,Up-Gram Sabha of village panchayat. Govt machinery should be set up to resolve inter and intra village conflicts arising due to the implementation of the programme.
10. The NGO can be involved for project implementation. The master degree students of local universities having sociology and agricultural extension backround can be introduced in these projects and they should be trained in PRA/RRA and other innovative techniques of participatory exercises for data collection and rapport building.
11. Sociological and anthropological studies relating to hill communities can also help us to understand the socio-cultural dynamics. The main land owing communities in the region are Gujjars,Bakerwals,Gaddies etc. The above study can help in understanding their socio cultural characteristics and based on it proactive development process can be initiated adopting a cluster approach for homogeneous communities groups point of view for the conservation and management of degraded forests.
12. Appropriate education films and field trips can be used to teach farmers about various methods of rain water

conservation and afforestation. Regular visits of field functionaries in watershed area and instituting awards and prizes for the sincere involvement of farmers in practising rain water harvesting techniques can motivate farming community in this regard.

13. Steps should be taken to popularise the Self Help Group concept among farmers so that they get loans subsidised from the banks and Govt. with marginal interest rates.

14. The Rural Development Agency should work systematically on improving attitude, communication, ensures devolution of power & resources to village institution and evolve a transparent system of cooperation and interaction. Training in modern participatory planning technologies like PRA/RRA must be given to govt functionaries so that they work as a facilitators by putting technical know how in the right perspective.

15. To ensure assimilation of improved indigenous soil and water technologies in the initial years,focus should be placed on building group and village level capacity through exposure visits, farmer to farmer sharing workshops and training of village leaders, para professionals and front line staff.

16. Extension activities under watershed development projects include rehabilitation of degraded terrain, demonstration of conservation and income generating works, field observations, extension meetings etc. The role of women in sharing ideas and experiences in these diverse activities on conservation can not be undermined. In this connection, efforts should be taken to develop leadership among women and encourage them to form groups.

17. A scientific study may be carried out on the use of different storage technologies (earthern pots,sacks,etc.) for different type of seeds and the results disseminated among the farmers.

18. To provide shelter for livestock a combination of modern and traditional low cost technologies must be evolved. The main problem with modern technologies is that they provide less protection from cold and heat due to stonewalls and tin roof. A survey of construction material may be made to find material which provides greater insulation than stone slab. The objective should be to provide relief to the farmers from the yearly labour of maintenance while also reducing cost & ensuring durability of the structure and its effectiveness in providing protection.
19. People-friendly uses of common lands should be promoted as grazing is now a low priority need in view of the decline usage of bullocks and maintenance of large herd of cows.

## Women Empowerment in Watersheds

Women constitutes an integral and a separate segment of stakeholders in any natural resources conservation, management & development project. Experience shows that lack of access to technical education & training; short of land, time & money; poor organisation, restricted access to political power & a limited ability to influence decision-makers etc. are the hindrances for their effective participation in watershed development projects.

Comparative employment generation in agri. & agri. allied activities for women in three WDPs of district Udhampur revealed that of the total employment generation, dairy sector topped in employment generation and constituted 63.40% (Sue-Chaker), 55.51% (Sundrani) and 39.14% (Kawa-Baryal). This was followed by agriculture 35.29% (Sue-Chaker),22.49% (Sundrani) and 37.10% (Kawa-Baryal).Mushroom and poultry were observed only in Sue-Chaker and percentage of post watershed mandays generated were 0.47 and 0.48 respectively. Horticulture created maximum mandays in Kawa-Baryal (23.76) followed by Sundrani (22.00) and least in Sue-Chaker (0.36).

Creation of assets in the form of house, land, animals & consumer durable purchased by women in post WDPs of district

Udhampur revealed that majority of women 18.5% (Sue-Chaker),32.0% (Sundrani) & 30.00% (Kawa-Baryal) renovated their houses followed by 17.00 % (Sue-Chaker),8% (Sundrani) and 30% (Kawa-Baryal) reported to be repaired. Land improvement through watershed technologies and improved agriculture inputs was practised more compared to purchase of land. Of the total, the percentage of respondents purchasing animals were 16.5(cow), 15.0 (buffalo),4.5 (pig), 2.0 (goat), poultry bird (2.0) and ass (0.5)in Sue-Chaker WDP.

In Sundrani, the percentage of respondents purchasing cow, buffalo and pig were 52.0, 22.0 and 8 respectively. The percentage of respondents purchasing buffalo was 30 compared to 20 for cow in Kawa-Baryal WDP. Among consumer durables, T.V accounted for 24.5% respondents followed by sewing machines(18.5)%, furniture (6.0)%, refrigerator (2.0)% and least household utensils (0.5)% in Sue-Chaker WDP. Similar trend was observed for Sundrani WDP. In Kawa-Baryal WDP, the percentage of respondents purchasing consumer durables in descending order were furniture (30)%, sewing machines (20)% and T.V(10)%.

Awareness regarding various watershed technologies showed that women of Sue-Chaker possessed moderate level of awareness regarding bench terracing & nallah bank erosion and low awareness regardin0g diversion drain & water harvest structures. Similarly majority of women falling under Sundrani WDP possessed moderate level of awareness regarding various watershed technologies. Awareness about nallah bank erosion, gulley plugging, diversion drain was found to be high where as regarding water harvest structures was found to be low among women in Kawa-Baryal WDP.

Satisfaction of existing and future family needs through WDPs revealed that in case of food, the average family deficiency figure came out to be 1.44qtls (Sue-Chaker), 0.78qtls (Sundrani) and 2.10qtls (Kawa-Baryal).In fodder, Sundrani (11.69qtsl) ranked first followed by 11.11qts l(Kawa-Baryal) and least by 5.73qtls (Sue-Chaker).Fuel deficiency needs of Sundrani was 3.25qtls ,Sue-Chaker 2.17qtls and Kawa-Baryal 2.00qtls.No existing and future needs in respect of agro-forestry and soil conservation were reported in three WDPs. Dairy, poultry and sericulture needs though quoted but the amount was found to be marginal.

Existing social, employment, communication & marketing needs were found to be deficient. The respondents of all the three WDPs emphasised on their empowerment and following suggestions may be made in this regard :

1. Initiating public investment on physical infrastructure like bio-gas plant, individual toilets etc. create demand for inputs which are manufactured by villagers. This in turn would create employment and in the process reduce poverty among women.
2. Women can be motivated to set up micro-enterprises. The products could be sold through Mahila cooperatives established in each block.
3. SHG-NGO Bank integration must be promoted as it is essential to credit delivery, for self employment and other business activities which could be effective vaccine against poverty. Such linkage could go all out for all round economic development (Sabyasachi Das,2005) by:
   a. Formation of homogenous SHGs in villages as per guidelines of GOI for SGSY scheme and due training /assistance in location specific activities for development of forestry and improvement in family income.
   b. Providing credit for consumption and production as and when required thereby preventing exploitation of the poorer sections from non-institutional credit sources.
   c. Development of group dynamics, building leadership quality to realise their potentiality and self-belief.
   d. Assisting the members to complete the formalities and documentation required to obtain credit from bank.
   e. Helping banks in recovery of credit by motivating members for prompt repayment of loans.

f. Building common infrastructure for the benefit of its members. In the model, the NGO works as financial intermediary responsible for lending to SHG/individuals and also bears the risk of non-payment. Being engaged at grass-root level, it has good information about borrowers thus, adverse selection and production of recovery is avoided. At the same time it helps rural poor, particularly women to bring them above poverty line and rural employment.

4. A Rural Women's Self Help Group should also be promoted as it enables members to become self-dependent and self-reliant. It also provides members for discussing their social & economic problems and equips women with the basic skills required for understanding monetary transactions.

5. People must be encouraged to set up formal NGOs as it besides helping in channelising funds, donations and subsidies from India & abroad, promotes supportive institutional linkages between official institutions and people's organisation. They are successful in propagation of low input sustainable agriculture production, bio-fertilizers, organic farming, dissemination of new technology in the process of cultivation, ways & means of manufacturing recycle products, selecting environmentally compatible materials, preservation and conservation of village common property resources etc.

6. Establishment of eco-clubs comprising of 20-30 member group for imparting environmental education and mobilising participation of people in various environmental conservation activities which indirectly would benefit the women.

7. Apart from finance, health and education are the areas which are needed in the process of empowering rural women. Gender equity and balanced representation of all caste groups in the health & family welfare committees formulated at the village level would benefit the rural women.

8. Women & youth belonging to artisans households like handlooms, handicrafts etc. find their future bleak as many traditional and cottage industries have lost viability. Development of cooperative marketing structure,skill upgradation institutions, building village infrastructure under PRIs would help the rural women in manucturing goods as per the demand of the markets.
9. A pre-requisite for speedy and orderly development of village lies in perspective planning through PRIs,which at present are constraint by lack of participation, bureaucratisation, non-observance of the election code of conduct, mal-development, corruption etc. It needs change at two levels. First, they have to be strengthen as legal and constitutional authorities. Second, the people who are involved in their working too need to change their attitude so that they work for empowerment of women and poor sections of the society.

In conclusion agriculture production can be improved by adopting an optimal combination of farm enterprises viz. cropping systems, alternative land use systems, livestock systems and means available with farmers to raise them profitable. Van-Panchayat, Van-Samities, Eco-clubs, SHGs, rural cooperatives, NGO etc. should be encouraged and women representatives must be included in them. SHG-NGO Bank integration must be promoted for credit delivery, self employment and other business activities.

# BIBLIOGRAPHY


Bailey, Conner and Charles E. Faupel: *Environmentalism and Civil Rights in Sumter County*, Colorado, Westview Press, 1992.

Barnum, Susan R.: *Biotechnology: An Introduction*, Belmont, Thomson/Brooks/Cole, 2005.

Burch, William R. Jr.: *Human Ecology: An Environmental Approach*, Belmont, Duxbury Press, 1994.

Campbell, R. R., and Wade, J. L.: *Society and Environment: The Coming Collision*, Boston, Allyn and Bacon, 1972.

Chrispeels, Maarten : *Plants, Genes and Crop Biotechnology*, Sudbury MA, Jones and Barlett Publishers, 2003.

Cox, Earl D. : *Beyond Humanity: Cyber Evolution and Future Minds*, Roackland, Charles River Media, 1996.

Daubenmire, R. F.: *Plants and Environment*, New York, Wiley, 1947.

Dixon, Dougal: *After Man-A Zoology of the Future*, New York, St. Martin's Press, 1981.

Dodds, John H.: *Plant Genetic Engineering*, New York, Cambridge University Press, 1985.

Edwards-Rees, D.: *The Service of Youth Book*, Wallington, Religious Education Press, 1943.

Erickson, Kai: *A New Species of Trouble: Explorations in Disaster, Trauma, and Community*, New York, W.W. Norton, 1994.

Gelobter, Michael: *The Distribution of Air Pollution by Income and Race*, Berkeley, University of California, 1989.

Gitman, Lawrence J.: *Principles of Managerial Finance*, MA: Addison Wesley Longman, 2000.

Johnson, Hazel: *Financial Institutions and Markets: A Global Perspective*, NY, McGraw Hill, 1993.

King, R.B., Mihony, G., and Sheldon, J.K.: *Practical Environmental Bioremediation*, Lewis Publishers, Boca Raton, 1992.

Kruvant, W.J.: *People, Energy, and Pollution*, Cambridge, Ballinger Publishing, 1975.

Martin, Justin: *The Man Behind Money*, Perseus Book Group, 2000.

Matthews, J. E.: *Working with Youth Groups*, London, University of London Press, 1966.

Milson, F.: *Growing With the Job*, London, National Assocation of Youth Clubs, 1968.

Murray, David: *Seeds of Concern: The Genetic Manipulation of Plants*, Sydney, University of New South Wales, 2003.

Petty, Keown, Scott, and Martin: *Basic Financial Management*, Prentice Hall, 1993.

Primrose, S.B.: *Principles of Gene Manipulation*, London, Blackwell Scientific Publications, 1989.

Retzer, W.J.: *Biotechnology Workbook*, Englewood Cliffs, Prentice Hall, 1991.

Schall and Haley: *Introduction to Financial Management*, McGraw-hill, 1988.

Shetty, Kalidas: *Food Biotechnology*, New York, Dekker/CRC Press, 2005.

Sontheimer, Sally: *Women and the Environment: Crisis and Development in the Third World*, New York, Monthly Review Press, 1991.

Vallette, J.: *The International Trade in Wastes: A Greenpeace Inventory*, Washington, Greenpeace, 1989.

Walden, Richard: *Genetic Transformation in Plants*, England, Open University Press, 1988.

# INDEX

□□□